W9-AZW-149

NIGEL
DEMPSTER'S
ADDRESS BOOK

NIGEL
DEMPSTER'S
ADDRESS BOOK

The Social Gazetteer

Weidenfeld and Nicolson
London

First published in 1990 by George Weidenfeld & Nicolson Ltd
91 Clapham High Street, London SW4 7TA

p. 3 Nigel Dempster with Jamie Blandford

Picture research by Tom Graves
Design by Nick Avery
Edited by Lesley Baxter

ISBN 0 297 83064 3

Printed in the UK by Butler & Tanner Ltd, Frome, Somerset

Introduction

The Sixties were heralded by the 'Never Had It So Good' General Election of 8 October 1959 when Harold Macmillan, dubbed 'Supermac', was returned to power with a majority of exactly one hundred. But, ironically, it was not until after Harold Wilson finally led the Labour Party to victory five years later that the so-called 'Swinging London' was christened – by *Time* magazine.

It was the era of the meritocracy when, notionally, actors, photographers, designers, models, dancers, even Italian restaurateurs, were liberated at last from their class roots and allowed to take their allotted places in the Halls of the Mighty.

The newly-married Princess Margaret and Lord Snowdon gave parties at Kensington Palace attended by a leather-suited Rudolf Nureyev and Peter Sellers and a somewhat subdued Britt Ekland.

The Earl of Lichfield suddenly preferred to be known as Patrick Lichfield, photographer. The Beatles took a Lord on the Board and beneath the leathers of many motorbikers was to be found the ermine of the aristocracy.

Budding politician, Jonathan Aitken, took LSD in a 'controlled' experiment for a newspaper report, after a Harvard Professor, Dr Timothy Leary, discovered the hallucinogenic drugs, was thrown out of the university and jailed (only to flee to Morocco). And Flower Power and the Woodstock Generation saw out the decade in a haze of marijuana and pacifism, rebelling against the Vietnam War.

Temporarily, the Establishment was forced to take an unaccustomed back seat. But *plus ça change, plus c'est la même chose ...*

Order was restored in the Seventies with a Prime Minister, Edward Heath, who extolled and practised the virtues of outdoor life and music. He won the rugged Sydney-Hobart yacht race, and performed with internationally renowned orchestras, in the process making a million by writing best seller books about his hobbies, which he promoted with such zest that an unsigned Edward Heath became a collector's item.

But waiting in the wings for his comeback was Harold Wilson who, aided by the chaos of the three-day week (as one German banker said waggishly, 'How will they get the British to work the extra day?'), returned to power in 1974 and, cocking a snook at his critics in the wake of the famous Ince-in-Makerfield slagheap furore, ennobled his controversial private and political secretary, Mrs Marcia Williams, who became Baroness Falkender.

The Seventies were a time for reflection and regrouping, awaiting the glory days ahead. Peter Jay, who became the son-in-law of the Prime Minister when James Callaghan succeeded Wilson after a surprise resignation in March 1976, which has never been explained fully, was named as a future leader of the world by *Time* magazine. Accordingly, Her Britannic Majesty's Secretary of State for Foreign Affairs, Dr David Owen, appointed Jay Ambassador to Washington, where he lost his wife to one of the two journalists who broke the Watergate scandal.

It was the decade that signalled the end of the career of Jeremy Thorpe, the Liberal Leader who had come within a whisker of being offered a Cabinet post after Heath failed to win an outright majority in the first 1974 General Election. A brilliant career, which began, as with so many others, with the Presidency of the Oxford Union, ended in an Old Bailey acquittal on the charge of attempted murder of a former male model, Norman Scott, whose Great Dane had been killed by a would-be hit-man.

Those searching for the true meaning of life dropped out to follow the squeaky-voiced Maharisha and other gurus, and self-awareness was marketed by Elmer Gantry figures who made personal fortunes out of the insecurity of the great and the good, finding unlikely disciples like Bernard Levin and Arianna Stassinopoulos.

Half way through the decade, the direction of the Eighties was decided when Mrs Margaret Hilda Thatcher won the leadership of the Conservative Party from an unforgiven Edward Heath, and the countdown to the Thatcher Years and the birth of the Thatcher Generation began.

With the Great Seal of Office came the age of Thatcherite entrepreneurism, liberating thousands of urgent young things from the prospect of humdrum office life, to become Yuppies with champagne tastes and Porsches to prove the merit of their calling.

It heralded the Wapping Revolution, which freed Fleet Street from the atavistic grip of print unions that embodied the ethos of heredity. It also unleashed the unscrupulous on the unsuspecting.

The Eighties ended with the Dockland Boom bust, albeit temporarily, and signs that the Thatcher Years were drawing to a close. It was a decade when 'Greed is Good' supplanted 'My Word is My Bond' as the motto of the Stock Exchange and Guinness was anything but good for a group of very rich, powerful men.

The Social Gazetteer

Aga Khan and his wife

A*a*

ABERCORN, Fifth Duke of, JAMES HAM-ILTON, (peerage of Ireland), *born* 4 July 1934, sits as the Marquess of Abercorn (peerage of Great Britain 1790), having succeeded father in 1979.

As Marquess of Hamilton was elected Ulster Unionist MP for Fermanagh and South Tyrone (succeeding the future Fifth Duke of Westminster) in 1964 with a majority of 13,872. He lost the seat to the Unity candidate in June 1970 by 1,447 votes, retiring from politics the following month to 'concentrate on business'. Married to the above is Alexandra 'Sasha' Phillips, granddaughter of Electrolux heir, Sir Harold Wernher, by his marriage to Lady Zia, daughter of a Russian grand duke at whose Luton Hoo estate the Queen and Prince Philip have spent nearly all their wedding anniversaries (the estate is now owned by Sasha's brother, Nicky). Prince Philip, a keen admirer of the Duchess, as was also Algy Cluff (q.v.) in the seventies, has been a regular guest, too, at Hamilton House – the villa owned by the Abercorns on the Bahamian island of Eleuthera, where the late Earl Mountbatten bought property for his family. Like father, Jamie Hamilton (Eton, Cirencester and the Grenadier Guards) is Lord-Lieutenant of County Tyrone, where he lives at Barons Court, Omagh, which was decorated by David Hicks. Developed shopping centre just outside Belfast and is a director of Northern Bank. Two sons, one daughter. Heir: James Harold Charles, Marquess of Hamilton, born 19 August 1969, a page-of-honour to the Queen 1982–4. What was said of a nineteenth-century ancestor applies today: 'He has not done much, but he has done nothing badly.'

His Highness Prince Katim, Aga Khan IV, *born* 13 December 1936.

Granted title His Highness by the Queen in 1957, His Royal Highness by the Shah of Persia in 1959. Son of Prince Aly Khan by his marriage to the Hon. Joan Yarde-Buller (now Viscountess Camrose). Educated Le Rosey and Harvard, became spiritual leader of twelve million Ismaeli Muslims spread across the world in July 1957 on the death of his grandfather, a toad-like voluptuary who lived in Cannes. After romances with Patricia Rawlins (q.v.) and Sylvia Casablancas, married, in 1969, model Sally Croker Poole (two sons, one daughter), former wife of the Marquess of Bute's younger brother, Lord James Crichton-Stuart. Co-founded the Costa Smerelda development in Sardinia, where his Italian girlfriend, Milena Maffei, had a clothes shop, Bella Blue, in Porto Cervo near his villa, and moved his operations from the Île St Louis to Aiglemont, in Chantilly, a £30 million purpose-built château and business complex near his training stables. In the eighties he won the Epsom Derby an unprecedented three times and has been leading owner in England, France and Ireland. In 1984, while visiting Spetsapoula, the private island of Stavros Niarchos (q.v.) on his yacht, **Shergar**, he met Austrian beauty, Pilar Goess, then the fiancée of Spyros Niarchos. She broke off the engagement and has been the Aga's close companion ever since and now runs an interior decoration business in Vienna – she appeared nude in a 1977 German edition of **Playboy** (now a collectors item). His followers voluntarily contribute a tithe (ten per cent of their income) to the Imamate, which funds hospitals and centres of learning where there are Ismaeli Muslim communities – mainly Pakistan, Bangladesh, East Africa, Britain, Canada and the United States. His personal wealth is put in excess of £2 billion.

AITKEN, JONATHAN WILLIAM PATRICK, *born* 30 August 1942, Conservative MP for Thanet South since 1983 (Thanet East 1974–83).

The great-nephew of the First Lord Beaverbrook (often mistakenly referred to as the Beaver's grandson), who, in the sixties, became private secretary to Selwyn Lloyd, was compared to William Pitt, and wrote a swinging sixties book called **The Young Meteors** (a source of subsequent embarrassment). Adopted for the safe seat of Thirsk and Malton in 1967, wrote in the London **Evening Standard** about experimenting with the hallucinogenic drug LSD, and was dropped three years later after he was sent for trial for publishing an article on the Biafran war that allegedly violated the Official Secrets Act – he was cleared in January 1971 and adopted for Thanet the next year. A business association with Prince Mohammed of Saudi Arabia led to a burgeoning financial career, which peaked when Aitken Hume, the company he ran with his cousin Timothy Aitken (a grandson of the Beaver), owned twenty per cent of TV-am. Both were, at different times, Chief Executive of the breakfast station. In 1979 married voluble Swiss Lolicia Azucki. They have one son (named William after grandfather, MP Sir William Aitken), twin daughters and live in a £2 million Westminster house, once owned by the Earl of Drogheda.

AITKEN, The Hon. Sir MAX, **baronet,** *born* 15 February 1910.
The elder son of the First Lord Beaverbrook (his brother Peter died in a mysterious yachting accident in Scandinavia in 1947), who disclaimed the peerage on the death of his father in 1964 with the words, 'There will only be one Lord Beaverbrook in my lifetime.' A noted Lothario – briefly engaged in the thirties to heiress Margaret Whigham, subsequently Mrs Charles Sweeny (q.v.) and later the Duchess of Argyll – he had a 'fine war', becoming Group Captain and gaining a DSO and DFC, and fighting in the early days of the Battle of Britain (a claim hotly denied by his sister, the Hon. Mrs Janet Kidd, in her autobiography). Owned The Prospect, the finest waterside house at Cowes (now a museum), where he indulged in his hobbies of yachting and, later, powerboat racing, with his mistresses, notably interior designer Rose Underdown, Verity Raymond, the Hon. Liz Allsopp and former Australian air hostess, Pat Tudor. Long-suffering wives

were left at the Garden House, Cherkley, on the estate near Leatherhead where the Beaver used to hold court (he left the main house to his widow Marcia Christoforides, who had already inherited a fortune on the death of her previous husband, Canadian magnate Sir James Dunn). After suffering a series of strokes, he sold out Beaverbrook Newspapers for £13 million in 1977 – its shareholding in Reuters was later found to be in excess of £150 million – and died, wheelchair bound and attended by twenty-four-hour nursing, in 1985. Only son Maxwell (by third and last marriage to Violet de Trafford) took on the Beaverbrook title, sold his part of Cherkley and is Deputy Treasurer of the Conservative Party.

ALEXANDER OF TUNIS, Second Earl, SHANE WILLIAM DESMOND, (and heir apparent to Earldom of Caledon).
Born 30 June 1935 and succeeded father, Field Marshal Earl Alexander of Tunis, Supreme Allied Commander Mediterranean 1944–5 and Governor-General of Canada 1946–52, in 1969. First marriage, in July 1971, to banana heiress Hilary 'Gussie' van Geest, was disrupted by some of the bride's relations, including her maternal aunt, protesting outside St Margaret's, Westminster because they had not been invited. The marriage was dissolved in 1976 (no children). In 1981 he married Princess Margaret's lady-in-waiting, the Hon. Davina Woodhouse, youngest daughter of Lord Terrington, and they have two daughters. His heir is his younger brother, the Hon. Brian Alexander, born 31 July 1939, who is in charge of property sales on the Caribbean island of Mustique and remains unmarried, although he has been close for twelve years to divorcée Johanna Morris, former wife of a Bahamas-based banker and whose uncle, Dr John Williamson, discovered and owned the fabulous Mwadu diamond mine in Tanganyika, leaving £14 million in 1958. Shane Alexander could do with a diamond mine – he is a substantial 'name' in the Lloyd's syndicates of Dick Outhwaite, which face losses esti-

mated at between £300 million and £1 billion, and is also involved in the Oakeley Vaughan syndicates, which have losses in excess of £25 million. He has an interest in the Alexander House Hotel near Gatwick.

AL-TAJIR, (MOHAMED) MAHDI, *born* 26 December 1931.
Educated Al-Tajir School, Bahrain, Preston Grammar School, Lancashire. Married, 1956, Zohra (five sons, one daughter). Made his fortune by becoming special adviser to the Ruler of Dubai after starting as a customs officer in Bahrain in the fifties. Appointed Ambassador to London for the United Arab Emirates in 1972 and resigned in 1986, during which time he availed himself of his diplomatic status to conduct deals between Britain and the UAE. In the eighties he announced he was worth between £2 billion and £3 billion and had bought Mereworth, an eighteenth-century Palladian villa in Kent, Keir, Stirlingshire with 15,000 acres, Dropmore House, Burnham, Windlesham Moor, Surrey (the Queen and Prince Philip's first home) and a large apartment in Carlton House Terrace overlooking The Mall. Sent his eldest son, Khalid (born 1959), to Harrow. Absent from London since, in 1985, his brother Sadiq was kidnapped in Knightsbridge and ransomed for £2 million. In January Dropmore, set in 200 acres and on the market for £12 million, was burgled and an estimated £10 million in treasure was taken. In June 1990 half the house was destroyed in a fire, causing an estimated £50 million damage.

AMBLER, JOHN KENNETH, *born* 1924, married, 30 June 1964, Her Royal Highness Princess Margaretha, eldest and tallest (5ft 11ins) granddaughter of the late King Gustav Adolf of Sweden and sister of King Carl Gustav of Sweden.
She was formerly involved with Robin Douglas-Home, nephew of the Earl of Home, sometime piano player (The Berkeley Hotel cocktail lounge, the Clermont Club), friend of Frank Sinatra and photographer and

journalist, who committed suicide in 1968. Known as 'Flash', Haileybury-educated Ambler served in the Coldstream Guards, including a wartime spell as bodyguard to Sir Winston Churchill, and was named as co-respondent when the late Earl Beatty obtained à divorce from his second wife, Dorothy. At the time of his marriage, he was a director of Atlas Air Express, a Bermondsey freight firm, and the controlling shareholder (1,320 out of 1,400) of the Bradford Cemetery Company Ltd., owner of one of the two private cemeteries in the north of England. The couple live in an Oxfordshire manor house and have two sons and a daughter.

AMIS, Sir KINGSLEY, *born* 16 April 1922.
The author of **Lucky Jim** in 1954, he is an enthusiastic drinker (and writer about drink) who took several days to locate a farewell note that his second wife, writer Elizabeth Jane Howard, had placed in a prominent position by the teapot informing him that she was leaving him for good – they were divorced in 1983 after eighteen years of marriage. The father of Martin, by his first wife Hilary, who later married the Seventh Lord Kilmarnock as his second wife. Amis and the Kilmarnocks bought a £200,000 house near Primrose Hill, Regent's Park and live together cosily, when he is not at the Garrick Club. He claims his favourite television programme is 'Coronation Street'.

ANDREWS, ANTHONY, *born* 1947, son of the late Stanley Andrews, conductor of the BBC Review Orchestra, and Geraldine, a dancer.
Miscast in 'Brideshead Revisited' but chose right co-star when he married, in December 1971, heiress Georgina Simpson (one son, two daughters), only child of the late Dr Leonard Simpson, an endocrinologist and owner of the Piccadilly store, who left the couple his Hyde Park Gate, Kensington home, which formerly belonged to Sir Winston Churchill. Anthony is best known for his supporting role to the Princess Royal,

which earned him the nickname 'Prince Annedrews' in royal circles. A former showjumper, who was once South of England champion, Georgina shares a love of horses with the Princess, who has been a friend since 1981, and has a country home near Andover, an easy drive from Gatcombe. The Princess is godmother to the couple's youngest child, Amy-Samantha, born April 1986.

ANDREWS, EAMONN, *born* 19 December 1922.
Before David Frost, Michael Parkinson and Terry Wogan, Eamonn was *the* TV chat show host, after starting as a boxing commentator aged sixteen (he was the All Ireland juvenile boxing champion) with Radio Eirann. Came to England in 1949 to tour with the Joe Loss Band Show as chairman of a 'double or nothing' quiz and began a television career with the BBC in July 1951 as chairman of the panel game, 'What's My Line?' Four years later he began his own programme, 'This Is Your Life', which eventually earned him £250,000 a year. He married Grainne Bourke in 1951 and they adopted a son Fergal, and two daughters Emma and Niamh. Andrews died in November 1987. He was ill-served by a biography by Tom Brennan, a consultant on 'This Is Your Life', which portrayed him as insecure, tightfisted, vain and a fluffer of lines.

ANNIGONI, PIETRO, *born* Milan, 7 June 1910, died in Florence in October 1988.
An artist in oil, tempera, etching and fresco, the twice married Annigoni (who has a son and a daughter by his first wife Anna), achieved fame with his 1955 portrait of the Queen, dressed in the deep blue and white satin-lined robes of the Order of the Garter, which hangs in the National Portrait Gallery and was commissioned by the Worshipful Company of Fishmongers. He was given fifteen sittings. Portraits of Dame Margot Fonteyn (1956), Prince Philip (1957) and Princess Margaret (1958) followed. Immortalized Patricia Rawlings (q.v.) as *La Strega*

(The Witch), which was exhibited at the Royal Academy Summer Exhibition in 1960.

ANSON, Lady ELIZABETH, *born* 7 June 1941, daughter of the late Viscount Anson (died 1958), sister of the Earl of Lichfield (q.v.), great-niece of Queen Elizabeth, the Queen Mother and goddaughter of King George VI. Founder of Party Planners, London's foremost firm for organizing grand balls. Personally gave parties at Claridge's for the Royal Family and friends after the weddings of the Prince of Wales and the Duke of York. Parental opposition (his) ended a proposed marriage to Lord Sudley (now the Ninth Earl of Arran) in the late sixties. In 1972 married photographer and baronet Sir Geoffrey Shakerley (whose first wife, actress Virginia Maskell, committed suicide in 1968) and they have a seventeen-year-old daughter, Fenella. The couple are now officially separated.

Lady Elizabeth Anson

Pietro Annigoni

Jeffrey Archer, his wife and double

ARCHER, JEFFREY HOWARD, *born* 15 April 1940.

Came to prominence at Oxford, where he gained a Blue for Athletics and Gymnastics in 1963 and held the Oxford 100-yards record at 9.6 seconds. Started financial career by organizing fundraising events at the university and was elected GLC Member for Havering in 1966, winning the ultra-safe parliamentary seat of Louth in 1969. Brief period in-between with the United Nations Association, which ended with a legal spat with Humphry Berkeley, the chairman, the details of the settlement of which have never been made public. Speculation in a Canadian company, with money lent by JCB heir Sir Anthony Bamford, led to the threat of bankruptcy and his resignation from Parliament in September 1974. There followed a highly successful writing career, beginning with *Not a Penny More, Not a Penny Less*, based on the Canadian swindle. A brief return to frontline politics as Vice-Chairman of the Conservative Party ended with the *News of the World* revealing that he had paid callgirl Monica Coghlan £2,000 although, as a High Court libel action later heard, he had never met her. He donated the £500,000 award, against the *Daily Star*, as well as a later £50,000 award against the *News of the World*, to charities. Lives with his wife, don Dr Mary Archer, in the Old Vicarage, Grantchester, where Rupert Brooke once lodged. Puts his own worth at £25 million.

ARGYLL, Eleventh Duke of, IAN DOUGLAS CAMPBELL, *born* 18 June 1903, died 1973.

Married firstly the Hon. Janet Aitken, only daughter of the First Lord Beaverbrook, secondly the Hon. Mrs Louise Vanneck, thirdly Mrs Margaret Sweeny and fourthly Mrs Mathilda Heller. Chief of the Clan Campbell, Admiral of the Western Coasts

Duke and Duchess of Argyll at Inverary

and Isles, he was forced to resign from White's, Britain's oldest gentleman's club, after he sold details to a Sunday newspaper of his marriage to Margaret, who had spent £2 million repairing his seat, Inverary Castle. Their 1963 divorce case, heard in Scotland but unable to be fully reported by the English press for legal reasons, featured nude photographs of a headless man and numerous other unidentified lovers. He was succeeded by his son from his second marriage, known as 'Wee Ian', who married Iona Colquhoun of Luss, whose family own Loch Lomond.

ASHLEY, APRIL, *born* George Jamieson, 29 April 1935 in Liverpool, the son of a bus conductor.
Ran away to sea at fifteen, becoming a deck boy with the Furness Withy Line on the *Pacific Fortune*. He underwent a £2,500 sex-

April Ashley

change operation in Casablanca in 1960 before meeting the Hon. Arthur Corbett, eldest son and heir of Lord Rowallan, the former Chief Scout and Governor-General of Tasmania. Their marriage took place in Gibraltar in September 1963, with the bridegroom receiving a telegram from his Eton and Christ Church educated brother, Bobby, reading, 'Congratulations. May I be a bridesmaid?' Arthur, who became Lord Rowallan in 1977, was running a nightclub in Marbella (later working on the Costa del Sol as a barman) and had a son and three daughters by his previous marriage to Eleanor Boyle, a cousin of the Earl of Glasgow. In 1970 Corbett successfully sued for nullity of the marriage on the grounds that his wife was a man. She retired to Hay-on-Wye after her Knightsbridge restaurant, AD 8, closed and has recovered from a heart attack. She was in the habit of recommending New Zealand butter to her lovers.

ASPINALL, John Victor, *born* 1926.
Educated at Rugby and Oxford, he was responsible for the legalizing of gaming after discovering a loophole in the law, and for holding 'floating' *chemin-de-fer* parties in London. He successfully defended a prosecution for illegal gaming in 1958 and the first London casino opened in 1961 at Les Ambassadeurs in Hamilton Place, Park Lane. He opened the Clermont two years later at 44 Berkeley Square, leasing the basement to his friend Mark Birley, (q.v.), who opened Annabel's nightclub. Among the regulars was his close friend the Earl of Lucan (q.v.), who has not been seen since the murder of his children's nanny in November 1974. Aspinall sold the Clermont for £500,000 to Victor Lownes (q.v.), head of Playboy, but had to return to gambling when he lost all his money on the Stock Exchange (advised, it was said, by his friend Sir James Goldsmith, q.v.). Backed by Goldsmith, he returned to

John Aspinall and friend

gambling with a small casino off Sloane Street, moving in April 1984 to the former Curzon Street home of Viscount Curzon. They sold out to Peter de Savary (q.v.) for £90 million just before the October 1987 stockmarket crash and £20 million has been put in trust for Aspinall's two pioneering zoo parks in Kent, where the feed bill is £4,000 a day. With his property millionaire son Damian, by his first marriage to model Jane Gordon-Hastings (dubbed 'The Spirit of Park Lane' in the fifties), and half-brother James Osborne, he bought the name back in May 1990 when the new owners, Leisure Investments, went into receivership and plans to reopen in 1991, also in Curzon Street. By his third wife, Lady Sarah Curzon, sister of the late Earl Howe, he has another son, Bassa Wulfhere.

ASTOR, Third Viscount, WILLIAM WALDORF, *born* 13 August 1907.
MP for East Fulham 1935–45 and Wycombe, 1951–2. Bill Astor was a keen racehorse owner who kept two dozen mares at the Cliveden Stud, and was a tenant of the nineteenth-century mansion built by Sir Charles Barry, the architect of the House of Commons. In the thirties Cliveden was a famous political centre when owned by Bill's father and mother Nancy, who were hosts to, among others, the German Ambassador Von Ribbentrop in the days leading up to appeasement. In the sixties Cliveden acquired a different notoriety when Bill sublet a cottage by the Thames to Stephen Ward, a Harley Street osteopath who had treated him. It was during a weekend in July 1961 that War Minister John Profumo and his wife Valerie were guests at Cliveden and met Miss Christine Keeler, who was staying with Ward, frolicking in the mansion's swimming pool. Astor was blamed for deserting Ward, who was prosecuted for living off immoral earnings and committed suicide in August 1963, before the trial ended. Astor married three times and his heir was his son William by his first wife, who succeeded to the title in 1966. His widow, judge's daughter Bronwen

Pugh, was a leading model before their 1960 marriage, and is now a recluse living in Surrey.

AYER, Sir ALFRED, (A.J. Ayer), *born* 29 October 1910.
The Wykeham Professor of Logic at Oxford who became the most widely read of the analytic philosophers in the tradition of Bertrand Russell. An atheist, Freddie Ayer became known to a wider public through his devotion to Tottenham Hotspur FC and to his second (and fourth) wife, American-born broadcaster Dee Wells. They married in 1960 and divorced in 1983 after she became involved with designer Hylan Booker, a coloured former US Air Force sergeant twelve years her junior. Ayer then married J. Lyons heiress, Vanessa Lawson (née Salmon), former wife of Treasury Minister Nigel Lawson, and who died in 1985. After revealing that he had 'died' for four minutes during an operation, Ayer remarried Dee in April 1989, just two months before his death.

B*b*

BAILEY, DAVID ROYSTON, *born* 2 January 1938.
The enduring sixties fashion photographer, known by all as just 'Bailey', and leader of the original triumvirate of (Terry) Donovan and (Brian) Duffy. Now married to model Catherine Dyer, his previous wives included model Marie Helvin and actress Catherine Deneuve, but not model Jean Shrimpton (q.v.), who rose to fame through his lens, nor another love, heiress Penelope Tree, who became a leading model in the seventies. A director of commercials and documentaries, he remains in the same cramped, dark-painted house near Primrose Hill, London that he has shared with all his wives and girlfriends and has a daughter Paloma, five, and a son, Fenton Fox, three, by Catherine.

Bb

David Bailey, Catherine Deneuve and Marie Helvin

BAKER, Sir STANLEY, *born* 28 February 1928.

Son of a Rhondda coal miner and knighted in Sir Harold Wilson's controversial resignation honours list in May 1976, he died in Spain of cancer six weeks later. Star of *The Cruel Sea*, *The Guns of Navarone*, *Zulu*, *Robbery and the Victim*, also a director with Richard Burton of HTV, Baker put part of his earnings into property, building Alembic House on the South Bank opposite the Tate Gallery, where Jeffrey Archer (q.v.) has one panoramic floor just below the penthouse.

BAKEWELL, JOAN DAWSON, *born* 16 April 1933.

Broadcaster and writer immortalized by Frank Muir, who described her as 'The Thinking Man's Crumpet'. Married, for the second time, in 1975, to actor–director Jack

Joan Bakewell

Emery, ten years her junior, whom she met when she interviewed him. A son and daughter by her first husband, television director Michael Bakewell.

BARCLAY, JOHN DONALD (JACK), *born* 7 February 1900.
After serving in the First World War in the Royal Flying Corps, he set up a car showroom in 1922 in Great Portland Street and started racing Bentley and Vauxhall cars, winning the first Brooklands 500-mile race in 1929 in a Bentley at an average speed of 107.42 mph. During the Second World War, when car production was suspended, he bought up Rolls Royces and Bentleys so that he would have a stock when the conflict ended and became their foremost salesman, with premises in Berkeley Square. He sold out to Lonrho subsidiary Dutton-Forshaw in 1967. He lived on a 1,000-acre farm near Oxford and died in August 1969. One of his two sons, Victor, is still a director of the business.

BARODA, The Maharajah of, *born* 1930.
In the days of the Raj, was one of five potentates to be accorded the highest salute of twenty-one guns. 'Jackie' Baroda, who died in September 1988, was a familiar figure in London, where he had a house in Old Church Street, Chelsea. He spent his summers watching cricket – he was President of the Board of Control for Cricket of India 1963–6 and managed the Indian team on three tours. Along with other Indian princes, his title was abolished by Mrs Indira Gandhi in 1971 but when his father had clashed with her father, Nehru, twenty years earlier, he transferred his property, valued even then at £15 million, to Jackie. In 1950 he married Princess Rajendra of Jodhpur, in one of the last princely ceremonies, with a mile-long procession headed by bejewelled elephants, through the streets of Baroda. The couple were separated for twenty-five years and, priding himself as a womanizer, he used to send friends abroad a voluminous annual newsletter chronicling his doings. In 1984 he declared, 'The world at large must be informed that at long last I

have joined the exclusive Mile High Club, making love to a Lufthansa air hostess while flying to America.'

BASUALDO, LUIS JUAN SOSA, *born* 5 September 1945.
Argentinian polo professional known as 'The Bounder', who ran off with eighteen-year-old Lucy Pearson, the heiress daughter of Viscount Cowdray (q.v.), and married her at Caxton Hall in 1972. They met when Basualdo was employed to play at Cowdray Park (six handicap) and for three years he had the Prince of Wales playing for his Golden Eagles high-goal team, financed by Lucy. He received a £220,000 payoff when they were divorced six years later (one son, one daughter). Between 1981 and 1983 Basualdo was employed as *homme d'affaires* by Christina Onassis (q.v.) at the rate of £20,000 a month, but left when she married her fourth husband, Thierry Roussel. The Austrian Police issued a warrant for his arrest after $1.2 million was transferred in 1985 from the St Moritz Credit Suisse account of Christina to the Bank of Tirol in Lanbeck, Austria. He has maintained his innocence but has remained in Argentina awaiting the resolution of matters.

BATH, Sixth Marquess of, HENRY FREDERICK THYNNE, *born* 26 January 1905.
Credited with having started the stately home business by opening Longleat, a renaissance house dating from 1568 with a park designed by Capability Brown, to the public. Later, in 1966, with the help of circus boss Jimmy Chipperfield, he installed a pride of lions. Henry Bath moved to nearby Job's Mill when he made over the house and 11,000 acres to his eldest son and heir, Viscount Weymouth, a former Life Guards officer who sports a ponytail, has a hippy existence and erotic murals painted in his private apartments. Married to Hungarian-born actress Anna Gael, with whom he spends six months a year, he sent his two children to local schools. His girlfriends are known as 'The Loins of Longleat'. Bath has a daughter, Lady Silvy Thynne, by his second marriage in

Luis Basualdo and Serge Kausov

1953, who was conceived after a visit to the phallus of the Cerne Abbas Giant. His youngest son, Lord Valentine, who once worked as a Butlin's redcoat, committed suicide in 1979 after a domestic argument at a party held on the estate.

BEARSTED, Third Viscount, MARCUS RICHARD SAMUEL, *born* 1 June 1909.
Head of the family property company that owned thirteen acres of Mayfair including Berkeley Square and Bruton Street (where the Queen was born) and chairman of the family firm of M. Samuel and Co. which, in 1965, merged with Philip Hill to become Hill, Samuel, the leading merchant bank

(now part of TSB). Served during the Second World War in the Middle East and Italy, where he was wounded, with his hands being badly burned. He turned as therapy to needlework, which remained a lifetime relaxation. He died in 1986 leaving £12 million to his daughter Felicity, wife of Robert Waley-Cohen, son of the former Lord Mayor, and a racehorse owner and trainer.

BEATTY, Second Earl, DAVID FIELD, *born* 22 February 1905.
Son of the victor of the Battle of Jutland, who was Commander-in-Chief of the Grand Fleet from 1916–18 and First Sea Lord of the

Admiralty from 1919–27, and raised to the peerage in 1919 when he received the thanks of Parliament and a grant of £100,000 for his services during the War, with which he bought Chicheley Hall, near Newport Pagnall. When he was fifty-four the Second Earl married, as his fourth wife, Diane Kirk, eighteen, daughter of a mushroom farmer, by whom he had a son and a daughter. Was heard to remonstrate in the Clermont Club with the Earl of Lichfield (q.v.), 'First you're after my wife, now you're trying to steal my butler. You've gone too far.' He died in 1972 with the title passing to his son David (Viscount Borodale) by his first marriage, while Chicheley was left to Diane.

BEAUFORT, Eleventh Duke of, DAVID ROBERT SOMERSET, *born* 23 February 1928.
Inherited the historic title, Badminton House and 52,000 Gloucestershire acres in 1984 from his distant cousin, who had been known as 'Master' since the age of ten, when he started with a small pack of harriers, and had been Master of the Horse (and thus rode beside the Sovereign's carriage during ceremonial processions) 1936–78. A descendant of John of Gaunt, Beaufort has been married since 1960 to Lady Caroline Thynne, daughter of the eccentric Marquess of Bath (q.v.). Their eldest son Harry, nicknamed 'Bunter' and able to sleep standing up, is the Marquess of Worcester and married to actress Tracy Ward (sister of actress Rachel), who is at the forefront of Britain's Green movement. David, best friends with Fiat chief Giovanni Agnelli, is co-owner of Marlborough Fine Art, the Mayfair gallery. His partner is Gilbert Lloyd (briefly the fiancé of ex-*Tatler* Editor, the Hon. Emma Soames), whose father Frank independently ran Marlborough Gallery in New York and was found by a US grand jury to have falsified and destroyed evidence in a battle over the estate of 798 paintings by Mark Rothko, who committed suicide in 1970. Frank, facing a twelve-year jail sentence and payment of a £5 million award against his gallery to the artist's son and daughter, retreated to his Nassau home, away from US jurisdiction.

BEDFORD, Thirteenth Duke of, JOHN ROBERT RUSSELL, *born* 24 May 1917.
Called Ian and brought up in South Africa, he did not know he had any connection with the Duke of Bedford (his grandfather) until he was sixteen. Inherited the title, a large area of Bloomsbury, London (Covent Garden was sold to meet the death duties of the twelfth duke) and Woburn Abbey in 1953 and gave over the running of Britain's most successful stately home to his eldest son Robin, the Marquess of Tavistock (q.v.) in 1974. Went into tax exile in Monte Carlo and Paris with his French-born third wife, Nicole, who wrote in her autobiography, ***Nicole Nobody***, of losing her virginity to a complete stranger who 'raped' her in a Manchester hotel in 1946.

BENSON, CHARLES RIOU, *born* 23 October 1935.
Noted horse-racing writer and tipster for the ***Daily Express*** for thirty years, originally understudying the legendary Clive Graham, whose by-line was 'The Scout', thereby earning Benson the nickname, 'The Boy Scout'. To augment income to pay bookmakers he became the 'Social Asset' at the Garrison, the discotheque in the basement of Les Ambassadeurs, after the previous greeter, brewing heir Mark Watney, shot himself. Another incumbent, Robin Douglas-Home (q.v.), also committed suicide but Benson survived, a testament to his education at Eton and National Service in the Green Jackets where, as an officer, he had to be saluted by Rifleman Anthony Haden-Guest (q.v.). Variously the best friend of the Aga Khan (q.v.) (also a former beau of the Aga's wife Sally) and Robert Sangster (q.v.), Benson has two sons by his first marriage and a daughter by his second wife, Chubby, whose father, Colonel William Gerard Leigh, commanded the Household Cavalry and was Silver-Stick-in-Waiting to the Queen and became known as Polo-Stick-in-Waiting to Prince Philip. Benson's philosophy may be summed up by

the title of his autobiography, *No Regard For Money*.

BENTINCK, Baron, Steven, *born* 3 May 1957, son of the late Baron Adolph Bentinck, Dutch Ambassador to London and Paris, and Baroness Gaby Bentinck, sister of Baron Heinrich Thyssen-Bornemisza (q.v.).

Youthful excesses included losing £75,000 on a glossy magazine, *Boulevard*, which folded in 1979 after three issues, and £140,000 on a stage musical on the life of the late James Dean. Dallied with Marilyn Cole (now married to Victor Lownes, q.v., former head of the Playboy empire) and *Majesty* magazine Editor, Ingrid Seward (former PR for Playboy), before marrying, in 1987, Italian-born Princess Nora Czartoryski, ex-wife of a Polish nobleman, who has three children from her two previous marriages. May be found daily in Kensington Gardens being pummelled by his personal exercise coach, Baptiste. His sister, Henriette, was the first wife of the Marquess of Northampton (q.v.), by whom she had a son and a daughter.

BENTLEY, John, *born* 19 February 1940.

Educated at Harrow, he was an early disciple of asset-stripper Jim Slater and, thanks to a timely takeover bid for his Barclay Securities (which had closed Triang toys, making a profit of £2 million and 1,200 workers redundant) in January 1973, left the City with £2 million before the crash later that year. When asked about the bid from the financial services group, J. H. Vavasseur, he replied when interviewed in New York, 'Vavva-who? I don't know much about them.' Various ill-fated ventures followed, not least with women – former child actress Viviane Ventura (q.v.), sued him for paternity of her daughter Scheherazade (which he later admitted), he was briefly involved with Dewi Sukarno, widow of the Indonesian dictator, and Nigerian chieftain's daughter Minah Bird. In 1982 he married Kitty Percy, daughter of the Marchioness of Bute, after a stormy five-year romance during which she

once fell from his second-floor Mayfair flat and since their divorce four years later, has been involved with Maria Niarchos, daughter of billionaire Stavros Niarchos. Now back in business as Chairman of the A. Brown Group, which is involved with satellite broadcasting.

BERLIN, Sir Isaiah, *born* 6 June 1909.

Order of Merit, former President of the British Academy and Chichele Professor of Social and Political Theory at Oxford (1957–67) who liked to give his tutorials after dinner. Worked during the Second World War in Intelligence in the Washington Embassy and so impressed Churchill that the Prime Minister instructed his staff to invite I. Berlin to lunch when he was next in London. By mistake they asked songwriter Irving Berlin when he was visiting, and after the meeting a confused Churchill, who, when he had asked Berlin what had been the most important thing he had done lately, received the reply 'White Christmas', opined, 'That fellow doesn't talk half as well as he writes.' Married since 1956 to Aline de Gunzbourg.

BERRY, Lady Pamela, *see* Lady Hartwell.

BIRBECK, Jane, *born* 1953.

Owner of Bodys, a keep-fit club in the King's Road, Chelsea and nicknamed 'Hottie' (short for hotpants) by her boyfriend James Hunt (q.v.), the 1976 world racing driver champion. Engaged to be married, the six-year affair ended in 1980. Three years later Jane became involved with Olympic gold medal decathlete Daley Thompson who, displaying all his prowess, jumped over a six-foot wall to escape the attention of press photographers who found the couple together. She is still unmarried.

BIRLEY, Marcus Oswald Lecky, *born* May 1930.

Son of portrait painter Sir Oswald Birley, whose style and taste he has inherited. Founded Annabel's (named after his then wife Lady Annabel, sister of the Marquess of

Londonderry, q.v.) in June 1963, followed by Mark's Club, Harry's Bar and, in 1988, the Bath and Racquets Club, next door to Claridge's, with membership set at £2,000 a year. His elder son Rupert was thirty when, in June 1986, he vanished off the coast of Togo, where he was on business; younger son Robin was severely mauled as a teenager by one of John Aspinall's tigers. After a ten-year affair with Jimmy Goldsmith, Annabel was divorced from Mark in 1975 and remarried three years later. For the last two years, Birley has been close to Chicago-born Joan Biskant, former wife of an Australian film-maker. In 1988 he showed his devotion to the Rio carnival by importing members of the Beija-Flor Samba School from Brazil for three weeks to celebrate Annabel's twenty-fifth anniversary.

BLACKWELL, CHRISTOPHER, *born* 1938.
Educated at Harrow and formerly aide-de-camp to the Governor-General of Jamaica (where his mother, Blanche, came from a leading white family) he discovered, promoted and managed local girl Millie, who had a worldwide 1964 hit with the song 'My Girl Lollipop'. He founded Island Records in 1962, supplying Jamaican music to West Indian customers in Britain, discovered Bob Marley, the King of Reggae, and sold the company to PolyGram for an estimated £180 million in August 1989. Twice married and divorced, Blackwell has homes in Berkshire, Nassau, Los Angeles and Jamaica, where he owns Goldeneye, the former house of Bond author Ian Fleming. For the last decade he has been involved with Nathalie Delon, the French actress and director and former wife of Alain Delon.

BLANDFORD, Marquess of, *see* MARLBOROUGH, Eleventh Duke of, John George Vanderbilt Henry Spencer-Churchill.

BLYTH, CHAY, *born* 14 May 1940.
A sergeant (the youngest to be promoted since the Second World War) in the Para-chute Regiment, he rowed the North Atlantic with Captain John Ridgeway in ninety-two days between June and September 1966, the first time he had ever been to sea. When interviewed afterwards, he said, 'Captain Ridgeway does the talking, I do the rowing.' Further heroics followed, including a solo circumnavigation of the world in 1970–1 and the successful Virgin Atlantic Challenge on the Blue Riband in 1986. Married with a daughter, Samantha, he lives in Fareham, where he is Managing Director of British Clippers, which plans to convert steamers into clippers.

BOND, ALAN, *born* 22 April 1938.
Brought up in Ealing and attended Perivale School, before, at the age of thirteen, joining his father who had emigrated to Australia to help cure a chest complaint. Left school in Perth to work as a sign writer (his large painting of a dingo on a flour mill in Fremantle is the only remaining example of his work) and made his first million before he was twenty, after marrying his first sweetheart, Eileen Hughes, a fourth-generation Australian, called 'Red' because of her hair. In 1983 became a national hero for winning the America's Cup off Newport, Rhode Island, on his fourth attempt, the first successful challenge in 132 years. His Bond Corporation grew with property, mineral, broadcasting and brewing acquisitions until it was valued at £2 billion. Made a fatal error attempting to take over Lonrho in 1988, causing Tiny Rowland to investigate Bond's creditworthiness and publish a damning seventy-page document stating Bond's company was 'technically insolvent'. Since then Bond has been fighting, to little effect, to save the business, which is controlled by Dallhold, his private company. Sold are Glympton, his Oxfordshire estate and village, for £11 million, and *Irises*, his Van Gogh painting, which was the world's most expensive when he bought it on the never-never, for £25 million to the Getty Museum. Both his yachts are for sale but his personal fortune, while dented, is not affected.

Alan Bond with Robert Maxwell

BOOTHBY, Lord ROBERT JOHN GRAHAM, (life peer), *born* 12 February 1900.
Enjoyed a forty-year affair with Lady Dorothy Macmillan, wife of his political rival Harold, who rose to become Prime Minister, and was the father of Lady Dorothy's daughter Sarah, born in 1930. Macmillan, later the Earl of Stockton, suffered a total collapse, spending months in a German sanatorium, but decided against a divorce lest it ruin his political career and, in 1958, ennobled Boothby. In 1935 Boothby had married Dorothy's cousin, Diana Cavendish, granddaughter of a Duke of Devonshire, but they were divorced two years later. Achieved notoriety by being photographed between the Kray twins at a 'private function', leading to innuendos of homosexuality. In 1967 he wed Sardinian Wanda Sanna, thirty-three years his junior, at Caxton Hall. They had met, he said, when she was working as a secretary in Monte Carlo five years previously. He died in 1986.

BOSANQUET, REGINALD, *born* 1932.
Educated at Winchester and New College, Oxford, the son of the Test cricketer who invented the googly. With his slightly slurred speech and a lopsided delivery, he was a cult newscaster with ITN for more than a decade until he suddenly quit in 1979, handing a poem, in tears, on-screen to fellow presenter Anna Ford, which read, 'If I suffer from eccentricity/Do I have eggcentricity/On my

Lord Boothby, his bride and her sister

face?/I may not be here tomorrow/Can I borrow/All of your best wishes?' He died of cancer, penniless, in 1984, a year after marrying his third wife, Mrs Joan Adams, and had a daughter by each of his previous marriages. He was once arrested in Covent Garden for his drunkenness and when asked in the police station to empty his pockets, produced a half-filled glass of red wine.

BRABOURNE, Seventh Lord, JOHN ULICK KNATCHBULL, *born* 9 November 1924. Film and television producer whose work includes **Sink the Bismark!**, **HMS Defiant**, **Murder on the Orient Express** and **The Mirror Crack'd**. In 1946 married Earl Mountbatten's elder daughter, Lady Patricia, who became Countess Mountbatten in her own right, with their eldest son, Norton Knatchbull, inheriting the title Lord Romsey and Broadlands, his grandfather's Romsey, Hampshire estate where the Queen and Prince Philip and Prince Charles and Diana spent the first part of their honeymoons.

BRADEN, BERNARD, *born* 16 May 1916. Married Barbara Kelly, one of the original panellists on 'What's My Line?' in 1942 and moved from Canada to England seven years later. BBC TV shows included 'On The Braden Beat' and 'Braden's Week', on which he employed Esther Rantzen as a reporter

1968–72. She copied his idea of a consumer reportage and in 1973 replaced his slot with 'That's Life' using the same format.

BRAGG, MELVYN, *born* 6 October 1939.
Head of Arts, London Weekend Television since 1982, presenter and editor of 'The South Bank Show', prolific author, and biographer of Richard Burton. In 1961, married Marie-Elizabeth (Lisa) Roche (one daughter), whose father was Rector of the Sorbonne. She committed suicide in 1971 and in 1973 he married television researcher Catherine Haste (one daughter, one son). When a Sunday newspaper revealed in 1987 that Bragg had enjoyed a passionate affair for eight years with Lady Jane Wellesley (q.v.), only daughter of the Eighth Duke of Wellington, he declined to sue for libel, claiming that litigation was 'too expensive'. The couple had met in a queue at the Edinburgh Festival. Bragg remains at his homes in Hampstead and his native Cumbria with his wife Cate who, at the time of the disclosure, was working on a book titled *Sexual Morals*.

BRAINE, JOHN GERARD, *born* 13 April 1922.
Author of *Room at the Top*, which was filmed in 1965, giving actor Laurence Harvey (born Larushka Skikne in Lithuania) his big break as Joe Lampton, the ruthless, randy young local government man on the make, starring opposite Simone Signoret (who won an Oscar). Braine was a £650-a-year branch librarian at the West Riding of Yorkshire County Libraries when he wrote the best seller, which he was never able to emulate although he wrote twelve more novels as well as a biography of J.B. Priestley. Married with a son and three daughters, he died in October 1986.

BRIDPORT, Fourth Viscount, ALEXANDER NELSON HOOD, also Duke of Bronte in Sicily (created 1799), *born* 17 March 1948. Descended from the brother of Admiral Horatio Nelson, through whom he inherited Maniace, a 1,000-year-old fortress and originally a 40,000-acre Sicilian estate at the foot of Mount Etna which he put up for sale in 1981 for £2 million. Married, for the second time, to Finnish-born Nina Martyn, who was widowed in 1970 when racing driver Jochen Rindt died at Monza (winning the world championship posthumously). A banker, he lives in Switzerland, and has a son and heir by his first wife, Linda Paravicini, and a son by Nina, also the ex-wife of former world backgammon champion Philip Martyn.

BRISTOL, Sixth Marquess of, VICTOR FREDERICK COCHRANE HARVEY, *born* 6 October 1915.
A member of the Mayfair Boys gang who was sentenced in 1939 to three years penal servitude for his part in the robbery of a Bond Street jeweller enticed with samples to the Hyde Park Hotel. He served nearly two years in Brixton, Wormwood Scrubs, Maidstone and Camp Hill prison, Isle of Wight and legend has it (falsely) that he was the last prisoner to get the cat-o'-nine-tails. He succeeded his father in 1960, inheriting estates in Suffolk, Lincolnshire and Essex. Married for the third time, to his secretary Yvonne, he went into tax exile, leaving his elder son and heir Earl Jermyn (John) at Ickworth, the eighteenth-century ancestral mansion owned by the National Trust, with an inheritance of 4,000 surrounding acres. He died in March 1985, three years before John, the Seventh Marquess, was sentenced to a year in jail for possession of cocaine. When Jermyn married Miss Francesca Fisher, twenty, at Ickworth in September 1984, his father took the unusual step of placing a notice in *The Times* stating that he and his wife had 'another engagement in London'.

BROCCOLI, ALBERT S., *born* 5 April 1909, known as 'Cubby'.
Formed Eon Productions with Harry Saltzman in 1962 to make *Dr No*, the first of seventeen James Bond movies – Saltzman dissolved the partnership after nine years, selling out to United Artists for £17.5 million. The nephew of the man who introduced to America a vegetable which was

Cubby Broccoli

named after him, thrice-married Cubby left Britain for Beverly Hills in 1977 because of soaring taxation.

BROCKET, Third Lord, Charles Ronald George Nall-Cain, *born* 12 February 1952.

Owner of Brocket Hall and 5,000 acres near Welwyn, Hertfordshire, which he has turned into a conference centre with attractions including his collection of forty Ferraris and Maseratis and beautiful American model wife Isa. Claiming it costs him £2,500 a day to live, he has applied to build a £30 million, 200-bedroom hotel and championship golf course on the estate. His wife is launching her own perfume shortly – named Isa. George Best's ex-wife Angie was given a £320,000 thirtieth birthday party at Brocket by her lover, American 'financier' Chris-

topher Carajohn, who was later jailed for seven years for masterminding a £2 million fraud.

BROPHY, Brigid Antonia, *born* 12 June 1929, author and playwright wife of Sir Michael Levey, who was Director of the National Gallery from 1973–87, until his resignation to look after his wife, who suffers from multiple sclerosis.

Married for thirty-six years, Levey proposed by telegram and Brophy accepted, giving her reason that she was an animal lover and he looked like a cat. One of the original campaigners for the Public Lending Right, she based the character of Antonia in her latest book, the lesbian novel **The Finishing Touch**, on her friend, the disgraced spy (Sir) Anthony Blunt.

BROWN, TINA, *born* 1953, daughter of George H. Brown, the independent producer of more than thirty films, including early Agatha Christie classics.

While at Oxford, writing for *Isis*, penned an adulatory letter to Auberon Waugh (q.v.), which led to a close friendship, an entrée to London literary circles and a job on the *New Statesman*. She met Harold Evans, then Editor of the *Sunday Times*, when she went to work for the award-winning newspaper and after, she claims, she took to walking up and down the corridor outside his office. Following a stint on *Punch* she became Editor of *Tatler* in 1979 at the invitation of Managing Director Johnny Elliott (who in the eighties served a jail sentence for fraud). Later the magazine changed ownership and was bought by Condé Nast, and turned into a profitable, upper-class comic. Married Evans (now sixty-two) in 1981 after his first marriage (three children) was dissolved. Fired by Rupert Murdoch as Editor of *The Times* with a £250,000 payoff Evans, with Tina, moved to New York, where she became Editor of *Vanity Fair* in 1984, turning it into a critical and financial success, while Harry became Editor-in-Chief of the Condé Nast *Traveler Magazine*. Son George was born five years ago, a second child arrived autumn 1990.

BROWN, Sir DAVID, *born* 10 May 1904.
The manufacturer of the first all-British tractor and owner of Aston Martin 1946–72, responsible for the DB marque. Went into tax exile in Monaco in 1978 after his Vosper shipbuilding company was nationalized without recompense. Divorced from his second wife Maggie in 1980 after twenty-five years (she remains at his 1,550-acre Chequers Manor estate near Marlow) so that he could marry his statuesque personal assistant Paula Benton Stone, forty-eight years his junior and half a foot taller. A noted ladies man, he liked to cruise his 255-ton yacht, *Charisma*, around the nudist Île de Levant and encourage topless sunbathing among his shapelier guests. Fortune, estimated in excess of £75 million, seems destined for Paula, although he has a son, David Brown Jnr, known as Bill, and grandchildren.

BROWNE, The Hon. GARECH DOMNAGH, *born* 25 June 1939, younger son of Lord Oranmore and Browne by his second marriage to brewery heiress Oongah Guinness – she later married Cuban dress designer Miguel Ferreras, dubbed 'The Fidel Castro of Haute Couture'.

Ponytailed Garech, owner of the Claddagh Records label, married Indian maharajah's daughter Princess Purna of Morvi in 1981 and is now engaged in costly litigation attempting to extract his share of the Guinness Trust. Lives at spooky Luggala in County Wicklow, where his younger brother Tara (born 4 March 1945) is buried beneath the lawn after being killed when he crashed his Lotus Elan in Earl's Court on 18 December 1966, spawning from his close friends the Beatles, the song 'Day in the Life'. Tara, the quintessential upper-class sixties hippy figure, left two young sons, Dorian and Julian, by his wife Nicky, daughter of a County Down farmer. The couple were estranged at the time of his death and his mother, Oonagh, gained custody of the boys.

Tara Browne

BUCCLEUCH, Ninth Duke of, WALTER FRANCIS JOHN MONTAGU DOUGLAS SCOTT, also Eleventh Duke of Queensberry, *born* 28 September 1923, succeeded in 1973.

As the Earl of Dalkeith, he was the main suitor for Princess Margaret and, says Lord Glenconner (q.v.), 'If the King had lived, he would have made Johnny Dalkeith marry the Princess.' Instead, he married one of Margaret's circle, Jane McNeill, daughter of a QC in Hong Kong, in 1953 and they have two sons and a daughter. Buccleuch lives between three stately homes, spending four months in each, and owns 247,000 acres in England and Scotland. He personally transports his favourite painting, the last Titian in private hands, from home to home. In a wheelchair since he broke his back hunting in 1971, he still shoots from a specially converted Range Rover.

BUNN, DOUGLAS, *born* 29 February 1928.

Former showjumper and owner of historic Hickstead Place, where he built the £2.5 million All England Jumping Course on his 1,000-acre estate. Educated at Cambridge and called to the Bar in 1953, he turned twenty acres at Selsea, Sussex, owned by his father, into a caravan site and expanded into other sites, making his fortune. Married three times with nine children, he pronounced on the steps of the High Court after his acrimonious divorce from wife number two, Susan, 'Women are twits.'

BURTON, SALLY HAY, *born* 1947.

The daughter of a former Fleet Street journalist, she married Richard Burton on 3 July 1983, after meeting him on the set of the television series 'Wagner' on which she worked on continuity. His fifth wife, she was widowed thirteen months later. Collaborated with Melvyn Bragg on his best-selling autobiography, ***Rich***, and earned opprobrium from his relations for selling the Swiss home where he died and near where he is buried, to move to a £1 million Bayswater house in 1988. Twice married to Elizabeth Taylor, for whom he deserted his first wife

Sybil, Burton ran off with Princess Elizabeth of Yugoslavia (q.v.), wife of Euro MP Neil Balfour, in 1974, but she left him after a year because of his drinking – he then married James Hunt's ex-wife and model Susan, in 1976, before divorcing six years later.

BUTLER OF SAFFRON WALDEN, Lord RICHARD AUSTIN, *born* 9 December 1902.

Married two Courtaulds heiresses – first wife Sydney, who died in 1954, was the granddaughter of the founder of the fibre firm and second wife Mollie, the widow of Augustine Courtauld. After failing to succeed Harold Macmillan as Prime Minister, Butler became Master of Trinity College, Cambridge, and was responsible for introducing the undergraduate Prince Charles to his first love, Lucia Santa Cruz, daughter of the then Chilean Ambassador to London, and who worked as a researcher for 'RAB'. In 1971 he sold his Gloucestershire estate, Gatcombe Park, to the Queen, who gave it as a wedding present to Princess Anne on her marriage to Mark Phillips (q.v.). When asked what he would do with the £500,000 he received, RAB replied: 'Half a million doesn't go very far these days.' He died in 1982 and his elder son Adam, MP for Bosworth, has been a Government Minister.

CABORN-WATERFIELD, MICHAEL 'DANDY KIM', *born* 1930.

A leader of the Chelsea Set that evolved in the late fifties and gathered in various restaurants, pubs and coffee bars along the King's Road, then a street of neighbourhood shops. Found guilty in his absence and sentenced to four years in jail for robbing the Antibes, South of France villa of Hollywood mogul Jack Warner, of jewellery worth £25,000. A former boyfriend of Warner's

C c

Lord Butler with Prince Charles

daughter, he was extradited in 1960 and released in July 1961, with remission for good behaviour. Always attracted to wealthy women, in 1972 he married twenty-one-year-old model Penny Brahms, who had inherited £500,000 when her husband, Clive Raphael, was killed in a crash while piloting his plane over France six months earlier – he had named nine men, including Dandy Kim, in the divorce proceedings he had begun before his death. They moved to Jacobean Sedgehill Manor, Wiltshire and bought an hotel in nearby Shaftesbury, but separated after having a daughter. A business partner of Diana Dors (q.v.), whom he had known since she was a teenage starlet, he was involved in a slimming business with her when she died in 1984.

CADBURY, PETER EGBERT, *born* 6 February 1918.

Thrice-married chocolate heir (grandson of the founder of the Bourneville empire) and wartime test pilot who practised as a barrister 1946–54 until taking over the Keith Prowse ticket agency. In 1960, after scouring the country for a suitable franchise, 'The Cad' was awarded Westward TV, based in Plymouth. He was ousted in a boardroom coup in 1980 by former Labour Minister Lord Harris of Greenwich, whom he had brought in to help renew the franchise. Harris, who claimed that the IBA would not deal with the controversial Cadbury, duly failed, and TSW took over Westward. With four sons and a daughter from three marriages, he remains close to his second wife Jennifer

Peter Cadbury

d'Abo, who went on to make her own fortune after their 1976 divorce, taking over Rymans and now owning Mayfair florists, Moyses Stevens.

CAINE, MICHAEL, *born* 14 March 1933.
Born Maurice Joseph Mickelwhite in the Old Kent Road. The resident star of Langan's Brasserie, in which he bought a 24.5 per cent stake for a bargain-basement £25,000 in 1976 after the impecunious owner, Peter Langan (q.v.) had been fleeced by a trusted employee. For several years Caine gave a Fourth of July party at the Brasserie and is a regular customer, receiving dividends in kind far in excess of his original investment. By his first wife, the late Patricia Haines, he has a daughter, Dominique 'Niki', thirty-three, who married Olympic showjumper, Rowland Fernyhough in 1981. In 1973 Caine married Shakira Baksh, who represented Guyana in the 1967 Miss World contest and came third. They have a sixteen-year-old daughter, Natasha, who has been attending a Knightsbridge school. Canny Caine made an estimated £3 million by emigrating to America with his fortune when the exchange rate was $2.60 to the £1, and returning when it was $1.50 to the £1. He lives between an apartment in the Chelsea Harbour tower just below the penthouse and a mill house in Wallingford, Berkshire, but is most proud of the Oscar he won for *Hannah and Her Sisters*.

CAMDEN, Fifth Marquess of, JOHN CHARLES HENRY PRATT, *born* 12 April 1899.
Prominent in the world of motor racing and yachting and aid to his close friend from schooldays, record breaker Sir Henry Segrave. 'Brecky' Camden married as his third wife Rosemary de Laszlo (née Pawle) in 1978 and died five years later leaving £3,288,298. Her first husband was Group Captain Peter Townsend (q.v.), by whom she had two sons, and who divorced her in 1952, citing banker John de Laszlo, before embarking on a romance with Princess Margaret to whose father, King George VI, he was Equerry. Their affair led to a Constitutional crisis in 1955 when Margaret told her sister she planned to marry Townsend, who, although the innocent party, was nevertheless a divorced man. Pressure from all sides, not least from the Archbishop of Canterbury and Prime Minister Winston Churchill forced her to give up.

CARRIER, ROBERT, *born* 1924.
The author of the ultimate best-selling cookery book, *Great Dishes of the World* (1963) and the man who introduced the concept of cookery cards. A New Yorker of Irish-German descent, Carrier came to London for the Coronation and discovered a country using ration books and serving soggy food. Started the Pickwick Club off Piccadilly in the early sixties (investors included Harry Secombe, Frank Sinatra and Wolf Mankowitz) and opened Carrier's in Camden Passage in 1967, having to cook himself because his Greek chef got cold feet and went home. His greatest love was Hintlesham Hall, where he spent £235,000 converting the stables into a country house restaurant, but he closed it in 1982 and Carrier's two years later and moved to Marrakech to write *Taste of Morocco*. He is occasionally visited there by his little-known French son (now thirty-eight), and wanders between other homes in Eaton Square, Paris, New York and Hintlesham, which he still owns.

CASSANDRO, MARIO, *born* 1921.
With his partner Franco Lagatolla (born 1930), began the Italian restaurant boom in Britain, opening the Trattoria Terrazza in Soho in 1959, with an investment of £1,200. The first year they lost £368, but the following year there was a small profit and business burgeoned after patronage by Frank Sinatra, Sophia Loren, Princess Margaret and the Earl of Snowdon, the Beatles and the Rolling Stones. The two, both with Neapolitan backgrounds, met as waiters in the Mirabelle, then London's most fashionable restaurant, in Curzon Street, and their inno-

vative menus, modest prices and cheerful Italian waiters were just waiting for the onset of swinging London and the eating-out boom. By the time the duo went public in 1968 (having spawned a host of imitators across the metropolis, owned by their former staff), there were four restaurants. Two years later there were eight, including one in Manchester, and they were each millionaires. They quit the business in 1973, when it was taken over by Spillers, best known for their dog foods. Mario came out of retirement to open an eponymous restaurant in the Brompton Road and Franco died at his home in Nice in 1980.

CAVENDISH, Lady ELIZABETH GEORGIANA ALICE, *born* 24 April 1926.
Daughter of the Tenth Duke of Devonshire (and sister of the Eleventh), who introduced Princess Margaret to her future husband, photographer Antony Armstrong-Jones, at a dinner party at her Radnor Walk, Chelsea house, eighteen months before they became engaged in 1960. She never married herself, being the mistress for twenty-six years of Poet Laureate Sir John Betjeman, and became his literary executor when he died in 1984 – he would never seek a divorce from his wife Penelope, daughter of the late Field Marshal Lord Chetwode. She has been an extra lady-in-waiting to Princess Margaret since 1960.

CAWDOR, Sixth Earl of, HUGH JOHN VAUGHAN CAMPBELL, *born* 6 September 1932. Also Thane of Cawdor and a direct descendant of Macbeth, 'Chalky' was cured of an irrational fear of knives by 'Professor' Ron Thatcher, also known as Dr Death, who taught the secretive martial art of Aikido, in which Cawdor became a black belt. Sold his 11,700-acre estate in Wales for £4.1 million in 1976 to concentrate on Cawdor Castle, Nairn with its 56,000 acres (now open to the public). Divorced from first wife Cath, daughter of a Major-General, by whom he has two sons and three daughters, he married Czech-born Countess Angelika Lazansky von Bukova in 1979.

CAZALET, PETER VICTOR FERDINAND, *born* 1907.
Trained racehorses at Fairlawne, his 1,500-acre estate near Tonbridge, where his house boasted Britain's only private Real Tennis court. A close friend of Queen Elizabeth, the Queen Mother, for whom he saddled 250 winners, although he professed dislike for her son-in-law. When the Earl of Snowdon attempted to cut in while he was dancing with the Countess of Westmorland at a sixties party given by Jack Heinz, Cazalet had two glasses of red wine tipped over him. His personal cook from 1958, Albert Roux, went on to become the owner of one of Britain's only two three-star restaurants, Le Gavroche. Twice married, Cazalet's eldest son is High Court judge, Sir Edward Cazalet. Fairlawne is now owned by Saudi Prince Khalid Abdullah, whose horses won the French and Epsom Derbys in 1990.

CAZENOVE, CHRISTOPHER, *born* 17 December 1945.
Educated at Eton and chose acting rather than the blue-chip family stockbroking business, Cazenove & Co., training at the Bristol Old Vic. Made film debut in 1970 in ***There's a Girl in my Soup***, and played Ben Carrington at the end of the 'Dynasty' soap series. Married to actress Angharad Rees, daughter of London University's Emeritus Professor of Psychiatry, Linford Rees, with two sons, Linford, sixteen and Rhys, thirteen. In 1980 the couple broke up, blaming pressures of cash, career and marital stress, but fell in love all over again four years later.

CECIL, HENRY RICHARD AMHERST, *born* posthumously 11 January 1943, third (and twin) son of the late Hon. Henry Cecil, younger brother of Third Lord Amherst of Hackney, and Elizabeth Rohays Burnett of Leys, who married secondly Sir Cecil Boyd-Rochfort, racehorse trainer to HM The Queen.
Educated Canford and married, in October 1986, Julia (Julie) Murless (one son, one daughter), only child of the late Sir Noel

Murless, racehorse trainer to HM The Queen. In 1973, when his father-in-law retired, Henry bought his historic New-market stables, Warren Place, and has been champion trainer seven times – in 1989 his 220-horsepower stable won £2,584,254 in prize money. The week before Christmas 1989 he left Julie to move in down the road with lawyer's daughter Nathalie Payne, whom he had met in the spring at a party for his staff, and celebrated her twenty-third birthday with her on 23 December. Divorce proceedings have been started by Mrs Cecil, who now plans to become a trainer in her own right after helping her husband since he gained his licence in 1969.

CHAPMAN, (ANTHONY) COLIN (BRUCE), *born* 19 May 1928.
Founder of Lotus cars, winning six Formula One World Constructors Championships between 1963 and 1978. Bizarre rumours followed his death of a heart attack in December 1982 that it had been faked and he was living in South America, having undergone plastic surgery – spawned because of his involvement in manufacturing the ill-fated John De Lorean sports car in Belfast. $17.78 million, including $5.15 million of British taxpayers money, had disappeared in November 1978 into a Geneva bank account controlled by Chapman.

CHARTERIS, (FRANCES) LAURA, *born* 10 August 1915, widow of the Tenth Duke of Marlborough (q.v.).
Formerly the wife of the Second Viscount Long and later the Third Earl of Dudley, she married, in 1960, publisher Michael Canfield, but he died in 1969. He was believed by the Duke of Windsor to be the natural son of his brother Prince George, the Duke of Kent. In January 1972 she married 'Bert' Marlborough. After the honeymoon he was quizzed in White's about his sex life. 'No good, I'm afraid,' explained the Duke, 'Mr Mouse won't come out to play.' Six weeks later he was dead. Laura left £2,585,516 when she died in February 1990.

CHELSEA, Viscount, CHARLES GERALD JOHN CADOGAN, *born* 24 March 1937.
Only son and heir of the Seventh Earl Cadogan and owner of 100 acres of London SW1, SW3 and SW7, stretching from Sloane Street in the east to Old Church Street in the west. Appalled at business magazine estimates of his London estate being worth £450 million. First wife Philippa, daughter of the Ninth Earl of Portsmouth, died of a heart attack in September 1984 after driving back from Chester races where she saw her colt win a race by a neck. Six years earlier her BMW, in the boot of which was her jewellery case containing £250,000 worth of gems including her engagement ring, was stolen from the forecourt of a Hungerford garage while she left it to have the aerial mended and went shopping for ten minutes. The two thieves were arrested two years later and jailed for six and three years. A racehorse owner and member of the Jockey Club, Charles married the club's cook, Jenny Rae, thirty-two, in July 1989. He is also a former chairman of Chelsea Football Club. His son and heir Edward Cadogan, an RAF pilot officer, became engaged in April 1990 to Katherina Hulsemann, daughter of a German rear-admiral who was naval attaché at their Embassy in London.

CHOW, MICHAEL, *born* 1938.
Changed the perception of the Chinese restaurant when he opened Mr Chow in Knightsbridge in 1968 with Chinese kitchen staff, Italian *maitre d'* and waiters, and state of the art decor. Three other restaurants and a nightclub followed, with branches in Los Angeles and New York. Brother of 'The World of Suzie Wing' actress Tsai Chin – their father Zhou Xinfang was the most celebrated actor of the Peking Opera, who died in the sixties purge – Michael was married, for the second time, to former top model Grace Coddington, who became an editor of *Vogue*. He lives in New York, where two years ago he successfully sued a food guide critic for $20,000 over an unfavourable review of his 57th Street restaurant, and is

separated from his third wife, Japanese-born Tina Lutz, by whom he has a daughter and son.

Michael Chow

CHRISTIE, JULIE, *born* 14 April 1940.
Daughter of a tea planter in India where she was brought up, she won an Oscar, New York Film Critics Award and British Film Academy Award for her role in *Darling*, the 1964 film which belatedly launched the swinging sixties. For seven years the fiancée of Warren Beatty (often to be seen doing calisthenics in the garden of her Selwood Terrace, South Kensington home) until the affair ended in 1975. Formerly unofficially engaged to Maidstone art teacher Don Besant and involved since 1978, as much politically as romantically, with left-wing Scots journalist Duncan Campbell of *Time Out*.

CHURCHILL, WINSTON SPENCER, *born* 10 October 1940.
MP for Stretford, Lancashire 1970–83, for Davyhulme since 1983. Son of the late Randolph Churchill and the Hon. Pamela Digby, who inherited a £75 million fortune when her third husband, American banking heir Averell Harriman, died in 1986. Married Mary Caroline (Minnie) d'Erlanger, daughter of the former Chairman of BOAC, in 1964 (two sons and two daughters). She remained constant in the face of downmarket newspaper revelations by Soraya Khashoggi (q.v.) of a lengthy affair while he was the Conservative Party spokesman on Defence 1976–8. Minnie's father, Sir Gerard d'Erlanger, commented, 'She has forgiven him his dalliance completely and is 100 per cent behind him.'

Julie Christie, Don Besant (left) and John Schlesinger, 1966

CLEESE, JOHN MARWOOD, *born* 27 October 1939.
Co-authored 'Fawlty Towers' with his first wife, American actress Connie Booth, in which they both starred, although Prunella Scales played his screen wife in the classic British comedy series. They were divorced in 1978 after ten years (one daughter,

Cynthia) and he married American actress Barbara Trentham, who co-starred in the futuristic film **Rollerball**, in Los Angeles in 1981 (one daughter, Camilla). The marriage ended in divorce in May 1990 after Cleese said, 'Our eighteen-month separation has gone so well, we have decided to make it permanent.' He is not amused by claims from fellow pupils at Clifton, the Bristol public school, that he was John Cheese, not Cleese in those days. Founder and director of Video Arts Ltd., with Sir Anthony Jay, writer of 'Yes, Prime Minister', and Michael Peacock, former BBC2 Controller, which was sold to its own management a year ago for £50 million. Cleese, who collected £10 million, started the company in 1972 with an invest-ment of £1,000 to make training films, the first of which was **Who Sold You This Then?**, a gem about how not to deal with customers.

CLORE, Sir CHARLES, *born* 26 December 1904.
The son of an immigrant Whitechapel cobbler turned tailor, Clore became the take-over king of the fifties and sixties, starting his property empire with the purchase of the derelict Cricklewood skating rink and the Prince of Wales theatre. Eventually his Sears Holdings encompassed Selfridge's, most of the British shoe industry and William Hill bookmakers. In a bid for gentrification he bought Stype Grange, near Hungerford and learned to shoot, eventually securing an invi-tation to Blenheim from the Tenth Duke of Marlborough (q.v.). Clore took the pre-caution of taking his instructor, a director of Holland and Holland, to load for him and after the morning's drives, when the eight guns adjourned to a lodge for lunch, asked Bert Marlborough if he could bring his 'loader' with him. 'Good God, Clore,' expostulated the Duke. 'You've had a man teaching you to shoot all morning, now I suppose you want him to teach you how to eat.' Despite going into tax exile in Monte Carlo sixteen months before his death in July 1979, the Inland Revenue successfully con-tested his £123 million estate, leaving just £56 million to be shared between three charitable trusts in Jersey and Israel, admin-istered by his daughter Mrs Vivien Duffield, ex-wife of Old Harrovian financier John Duffield.

Charles Clore and Cathy McGowan, 1966

CLORE, ALAN, *born* April 1944.
Only son of the 1943 marriage of Charles Clore to French resistance heroine Françine Halphen, which was dissolved in 1957. Attended Le Rosey and Lincoln College, Oxford and inherited, with his younger sister Viven, £7 million trust fund. Went into tax exile in Switzerland in 1968 when the Labour Government suggested a top ceiling tax of 137 per cent (27s 3d in £1). In 1985 he gave a five-year legal battle to contest his father's will, from which he was excluded. Known as an 'all on' gambler, whereby all profits went on his next project, Clore once owned

350 racehorses and brood mares in training in France and England. A confirmed bachelor, he lives in Paris and was in the habit of conducting board meetings from the telephone beside his bed with Gulf Resources, the Texan company of which he used to be Chairman.

CLUFF, JOHN GORDON (ALGY), *born* 19 April 1940.

Educated at Stowe, the son of a Lancashire businessman, Cluff achieved the social breakthrough when he was commissioned into the Grenadier Guards and became friends with brother officers like Viscount Anson, the future Earl of Lichfield (q.v.). Captain in the SAS, he was invalided out with amoebic dysentery, stood as a Conservative candidate in Manchester in the 1966 general election and went into the oil exploration business in 1971, backed by the Duke of Marlborough and Lord Lambton (q.v.), among others. Regarded as a confirmed bachelor, he surprised his friends by forming a passion for the Duchess of Abercorn, to whom he was close for two years. In 1981 he bought the *Spectator* for £75,000, selling it four years later to the Australian Fairfax Group for £1.2 million. Briefly owned Brownsea Island in Poole Bay. Cluff Oil, now renamed Cluff Resources, has a profitable gold mining enterprise in Zimbabwe. He remains a batchelor.

COLERIDGE, NICHOLAS, *born* 4 March 1957.

Eton and Cambridge educated son of David Coleridge, the new Chairman of Lloyd's and Chairman of Sturge Holdings, a leading underwriting company. After editing *Harpers and Queen* for three and a half years, moved to Condé Nast in July 1989 to become Editorial Director of its rival, *Tatler*, and other Condé Nast publications, including *Vogue* and **GQ**. Ten months later he fired *Tatler*'s Editor, Emma Soames, who in February had published an offensive profile of the Duchess of York that had reduced her father, Major Ronald Ferguson (q.v.) to tears

with its four letter word content in descriptions of his daughter. Just before his move, Coleridge married journalist Georgia Metcalf, twenty-two, whom he had met before she went to Oxford, when she was otherwise involved. He followed her and her boyfriend to India, taking a suite in the Rambagh Palace Hotel in Jaipur where he knew they would be staying. Coleridge managed to lure Georgia off alone on a rickshaw ride during which he kissed her and said, 'One day you are going to marry me.' And lo, so it came to pass. . .

Nicholas Coleridge

COLLINS, CHRISTOPHER DOUGLAS, *born* 19 January 1940.

Educated at Eton, where he was mercilessly ribbed for being 6ft 2ins tall and very fat and became an amateur champion jockey, coming third in the 1965 Grand National and winning the Swedish Grand National twice and the Velka Pardubicka in Czechoslovakia, the world's toughest race, in 1973. The son of perfumier, Douglas Collins, who founded Goya and twice sold the company, making a seven-figure fortune on each occasion. He finally bought it back in 1968, when Chris was made Managing Director, relying on his nose (broken three times) to produce new scents which would be commercial. Briefly edited Sir William Pigott-Brown's (q.v.) magazine **Look of London** in the sixties, having passed out in the top five in the national chartered accountancy exams. Sold Goya to ICI in 1975. Elected to the Jockey Club in 1972 and helped save the Grand National when the developers threatened to sell Aintree. Became a wine merchant and now lives in Australia with his wife, three-day eventer Suzanne Lumb, a niece of Lord Hanson, their son Edward and daughter Lorna, giving up the chance to become Senior Steward of the Jockey Club.

COLLINS, JOSEPH, *born* 1 November 1902.
Son of a Whitechapel fishmonger called Isaac Hurt, who became a theatrical agent, and his dancer wife, Henrietta, one of nineteen children of an ice cream stall owner. Doyen of London's theatrical agents before his death in April 1989, whose books, when he started in the thirties, included **Lew Grade, a Champion Charleston Dancer**, he went on to launch the careers of Vera Lynne, Roger Moore, Shirley Bassey and Tom Jones. In 1950 he took a page in the Spotlight Casting Directory to launch his daughter Joan, then a seventeen-year-old drama student and within weeks she had her first film offer. His second daughter, Jackie, younger by five years, was placed as a stage presenter for 'Carroll Lewis and his Discoveries' (a talent-spotting show) and although she had a reasonably successful stage career, her ambition was to write. Joan went on to have four marriages, with a son and daughter by her second husband, Antony Newley, and a daughter by her third, the late Ron Kass, one-time record boss of the Beatles empire, and made an estimated $20 million after a career comeback in 'Dynasty'. Jackie has three daughters by her second husband,

American Oscar Lerman, a co-owner of the Jermyn Street club, Tramp, and they live in Los Angeles, where she writes steamy best sellers like **Hollywood Wives** and **Rock Star**. Joe also had a son, Bill, by his first wife, Elsa, and a daughter, Natasha, by his second wife, Irene. While Joan was prominent at her father's funeral in Golders Green, Jackie stayed away, citing 'business commitments'.

COLQUHOUN, ANDRINA, *born* 1952.
The last girlfriend of the Earl of Lucan (q.v.). She was waiting for him at the Clermont Club, where he had a dinner reservation for four, on the night in November 1974 when his children's nanny, Sandra Rivett, was murdered. He never showed up (fellow guests Greville Howard and his wife, Zoe, did) and has not been seen since a visit later that night to the Uckfield home of fellow gambler Ian Maxwell-Scott. Andy was formerly involved with Philippe Niarchos and in 1982 became the personal assistant of Jeffrey Archer (q.v.), organizing his social life. She left (with the gift of the personalized car number plate, ANY 1, on a blue BMW) when he was appointed Deputy Chairman of the Conservative Party in 1985, to become Deputy Director of the Boilerhouse design project at the Victoria and Albert Museum. In April 1990, she married Robert Waddington, a well-known golfing gambler at Sunningdale.

CONNERY, SEAN THOMAS, *born* 25 August 1930.
Married first Diane Cilento, daughter of Australian physician Sir Raphael Cilento (dissolved 1974), by whom he has a son Jason, and secondly French-Moroccan Micheline Roquebrune – they shared a love of golf. **Dr No**, in which he introduced James Bond, was his tenth film (previous ones included **Tarzan's Greatest Adventure**) and he won an Oscar for best supporting actor in **The Untouchables**. Worth an estimated £20 million, he sued successfully his former financial adviser Kenneth Richards in the High Court for the return of £2.8 million in 1984. But Lausanne-based Richards, who

claimed he had lent the money to a property developer without security, was unable to pay and died, a bankrupt, in 1989.

Jason, Micheline and Sean Connery

COOK, PETER EDWARD, *born* 17 November 1937.

With Dr Jonathan Miller, Alan Bennett and Dudley Moore (q.v.), was one of the comic geniuses behind *Beyond the Fringe*. Majority shareholder (sixty-eight per cent) of the satirical magazine *Private Eye*, his own private life is less than funny: his marriages, in 1964 to Wendy Snowden (two daughters) and in 1973 to former debutante Judy Huxtable, widow of stage designer Sean Kenny, have been dissolved. Last year he married Malaysian-born Lin Chong, his companion of seven years. Divorced herself, with a thirteen-year-old daughter, she is a canny theatrical investor who has made small fortunes from *Cats*, *Les Misérables* and *Phantom of the Opera*. Either a teetotaller or a heavy drinker, Cook lost his licence for twelve months in 1986 after crashing into a police car. He explained to the officers, 'It's my birthday.'

COOPER, JILLY, *born* 21 February 1937, wife of publisher Leo Cooper, who became 'detentacled' from Octopus Publishing this year when they decided his military imprint was not for them.

Their thirty-year marriage (an adopted son and daughter) has been infused with all the drama of one of Jilly's thirty-six books – the first was *How to Stay Married* – not least when she discovered a year ago that Leo was being pursued by a female colleague. 'There was someone else, but the idea of us splitting up is ridiculous,' says Leo, who cheerfully admits he has read none of his wife's fiction. Living in a thirteenth-century house near Stroud, Gloucestershire, Jilly says of the female characters in her romantic novels, 'Leo is the hero of them all, with blonder hair, twenty years younger, but it's always Leo, the greatest love affair of all time.'

Judy Huxtable, Peter Cook and Dudley Moore, 1971

Jilly Cooper

CORDET, HÉLÈNE (née Founounis), *born c.* 1920.

Cabaret singer and presenter of an early fifties TV show, 'Café Continental'. Achieved social prominence through a close friendship, dating from childhood, with Prince Philip. He was best man at her wedding and became godfather to her children, Max and Louise Boisot (their father, Marcel, was a French Officer), who were invited to watch the Coronation from the Buckingham Palace balcony. Now an economics professor in Peking, Max felt impelled to make a statement in 1988 denying that the Prince was his father. In 1961 Hélène opened London's first discotheque, the Saddle Room, in Hamilton Place, Mayfair opposite Les Ambassadeurs. She now lives in Switzerland.

CORNFELD, BERNIE, *born* 1928.

Asking the searing question 'Do You Sincerely Want To Be Rich?', Brooklyn-born

Helene Cordet, 1955

Bernie moved into No.1 West Halkin Street, Belgravia, and unleashed hundreds of unprincipled life insurance salesmen on an unsuspecting European public (GI's in Germany were especially targeted) and by 1970 his Swiss-based company IOS (Investors Overseas Service) had raked in £1,000 million – at which point the pyramid collapsed. Cornfeld, whose harem included teenage actress, later to be 'Dallas' star, Victoria Principal (he paid for her nose job) spent eleven months in a Swiss jail in 1979 before fraud charges were dropped and he moved to a thirty-seven-room mansion in Los Angeles (once the home of Douglas Fairbanks) with his wife, American model Lorraine Armbruster, by whom he has a fourteen-year-old daughter, Jessica. He is now based mostly in Europe, where he has a home in Paris and a twelfth-century château near Geneva with 200 acres on which he plans to build a golf course and medieval village. One of his most recent business ventures: a potency pill.

CORNWELL, DAVID JOHN MOORE, *born* 19 October 1931, (John le Carré).

Lasted just three years at Sherborne, the Dorset public school which he says he hated, before going on to Berne University and Oxford to study languages. He then entered the Foreign Office, where he worked for MI6, quitting in 1964 after the international success of his third novel, ***The Spy Who Came In From The Cold***. Took the *nom de plume* because Foreign Office rules forbade officers to publish under their own name. Three sons by his first wife, Alison, and one by second, Valerie. Brought up in Bournemouth, where his father was a solicitor who went to jail for financial impropriety.

Bernie Cornfeld

His half-sister is actress Charlotte Cornwell (born 1950), who has an eight-year-old daughter, Nancy, by Kenneth Cranham, former husband of Diana Quick. She made history by suing **Sunday People** journalist, Nina Myskow, for libel over comments about her performance in the 'No Excuses' television series. After being awarded £10,000 over the slur, which stated that her 'bum was too big', the decision was overturned on appeal. When the case was heard again in 1987 she was awarded £11,500, but faced costs estimated at £50,000. She is now writing a book about libel and the law.

COWDRAY, Third Viscount, WEETMAN JOHN CHURCHILL PEARSON, *born* 27 February 1910.
Grandson of the Victorian entrepreneur known as the MP for Mexico (where he made a fortune) who was MP for Colchester from 1895–1910. With his family, speaks for around twenty per cent of the £2 billion Pearson conglomerate which owns the **Financial Times**, Westminster Press provincial newspapers (Chairman, his nephew, the Duke of Atholl), Penguin Books, Royal Doulton China, Lazards bank and Madame Tussauds, Warwick Castle, Alton Towers and Chessington Zoo. After losing an arm in a wartime accident, singlehandedly engineered the revival of British polo at Cowdray Park, his 17,000-acre Sussex estate, which has been left to his elder son and heir, Michael Pearson (q.v). By his second marriage, John Cowdray has a son, Charles, who has been left Dunecht, his 60,000-acre Aberdeenshire estate. Daughter Lucy was married to Luis Sosa Basualdo (q.v.) and her younger sister, Rosie, formerly a journalist on **The Economist**, wed Rastafarian reggae musician Palma Taylor two years ago. She gave birth to a daughter, Annie Glennah, in April 1990 in Montego Bay, Jamaica, where she now lives.

COWLES, FLEUR, (Mrs Tom Montague Meyer), *born c.* 1912.
The quintessential London hostess with trademark shaded glasses, who has lived for thirty-five years at Albany, the eighteenth-century chambers set back from Piccadilly and running up to the beginning of Savile Row, but who also spends time at a sixteenth-century Sussex house and a tenth-century Spanish finca. Represented President Eisenhower at the Queen's Coronation and returned to live here permanently when she married Tom Montague Meyer, head of the family timber firm. She was previously married to Gardner Cowles, who owned **Look** magazine, (the longtime rival of **Life**) and her drawing-room photographs show her range of friends – Ron and Nancy Reagan, Prince Rainier and Princess Grace of Monaco, several popes. A writer and artist – thirty or so one-man exhibitions – she once disturbed the cloistered peace of Albany when dinner guest Judy Garland literally sang for her supper. A uniformed porter in top hat banged on the door and demanded she cease. 'Stop? Anywhere else I'd get $10,000 for doing this,' replied Miss Garland.

CREER, ERICE, *born* 1948.
Model and photographer, whose parents bred budgerigars in Maidenhead. A much sought after doll – lengthy affairs with John Barry, composer of the James Bond theme and winner of two Oscars for his movie music; Albert Finney, Mark Birley (q.v.), and American film director Richard Moore. Owned the Kissing Tree House, the former home of J. B. Priestley, and thirty-one acres near Stratford upon Avon, which she sold to a development company in February 1989 for £1.2 million. Never married, she has a six-year-old son by a secret liaison with a leading City banker, and a daughter by an undischarged bankrupt, an order for whose eviction from Kissing Tree she obtained from the High Court in April 1989.

CREWE, QUENTIN HUGH, *born* 14 November 1926.
The elder son of Major Hugh Dodds, whose wife, Lady Annabel, was the heiress elder daughter of the first and last Marquess of

Crewe. After Eton, changed name by deed poll to inherit his grandfather's estate, prompting the doggerel, 'How odd of Dodds to choose the Crewes.' Three marriages, all dissolved, and five children, including a daughter, Candida, by his second wife, author and playwright, Angela Huth. Briefly the gossip columnist for the *Daily Mail* (using the pseudonym Paul Tanfield), a columnist for the *Sunday Mirror* and contributor to *Queen*, where he was original restaurant critic, *Vogue*, the *Sunday Times* and *Sunday Telegraph*. Confined to a wheelchair with muscular dystrophy since 1962, he has become an intrepid traveller, spending eighteen months, driving 25,000 miles, researching *In Search of the Sahara*, during which time he was blown up by a landmine. Other journeys for books have been to India (*The Last Maharajah*), through the Caribbean (*Touch the Happy Isles*) and the ten South American countries (*In the Realms of Gold*). A founding partner in the Knightsbridge group of St Quentin restaurants and patisseries, he now lives in France.

CURZON, Lady MARY GAYE GEORGINA LORNA, *born* 21 February 1947, and **Lady** CHARLOTTE ELIZABETH ANNE, *born* 5 July 1948.
The pulchritudinous heiress daughters of the late Sixth Earl Howe, a former motor-racing driver, by his second wife, South African-born Grace Lilian Wakeling, who were brought up in splendour at Penn House, set in 1,500 Buckinghamshire acres. Mary Gaye was first married to Esmond Cooper-Key, the son of Viscount Rothermere's sister Lorna, (one daughter), then to baronet's son John Anstruther-Gough-Calthorpe (one son, two daughters), whose family own the choicer bits of Birmingham, and now to Old Harrovian Jeffrey Bonas (one daughter). Charlotte, after lengthy liaisons with Charles Benson (q.v.), Rupert Deen (q.v.), car-trader George Wright, a minor gangster who died mysteriously in the Knightsbridge flat of the Duke of Bedford's son Lord Rudolph Russell, and the late powerboat racer Michael

Doxford, married born-again Christian Barry Dinan (one son). The title passed to Howe's cousin, Richard Curzon, a bank manager.

D*d*

D'ABO, MICHAEL, *born* 1944.
The son of a city stockbroker, he was educated at Harrow, where he formed the school's first rock band, The Band of Angels, which continued to perform with modest success at debutante parties until it broke up in April 1966. Three months later the Manfred Mann pop group lost their lead singer, Paul Jones, and d'Abo became the replacement, singing the hits 'Mighty Quinn' and 'Fox on the Run' among others. In December he married model Maggie London and their daughter, Olivia, twenty-one, is an actress who works in Hollywood (actress Maryam d'Abo is a cousin). D'Abo became a songwriter and moved to America in 1977, divorced and married again, and formed a new group, Mike d'Abo and his Mighty Quintet, in 1988. He is now a radio show host in Gloucestershire.

DAHL, ROALD, *born* 13 September 1916.
The world's highest paid writer of children's stories and *Tales of the Unexpected*, who told his wife Patricia Neal (Oscar for *Hud*, 1963) that he had been having an affair with her best friend, Felicity Crosland, for nearly twenty years. They divorced in 1983, and Dahl married 'Lissie', as he calls her. During their thirty-year marriage, their daughter Olivia died, aged seven, of measles, only son Theo was brain-damaged after his pram was run over in New York by a taxi and, in 1956, Pat almost died of an aneurism that led to two massive strokes from which doctors did not expect her to survive – Dahl patiently nursed her back to health. Dahl is closest to their eldest daughter Tessa, who lives in her

Roald Dahl and daughter, Tessa

mother's Martha's Vineyard, Massachusetts house and has written several books. She has a daughter by a liaison with actor Julian Holloway and a son by her marriage (dissolved 1988) to Bostonian James Kelly, head of an international magazine consultancy.

DASHWOOD, Sir Francis John Vernon Hereward, **eleventh baronet,** *born* 7 August 1925, and Premier Baronet of Great Britain.

Owner of West Wycombe Park, 4,000 acres and the legacy of the Hellfire Club, made notorious by his eighteenth-century ancestor, also Sir Francis. Arguably the most successful agent for names at Lloyd's, where he has been an underwriting member since 1956. First wife Victoria (one son, three daughters) died in 1976 and a year later he married Italian Marcella Scarafia.

DAVIES, David, *born* 1 April 1940.

Winchester and Oxford educated banker whose women, coincidentally, have all been wealthy. After taking a course at Chase Manhattan in New York he married banking heiress Debbie Loeb (one son) in 1967. After they separated, Princess Margaret's lady-in-waiting, Jane Stevens, left her husband Jocelyn for Davies, in anticipation of a marriage that did not happen. Instead he bought her a Chelsea apartment. There was a brief fling with Sir Charles Clore's daughter, Vivien (now with Jocelyn Stevens, q.v.) and he has a seven-year-old daughter by Amanda Denman, whose grandfather was a Hong Kong Taiping. In 1985 he married Linda Wong, eldest child of a Malaysian multimillionaire, with three wedding receptions costing an estimated £500,000, and they have a daughter, Alissa. Former Chairman of Hill Samuel, which he sold to TSB, and now head of Johnson Matthey, the metals processing and marketing group. He inherited a County Wicklow estate from his father, Kenneth (who had a rope manufacturing business in Wales) and maintains a home in Hong Kong, where he spent three years rescuing the Hong Kong Land Co., a subsidiary of Jardine Matheson.

DAVIS, Sir John Henry Harris, *born* 10 November 1906.

The ruthless former Chairman of the Rank Organization, where he was kept in power by the shareholding of the charitable trusts of the late Lord Rank. Sacked so many members of senior management that they formed a club, calling themselves 'The Rank Outsiders'. Married six times, he was famously depicted on a cover of *Private Eye*, in a Scarfe cartoon, wearing a girdle and suspenders and wielding a whip after the satirical magazine discovered details of his divorce on the grounds of his cruelty from his fifth wife, actress Dinah Sheridan (1954–65). Now married to former public relations officer Felicity Rutland (whose coming-out dance was attended by the Duke of Kent), thirty-two years his junior, they live in a South Kensington terrace, three doors away from Lady Sarah Armstrong-Jones and he goes to work every morning as Director of the Rank Foundation and writes his memoirs. Sold his Crowhurst, Sussex estate to Adam Faith.

DAWSON, Sir Hugh Halliday Trevor, **third baronet,** *born* 6 June 1931.

A lofty (6ft 4ins tall) former Scots Guards officer known as the 'Galloping Major', who was a close friend of, and gambling mentor to, Sir Hugh Fraser (q.v.) who inherited the Harrods empire. Although married (in 1955 to Caroline Acton), Dawson was always to be found, wearing a white suit, in London's West End clubs and restaurants escorting pretty young women (such as debutantes Sybilla Edmonstone, q.v., and Venetia Cunninghame), being chauffeur driven in a Cadillac with a TD 1 number plate. In September 1981 he was forced to resign from merchant bankers Arbuthnot Latham, where he was investment chief, after he took personal advantage to funnel £350,000 share profits into private accounts, rather than to put the transactions down to bank clients. Despite committing suicide in 1983, his insurance policies paid out £137,000 to his wife because their twenty-six-year old spastic son might not be cared for. His sister, Pat, is married to John Menzies, Chairman of the eponymous newsagents chain of high-street shops.

DAY, Sir Robin, *born* 24th October 1923.
High-profile President of the Oxford Union 1950, barrister and broadcaster who, after a distinguished career spanning thirty-seven years with the BBC and ITV, is giving credibility to the new satellite station, BSB, with a weekly hour-long programme. Married Australian Katherine Ainslie, in 1965 (two sons) and divorced in 1986 after a lengthy separation. Among his dates since has been Australian Ainsley Gotto, who, in 1969, when she was secretary to Australia's Premier John Gorton, became a public figure when Dudley Erwin, sacked as Air Minister, claimed he was a victim of a political manoeuvre. Asked to describe the manoeuvre he replied, 'It wiggles, it's shapely and its name is Ainsley Gotto'. In 1981, after moving to London, she was signed by Granada TV as a reporter and presenter. Author of a best-selling autobiography, Day remains a bachelor and his children, who live with their mother in Perth, Western Australia, make annual visits.

DE BENDERN, Count John Gerard, *born* 1907.
Younger son of Baron Maurice de Forest, adopted son of Austrian Baron Hirsch, the vastly rich financier to King Edward VII. In 1932, after resigning as Liberal MP for West Ham, he relinquished his British citizenship and moved to Liechtenstein, taking the title of de Bendern. Educated at Eton, John won the British Amateur Golf Championship at Muirfield in 1932. When he became engaged to Lady Patricia Douglas, elder daughter of the Eleventh Marquess of Queensberry, he was told by his prospective father-in-law, 'Your family is mad, mine is barking, God help the children.' There was a son and two daughters by that marriage, a son by his second wife, Spanish beauty Mercedes Gorina, and a daughter by his third, Barbara

Allen, a Clapham hairdresser. When his father died in October 1968 in Biarritz, only £10 million of his fortune could be traced. John, who had been estranged from his father and left virtually penniless until his inheritance, walked into White's, went to the bar and ordered a bottle of Krug, the most expensive champagne. He was told that the club had run out. 'Twenty years I've been waiting to touch it, and the Krug's off,' he wailed.

DEEN, Rupert, *born* 24 November 1938.
Harrow-educated member of the Wright, Deen underwriting family, an underwriting member of Lloyd's and agent for names. The subject of various television documentaries, in which he is given to making inflammatory right-wing statements such as, 'a labrador is bred to retrieve pheasants and Welshmen are born to go down mines.' Once worked in The Room at Lloyd's, but for the last thirty years has lived the life of a gentleman of leisure without the means – gone are Harry, his chauffeur-cum-valet, the Bentley, the annual Royal Ascot party he used to host on the Wednesday of the royal meeting, and the chartered yacht for the Monaco grand prix. A bachelor, he was 'engaged' to Lady Charlotte Curzon (q.v.) for a decade, during which time she was involved with other men. 'I'm just lending her,' Deen, nicknamed 'The Poodlefaker', would explain.

DE FERRANTI, Sebastian Basil Joseph Ziani, *born* 5 October 1927, married 1953 (dissolved 1982) Mona Cunningham (one son, two daughters), secondly, in 1982, Naomi Rae.
Built, at an estimated cost of £5 million, Henbury Hall near Macclesfield, a version of the sixteenth-century Villa Capra by Palladio, known as Le Rotunday. Quinlan Terry, the original architect, was replaced by Julian Bicknell, whose design was based on a painting by Felix Kelly. Resigned abruptly as Chairman of the family company in 1982 after nineteen years and voted, as head of family trusts, against the 1987 takeover by

Ferranti of the American International Signal and Control, in which a £215 million fraud by its previous owner, James Guerin, was discovered in 1989. Younger brother, Basil Reginald Vincent Ziani de Ferranti, born 2 July 1930 (died 1988) was Chairman of Ferranti 1982–7, and Euro MP for Hampshire Central from 1984. Married first, in 1956, Susan Gore (three sons), secondly, in 1964, Simone Nangle and thirdly, 1971, Hilary Laing, former British ski champion and one-time love of Sir Max Aitken (q.v.) and Tommy Sopwith (q.v.).

DENBIGH, Eleventh Earl of, WILLIAM RUDOLPH MICHAEL FEILDING, also Tenth Earl of Desmond, *born* 2 August 1943.
Known as 'Rollo', he was among the first of the motorbiking peers (along with Lord Eliot, q.v.). One of his forebears was Henry Fielding, eighteenth-century barrister and journalist who wrote **Tom Jones**. Inherited a 2,000-acre Warwickshire estate near Rugby and threatened to emigrate to New Zealand with his wife Judy, their son and two daughters, in 1978, because his trustees were being less than generous. New Zealand immigration authorities turned down his application, saying that being an earl was not a category they sought, but there was a dearth of plumbers.

DERBY, Nineteenth Earl of, EDWARD JOHN STANLEY, *born* 21 April 1918.
Married, 22 July 1948, Lady Isabel Milles-Lade, sister of the Fourth Earl Sondes (no children). Direct descendant of the Twelfth Earl, who gave the family name to Britain's premier horse race (Disraeli called it the Blue Riband of the turf) when he won the toss in 1784 against baronet Sir Charles Bunbury as to what the one-and-a-half-mile race should be called. In 1952 the couple were involved in a much-publicized incident at Knowsley, the Stanley family seat near Prescot, Lancashire, when a trainee footman, nineteen-year-old Harold Winstanley, went beserk with a Schmeisser gun (apparently acquired with ammunition for £3 and a pair of trousers).

On the evening of 6 November, Winstanley, smoking a cigarette, entered the smoking room from the library to find Lady Derby dining alone. Taken by surprise, she rose to face him and noticed that he was holding a sub-machine gun, which was pointing directly at her. He told her to turn round and then shot her in the neck, the bullet coming out just below her left ear. Leaving her for dead, he then fired a further thirty-six shots, killing the butler, under-butler and wounding Lord Derby's valet and the French chef. Winstanley was found guilty of murder but insane and the case caused a sensation, not least because it made public the amplitude of servants in the Derbys' employ in austere, post-war Britain. The Prime Minister, Winston Churchill, is said to have remarked, 'It's nice to hear of a house where you can still get a left and a right at a butler.' Lady Derby died in March 1990.

DE SAVARY, PETER, *born* 11 July 1944.
Claims to be descended from one of Napoleon's generals. Educated at Charterhouse, from where he was expelled at the age of sixteen for interfering with a maid. An entrepreneur who is revered for having got a £25 million interest-free loan from Blue Arrow, the beleaguered employment agency company where his friend Tony Berry was Chairman (the company has written off the investment, which was earmarked for the proposed development of Canvey Island). After a rocky start, made his first fortune in Africa and then the Middle East, before basing himself in the Bahamas with Karen Hanson, stepdaughter of Lord Hanson, who introduced him to the finer things in life, including Savile Row suits and Turnbull and Asser shirts and ties. Mounted Britain's challenge for the America's cup in 1983 (Australia won) and now puts his own worth in excess of £75 million. Owns Littlecote near Hungerford, which is open to the public, Land's End and John O'Groats. Had a brainstorm in 1985 when he dumped his longstanding American fiancée, Lana Paton, and married his secretary, Alice Simms, in Gibraltar. Six

Peter and Lana de Savary

weeks later he left Alice and returned to Lana and, after a divorce, they wed in 1986 and have two daughters. He also had two daughters by his first wife Marcia, a sculptress, who is now married to Sir John Astor, younger brother of the late Viscount Astor (q.v.).

DE SOLA, RAPHAEL, *born* 1903.

Always to be found extravagantly dressed at events like the Derby, Royal Ascot and Cowes (he was a member of sixteen yacht clubs), his only claim to fame was that his sister Esther, a talented artist, married shipping heir Sir John Ellerman, a recluse who was not photographed for fifty years. De Sola acted as agent for his deeply shy brother-in-law (to whom he once gave a baby elephant as a birthday present) and celebrated his fifty-sixth birthday by riding in full hunting costume on a carousel in Ryde, Isle of Wight. He sailed his own boat to Dunkirk to rescue the British expeditionary force, exquisitely attired in the uniform of the Royal London Yacht Club. Canadian-born and a lifelong bachelor, he died in 1989.

DETERDING, OLGA, *born* August 1928, the daughter of Sir Henri Deterding, a co-founder of Royal Dutch Shell who died when she was nine, leaving £2 million.
Captured the imagination of society when she went to Lambarene in 1959 to work for

Professor Albert Schweitzer, as an unpaid nurse, in his leper colony. She returned and fell in love with Alan Whicker, whom she accompanied on his worldwide TV travels, becoming engaged to him in Monte Carlo in 1966. Four years later she fell in love with Jonathan Routh, the prankster star of ITV's 'Candid Camera', who would seduce her only (her BO was famous) after immersing her in a bath of Dettol in her duplex Piccadilly apartment overlooking Green Park. They split up after five years. Before she died, on New Year's Eve 1978 (choking on a large piece of steak on the stroke of midnight), she achieved publicity in making bids for newspapers – £5 million for the **Observer** in 1976 and unspecified amounts for **The Times** and the London **Evening Standard**. Six months before her death she was banned from Langan's Brasserie, her local restaurant, for being sick over the proprietor, Peter Langan (q.v.), and using the men's urinals.

Jonathan Routh with Olga Deterding, 1970

DEVONSHIRE, Eleventh Duke of, ANDREW ROBERT BUXTON CAVENDISH, *born* 2 January 1920.

Married 19 April 1941, the Hon. Deborah Freeman-Mitford, youngest daughter of Second Lord Redesdale and sister of writer Nancy (**The Pursuit of Love**), Pamela, Diana (who married Sir Oswald Mosley), Unity (friend of Hitler) and author of Jessica (**Hons and Rebels**, **The American Way of Death**). Their son Peregrine Andrew Morny, Marquess of Hartington, is the Senior Steward of the Jockey Club and will succeed Sir Piers Bengough as Her Majesty's Representative at Royal Ascot. Owner of Pratt's, the St James's club that is only open in the evenings, Andrew Devonshire inherited Chatsworth, Britain's finest treasure-laden stately home, with 38,000 Derbyshire acres, 30,000 acres of Yorkshire and 1,200 acres around Eastborne and has sold £31 million of drawings and Old Master prints to provide for the future of the mansion, built for the First Duke between 1687 and 1707 by William Talman. A noted ladies man (he once shared a mistress with his close friend, Newmarket trainer Bernard van Cutsem), he bravely gave evidence in 1985, when the son of his butler was accused of stealing three cheques worth £150,000 and was cross-examined about his women. The younger son of the Tenth Duke, his elder brother, William John Robert, Marquess of Hartington, who married the daughter of Joseph Kennedy (and sister of President John F.) in May 1944, was killed by a sniper in Belgium four months later.

DEXTER, EDWARD RALPH (TED), *born* 15 May 1935.
As good a golfer as cricketer (he has been round Sunningdale in sixty-three), who was captain of Sussex 1958–68 and England, 1962–5. Married fashion model Susan Long-field in 1959 (one son, one daughter). She once broke his leg, running him over in her car when she reversed by mistake. Now the first ever salaried Chairman of the England cricket selectors (£20,000 a year).

DIMBLEBY, DAVID, *born* 28 October 1938, broadcaster and newspaper proprietor. Inherited the **Richmond and Twickenham**

Times from his late father, Richard (in whose television footsteps he and his brother Jonathan have followed). In 1967, married Josceline Rose Gaskell (one son, two daughters), Cookery Editor of the **Sunday Telegraph** and author whose first book, *A Taste of Dreams*, was published in 1976. Weekend cottage in Dittisham, Devon, where tranquillity is being threatened by a playground development close to the front garden.

DI PORTANOVA, Baron ENRICO, *born* 1928.

Educated Hollywood High School. Married first, 1963 (dissolved 1972), Yugoslav actress Ljubica, secondly, 1975, Sandra Hovas, Houston stores heiress. In 1968 inherited £7.8 million from his Texan grandfather Hugh Roy Cullen, founder of a Quintana Petroleum Company, which he invested in oil, making a further fortune. In 1983 he sued for a greater share – Quintana, which also owns the Cullen Centre in Houston, was making profits of £300 million a year – after claiming that he and his brother, Ugo, had been cut out because Cullen disapproved of his daughter marrying Paolo di Portanova, a Neapolitan of dubious aristocratic ancestry. 'Ricky' di Portanova's Acapulco mansion has thirty-two bedrooms, twenty-six bathrooms, five kitchens, three swimming pools and two indoor waterfalls. It can seat 1,000 for dinner. The couple spend their summers in a second floor suite at Claridge's, where they used to entertain Prince and Princess Michael of Kent, flying the couple around Europe in their private jet. But in June 1981, following the birth of Princess Gabriella Windsor, the di Portanovas arrived for the Royal christening only to find that Buckingham Palace had crossed their names off the invitation list. They crossed the Kents off their invitation list.

DOCKER, Sir BERNARD DUDLEY FRANK, *born* 1896.

Educated at Harrow, in 1949 he married Norah Turner (one of four children of a car salesman, and born in a flat above a butcher's

Lady Docker

shop in Derby), the widow of Sir William Collins, the head of Cerbos Salt and Fortnum and Mason, who was twenty-nine years her senior. Norah, whose mother ran a public house in Birmingham, became a dancing partner in the Café de Paris in London, where she met her first husband, Clement Callingham, Chairman of Henekey's, the wine and spirit merchants, and was cited in his divorce (because of which she was later banned from the Royal Enclosure at Ascot). They had a son, Lance, who was educated at Harrow. With Sir Bernard, who was a senior director of Midland Bank and Chairman of BSA, which made Daimler cars among other products, she was an early example of conspicuous consumption, suggesting the Daimler that was to appear in the 1951 motor show be covered in gold leaf because there was a chrome shortage. Docker owned the 863-ton yacht *Shemara*, on which they cruised the Mediterranean, but in 1958 they were banned from Monte Carlo and, by treaty, the rest of the Côte d'Azur after she tore up a small Monaco flag in the casino nightclub because she could not take Lance to the christening of Princess Caroline. Sir Bernard was sacked by BSA in 1956 after bills were produced showing Norah had spent £7,910 on dresses for the Paris motor show, and the couple moved into tax exile in Jersey, later going to live in Majorca after she called the Jersey people, 'The most frightfully boring, dreadful people that have ever been born' – she had been banned from a St Aubin pub and restaurant for insulting busty cabaret star Yana, the owner's wife. Sir Bernard died in 1978 and Norah five years later.

DONOVAN, TERENCE, *born* 1937.

Son of a lorry driver and a Woolworth's manageress who became a leading fashion photographer and commercials director. A judo fanatic (fifty-two-inch chest, twenty-inch collar), he has three children by his second marriage to former debutante Diana St Felix Dare, whose family owned plantations in British Guiana. She is a tennis partner of the Princess of Wales at the Vanderbilt Club. His son Dan, by his first wife, a Sussex schoolteacher, is a musician.

DORS, DIANA, *born* 1932.

Real name, Diana Fluck. Trained at a stage school, made her film debut at the age of fifteen and by the early fifties was being hailed as Britain's answer to Marilyn Monroe. At twenty-one she was one of the best-known faces and figures in the country, with a Chelsea flat, Rolls Royce and earnings of £12,000 a year. Her first husband was the Svengali-like property tycoon Dennis Hamilton at whose riverside home in Maidenhead Hollywood-esque orgies (two-way mirrors, strip poker) took place, which shocked a prurient Britain still experiencing post-war austerity. He died of syphilis in 1959 having mismanaged her affairs and in 1968 she was declared bankrupt, owing £53,000, most of it to the Inland Revenue. With her second husband, comedian Dickie Dawson, she moved to Los Angeles and made several films, including a starring role opposite Jerry Lewis. The couple had two sons before the marriage ended in 1967 after she had a romance with Rod Steiger. A year later she married actor Alan Lake and had a son, Jason. Six months after her death from cancer, Lake shot himself on the seventeenth anniversary of the day they met.

DOUGLAS-HOME, (CECIL) ROBIN, *born* 8 May 1932, elder son of ornithologist Henry Douglas-Home, brother of the Fourteenth Earl of Home (former Prime Minister, Sir Alex Douglas-Home).

Married 1959 (divorced 1964) model Sandra Paul (now the wife of Michael Howard, the Secretary of State for Employment) and their son Sholto was heir-presumptive to the title. In 1958 it was generally expected that Douglas-Home, who worked as the pianist in the Berkeley Hotel cocktail lounge, would announce his engagement to Princess Margaretha of Sweden (now Mrs John Ambler, q.v.) but her grandfather, King Gustav Adolf, banned the union. A freelance journalist and photographer, his first book, **Hot For Certainties**, was published in 1964, but lasting success eluded him and he was back playing the piano two years later in the Society restaurant (now the discotheque Tramp). In 1967 John Aspinall gave him a job, playing at the Clermont Club for three evenings a week at £15 a night, but he was sacked after a photograph of Aspinall cavorting in his swimming pool with a Siberian tiger found its way into the William Hickey column of the **Daily Express**. Douglas-Home died of a drugs overdose in October 1968 in his cottage in West Chiltington, Sussex. His younger brother, Charles, Editor of **The Times**, died in 1985.

DOURO, Marquess of, ARTHUR CHARLES VALERIAN WELLESLEY, *born* 19 August 1945, heir of the Eighth Duke of Wellington.

In his own right, is the Duke of Cuidad Rodrigo and a Grandee (First Class) in Spain, where he owns an estate near Granada (a gift to his ancestor, the Iron Duke, for chasing

Diana Dors

Napoleon out of the Iberian peninsula). He has been host there to the Prince of Wales, a one-time escort to his only sister, Lady Jane Wellesley. Married to Guinness heiress Princess Antonia of Prussia, whose father, Prince Friedrich (grandson of Kaiser Bill), committed suicide in 1966 by jumping into the Rhine when his wife, the former Lady Brigid Guinness, left him. Charlie Douro, whose former girlfriends include actresses Gayle Hunnicutt (Mrs Simon Jenkins) and Alexandra Bastedo (Mrs Patrick Garland) as well as Lady Leonora Grosvenor (the Countess of Lichfield), was Euro MP for Surrey 1979–89, resigning because he wanted to spend more time with his family – a son and two daughters. The gifted Antonia, who is close to the Princess of Wales, caused Peter Schaufuss to be sacked as Artistic Director of the English National Ballet because he supported her to become Chairman rather than Pamela, Lady Harlech (q.v.), who was eventually elected in January 1990.

DRUMMOND, GEORGE ALBERT HARLEY, *born* 1943, son of a banker who sold the family business, founded 1717, to the Royal Bank of Scotland (it is now their Drummond's branch on the corner of Whitehall and Trafalgar Square, incorporating Britain's first drive-in window).
Godson of King George VI and educated at Gordonstoun, Drummond flashed through the sixties in a series of expensive cars – a Lamborghini Muira, Ferrari, Cadillac Eldorado – and backed a film project, *La Motorciclette*, to star Alain Delon and Marianne Faithfull. His racing team had the Earl of Denbigh (q.v.) among its drivers and it was he who offered to stand bail when Drummond was arrested for dishonestly handling £41,000 of stolen travellers cheques – in May 1971 he was sentenced at the Old Bailey to four years in jail. Known as 'The Ferret', he married Rachel Manley, daughter of the Prime Minister of Jamaica, in 1970, and they have a son, Drum. That marriage ended in divorce and he moved to Barbados, where his mother owned a plantation house in the

middle of the island, marrying again when he met a girl called Debbie from the Midlands, who was on a package tour.

DUDLEY, Fourth Earl of, WILLIAM HUMBLE DAVID WARD, *born* 5 January 1920, married in 1961, as his second wife, actress Maureen Swanson (one son, five daughters), a graduate of the Royal Ballet School whose break came playing the juvenile lead in *Carousel* at the Theatre Royal, Drury Lane. Given a Rank contract, she starred in five films, including *The Spanish Gardener* opposite Dirk Bogarde, and was once offered a contract by Howard Hughes when he owned RKO Pictures. Known as 'Little Mo', her close friendship with Michael of Kent ended after a trip to Washington in 1986, where she acted as unofficial lady-in-waiting, and an argument which involved Senator John Warner (a husband of Elizabeth Taylor). This led Billy Dudley to pen a wicked poem about the Princess, which he would render at social gatherings causing, it was said, Princess Margaret to fall off her chair with laughter when she heard it. The poem became the subject of legal proceedings and a private, written apology from Dudley to the Princess. There was a brief estrangement between the Dudleys two years ago when Maureen moved to San Francisco to be near her friend, Paul Miller. But spurred on by the fact that Dudley had made over both his houses (in Kensington and Devon) to his wife, she returned.

DUFFERIN AND AVA, MAUREEN, **Marchioness of,** *born* 31 January 1907, one of the three daughters of Arthur Guinness, younger son of the First Earl of Iveagh.
Married the Fourth Marquess of Dufferin and Ava (who was killed in action in Burma in March 1945) and they had a son, Sheridan (q.v.) and two daughters, Caroline and Perdita. In 1955 she married Judge John Maude, but announced she preferred to be addressed by her title (he died in 1986). At one stage she spoke for family trusts that controlled eight million shares in Guinness

Countess of Dudley (Maureen Swanson) with Stephen Ward, 1954

and made over her own trusts to her three children to be tax-effective. But by 1989 she was receiving income from her trust of just £1,700 a year and was not mentioned in the £15 million will of her son. She resorted to selling her old clothes at auction and was confined to the third-floor bedroom of her Knightsbridge house because she could not afford £40,000 for the installation of a lift – she has a permanent injury to her right ankle.

DUFFERIN AND AVA, Fifth Marquess of, SHERIDAN FREDERICK TERENCE, *born* 9 July 1938.

Married his distant cousin Serena Belinda Rosemary (Lindy) Guinness, a painter, in October 1964 (no children), to whom he left his £15 million fortune when he died, of Aids, in May 1988. Inherited Clandeboye, a 3,000-acre Irish estate in County Down, and was a leading figure in the London art world, a close friend of gallery owner Kasmin with whom he opened a Bond Street gallery in 1961, and a trustee of the Wallace Collection and the National Gallery. He also made successful films about Liberace and Playboy founder Hugh Hefner, backed a film about the death of St Sebastian in which the Roman Catholic martyr was portrayed as a homosexual. He was a Real Tennis champion and did his National Service in Cyprus with the Royal Horse Guards, first as a trooper, then as a cornet. Lindy, the daughter of the late Group Captain Loel Guinness, a Swiss-based banker and one-time MP for Bath, lives in New York.

DU MAURIER, Dame DAPHNE, *born* 1907, second daughter of Sir Gerald du Maurier, the actor-manager.

In 1932 married Lieutenant-General Sir Frederick 'Boy' Browning, one of the heroes of Arnhem (one son, two daughters). She wrote her most famous novel, ***Rebecca***, later filmed with Laurence Olivier and Joan Fontaine, in Egypt while her husband was commanding the Second Battalion of the Grenadier Guards in Alexandria. Her short story, ***The Birds***, was filmed by Alfred Hitchcock in 1963. She

spent twenty-six years lovingly restoring her Cornish home, Menabilly, (the model for Manderley in ***Rebecca***) only to have her landlord, Philip Rashleigh, reclaim it from her in 1969. She moved to Kilmarth, the dower house, a mile away. Her younger daughter Tessa, formerly the wife of Peter de Żulueta, is married to Viscount Montgomery of Alamein, son of the wartime Field Marshal. Dame Daphne died in April 1989.

EDMONSTONE, (ANNE) SYBILLA, *born* 18 November 1943.

Daughter of Sir Archibald Charles Edmonstone, sixth baronet, and Gwendolyn Mary Field, whose father was the Chicago newspaper and stores tycoon, Marshall Field. The most beautiful debutante of her year (1961) she had a Piccadilly nightclub in Swallow Street, which opened in 1965, named after her (her then boyfrend, advertising copywriter Terence Howard was a co-owner). In 1970 she married former Welsh Guards officer Jamie Robertson (one son, Dickson) but they separated four years later. Back in her native Scotland, she died suddenly after lunch, of a brain tumour in March 1986.

EGREMONT, First Lord, JOHN EDWARD REGINALD WYNDHAM, also Sixth Lord Leconfield, *born* 5 June 1920.

Owner of palatial Petworth House in Sussex and Private Secretary to Harold Macmillan when Prime Minister, 1957–63. When Macmillan retired, so did Wyndham (who was ennobled with an hereditary peerage) although he was only forty-three. While at Number Ten, he used to enjoy playing practical jokes on government colleagues. Sir Dick White, head of MI6, was a favourite target, and when Egremont grew merry late at night he would dial the deeply secret home number of 'M' and coo down the telephone,

'Aha, villain, I know your secret.' Soon the full technology of MI5 was brought to bear and the incessant calls were eventually traced. When the report arrived on the desk of the director of security services, it revealed that the calls came from the direct line of the Prime Minister in Downing Street. Married to noted beauty Pamela Wyndham-Quin, a cousin (two sons, one daughter), he died of cancer in June 1982.

EKLAND, BRITT, *born* 1943.
Swedish actress who married Peter Sellers (q.v.) in 1964 (one daughter) after she was cast in his film *The Bobo*, and through him became a close friend of Princess Margaret and the Earl of Snowdon, sharing several holidays with them, including one in Sardinian waters on the Sellers' yacht, *The Bobo*. After her divorce in 1969, she moved in with the Princess's cousin, the photographer the Earl of Lichfield (q.v.), entertaining at Shugborough, his stately home in Staffordshire. When that broke up after two years, Lichfield gave as a reason that Britt 'was not good in the country', to which she answered with a riposte, 'He wasn't good in the sack.' In 1973 she gave birth to a son, Nicholai, whose father is Lou Adler, a record company owner who made $10 million out of the Carole King LP 'Tapestry'. They never married and in 1975 Britt became the live-in-lover in Los Angeles of Rod Stewart, claiming £12 million in a palimony suit when they broke up three years later. She later settled for less than £1 million. In 1984 she married 'Slim' Jim MacDonnell, the former drummer of the Stray Cats and seventeen years her junior. Their son, Thomas Jefferson, was born in April 1988.

ELDON, Fifth Earl, JOHN JOSEPH NICHOLAS SCOTT, *born* 24 April 1937.
Formerly Viscount Encombe, and 6ft and 6ins tall. Educated at Ampleforth and Trinity College, he was sent down from Oxford in 1958 for shooting a tame deer in the grounds of Magdalen College. He told the authorities that it was a 'family tradition' and that his grandfather and uncle had both shot deer, but had not been sent down. A sometime photographer who trained in the studios of the Earl of Lichfield (q.v.), he married Austrian Countess Claudine de Montjoye-Vaufrey et de la Roche in 1961 (one son, two daughters). His side of the family lost Encombe, a 10,000-acre Dorset estate near Corfe Castle, when his grandfather married a Catholic and the property went to the son of a younger brother.

ELWES, DOMINIC, *born* 1931.
The son of royal portrait painter Simon Elwes, RA, he captured the imagination of the world in November 1957 when he eloped to Scotland with nineteen-year-old shipping heiress Tessa Kennedy after a High Court judge ordered her return to the court's jurisdiction. Her father, however, successfully gained an order from the Court of Session in Edinburgh forbidding the union and the couple flew on, in January 1959, to Cuba (courtesy of a French magazine which had bought their story). They were married in Havana and after a stay in the United States returned to Britain on the French liner *Liberté* when Dominic's visa ran out. He was arrested for contempt of court, taken to Brixton prison, but discharged two weeks later. The couple had three sons and divorced in 1969 (he left their Kensington house one evening saying he was going to buy a packet of Gauloises and disappeared for a year). A close friend of the Earl of Lucan (q.v.), he moved to Spain, where he was involved with the development of Cuarton near Gibraltar. Attempts to emulate his father as a portraitist failed and when a painting of the Clermont Club with various prominent members found its way into *The Times*, in an article about the Lucan mystery, he was ostracized by his friends, mainly Sir James Goldsmith, John Aspinall and Mark Birley, for 'disloyalty'. He committed suicide in his small Chelsea *pied-à-terre*, where his body and a note were found by his last love, Melissa Wyndham, a cousin of Lord Egremont (q.v.). At his memorial service John Aspinall

gave a robust address criticizing suicide and was punched on the jaw afterwards by Dominic's cousin, Lord Rennell of Rodd, a former Scotland rugby scrum half, with the words, 'That's what I think of your bloody speech, Aspinall.'

EXETER, Sixth Marquess of, DAVID GEORGE BROWNLOW CECIL, Hereditary Grand Almoner, *born* 9 February 1905.
As Lord Burghley, he won the 400-metres hurdles in the 1928 Olympics in Amsterdam and won a silver medal in the 4 x 400-metres relay in the 1932 Olympics in Los Angeles. In 1958 he inherited Burghley House, near Stamford, begun in 1552 by his ancestor Sir William Cecil, one of Queen Elizabeth I's ministers. The building, with 240 rooms, was completed in 1587. He married twice, and by his first wife, daughter of the Seventh Duke of Buccleuch, had a son and heir, John William Edward, who died after thirteen months, and three daughters. By his second marriage there is a daughter, Lady Victoria, who lives in the house, set in 27,000 Lincolnshire acres, with her husband, stockbroker Simon Leatham, and their two children. When Exeter died in 1981, the title passed to brother Martin (born 27 April 1909), who founded a religious sect, the Emissaries of Divine Light, on his 12,000-acre ranch in British Columbia. He died in 1988 and his son Michael (born 1 September 1935) became the Eighth Marquess. His son and heir Anthony, Lord Burghley, who was educated at Eton, will eventually take over Burghley.

EYRE, RICHARD CHARLES HASTINGS, *born* 28 March 1943.
Succeeded Sir Peter Hall as Director of the National Theatre in 1988 (Associate Director 1981–8). Expelled from Sherborne for subversion in his last term before going to Peterhouse, Cambridge. Married to producer Sue Birtwistle (***Hotel du Lac, Scoop***, etc.) with a daughter at St Paul's. The only son of notably eccentric parents – his mother Minna (the daughter of the Commander of Scott's ***Discovery***) collected Pekinese dogs and his

father Snowy, a former Royal Navy Lieutenant-Commander, farmed in Dorset. He kept a Poll Hereford bull, Mr Nyung Nyung, in the garden of his Maiden Newton house, feeding it shredded wheat and other delicacies whenever it put its ringed nose through the open kitchen window.

FAIRBANKS, DOUGLAS ELTON, *born* 9 December 1909.
Son of the legendary Hollywood star. Married first, in 1929, Lucille le Sueur, who became better known as the actress Joan Crawford. In 1939 he married Mary Lee Epling, the former wife of Huntington Hartford, heir to the American Atlantic and Pacific grocery chain fortune (three daughters). In 1950, a year after he was awarded an honorary knighthood, he bought, from the Eleventh Duke of Leeds, the largest private house in the Boltons (now owned by the Ruler of Abu Dhabi) and would spend half the year in England and the other six months in a permanent top-floor suite in the Blackstone Hotel, New York. Long rumoured to have been the 'headless man' in the photographs which featured in the divorce case of the Eleventh Duke of Argyll (q.v.), which he has always denied, he was claimed in the autobiography of Mandy Rice Davies to have been one of her lovers during the Profumo scandal. Mary Lee died in 1988.

FAITHFULL, MARIANNE, *born* 29 December 1946.
Daughter of Eva Sacher-Masoch, Baroness Erisso, whose novelist forebear gave his name to the medical condition. A symbol of the swinging sixties who had a No.1 record ('As Tears Go By', written by Mick Jagger, q.v.), she became involved with the lead singer of the Rolling Stones after her marriage in 1965 to Cambridge undergraduate John Dunbar

(one son). When police raided Keith Richards' home searching for drugs, they found Marianne in the famous 'Mars Bar' pose, wearing nothing but a fur rug. Mick Jagger took the rap for the amphetamines found in her jacket pocket. After a miscarriage she attempted suicide on a Stones tour of Australia and when Jagger ditched her, turned more to drugs, spending much of the seventies and eighties on heroin. In 1979 she married, briefly, Ben Brierley, a punk rock musician who performed under the name Ben E. Ficial. Now living in Ireland, she resumed her career with a much-applauded performance at the Dominion Theatre in London in May 1990, her first concert since 1981.

FALKENDER, MARCIA MATILDA (née Field), *born* March 1932 and created Baroness Falkender, 1974.
From 1956 to 1983 was the Private and Political Secretary to Harold Wilson (later Lord Wilson of Rievaulx) and widely held to have been the major influence of his two terms as Prime Minister, 1964–70, and 1974–6. Credited with having drawn up, on lavender writing paper, the honours list on Wilson's resignation, which was sent back by Buckingham Palace as unacceptable. The so-called Lavender List gave David Frost (q.v.) and James Goldsmith (q.v.) life peerages and boxing promoter Jarvis Astaire a knighthood. Only Goldsmith survived the amendments, ending up with a knighthood. An honours graduate (history) of London University, she married the Chairman of the college's Conservative Association, Edmund Williams (dissolved 1960), an aero-engineer who later worked for Pan Am in America. Once involved with Lord Kagan (q.v.) she has two sons by Walter Terry, former Political Editor of the ***Daily Mail***, who were educated at Westminster and who have not seen their father for many years. Lives in a Marylebone mews house with her sister,

Marcia Falkender and Harold Wilson

Peggy Field, who acts as her personal assistant.

FENSTON, FELIX DONOVAN, *born* 1915.
Son of impresario Joseph Fenston, and a gifted pianist, he started a property empire with £50 he was given when he was invalided out of the Army during the Second World War after losing a leg. His first purchase was a shoe shop in Watford and the fifties property boom made him a multimillionaire, with homes in Mayfair, formerly the house of the Tenth Duke of Devonshire, the Island of Tyree (which he owned) and the 3,046-acre Druids Lodge estate on Salisbury Plain. He was a friend of Ernest Hemingway, hunted bear in Alaska and shot tigers with the Maharajah of Cooch Behar in India. His partner in Metropolitan Provincial Properties was Prince Stanislas Radziwill (q.v.), the brother-in-law of Jacqueline Bouvier Kennedy, wife of the US President. By his first wife, Betty, he had a son, Timothy, who died in an accident in October 1965, when a BEA Vanguard, flying from Edinburgh, crashed in fog at London Airport killing all thirty passengers and six crew. There was a son by his second wife, Lucienne (their marriage was dissolved after sixteen years in 1959) and in 1963 he married his third wife, Greta Borg, who was twenty-eight and whose father commanded the Royal Malta Artillery during the Second World War. He died in September 1970, leaving £4,686,516.

FERGUSON, Major RONALD IVOR, *born* 10 October 1931.
Married Susan Wright, niece of Viscount Powerscourt, 10 January 1956 (two daughters), dissolved 1974, after he encouraged Hector Barrantes, Argentinian polo professional to Lord Vestey (q.v.) and his brother, the Hon. Mark Vestey, to look after her while his eyes wandered elsewhere (Susie heard that he had even proposed marriage to one lady). Married, 1975, Susan Deptford (one son, two daughters), daughter of a Norfolk landowner who is said to have bought Ferguson's 800-acre Hampshire estate, Dummer Down House, in trust for his grandchildren. Commander of the Sovereign's Escort when in the Life Guards, retiring from the Army to go into Public Relations and be Director of Polo at the Guards Polo Club. He left the £25,000-a-year job at the Guards after thirty-three years building up Smith's Lawn as a major polo centre when he was not re-elected in September 1988. He refused a lesser role of running polo at the club and it was wrongly construed that the matter had come to a head following revelations in a Sunday newspaper that the major was a member of the Wigmore Club, where masseurs performed various sex acts for additional remuneration. Ferguson moved to the Royal County of Berkshire Polo Club and remains polo manager to the Prince of Wales. The Wigmore Club was forced to close its doors, much to the sorrow of other members, including the Hon. Nigel Havers and David Puttnam.

FERMOY, Fifth Lord, EDMUND JAMES BURKE ROCHE, *born* 20 March 1939.
Son of American-born fourth baron who was left £600,000 in 1956 by his maternal grandfather on the condition that he never set foot in England. He and his twin brother defied the wishes but each received £543,000 under a family agreement. Brother of the Princess of Wales's mother, Frances, and son of Ruth, Lady Fermoy, who has been Woman of the Bedchamber to Queen Elizabeth, the Queen Mother since 1960 and is two years older than Her Majesty. Fermoy killed himself with a shotgun in his stables in a fit of depression in August 1984 and his widow, Lavinia (two sons, one daughter), put their 900-acre Hungerford estate on the market for £3.5 million.

FIFE, Third Duke of, JAMES GEORGE ALEXANDER BANNERMAN CARNEGIE, *born* 23 September 1929.
Descended from HRH Princess Louise, the Princess Royal, eldest daughter of King Edward VII. A cousin of the Queen and in

Major Ronald Ferguson

line of accession to the throne. First marriage to whisky heiress Caroline Dewar, daughter of Lord Forteviot, was dissolved in 1966 (one son, one daughter) and three years later he fell in love with Davina Galica, daughter of a former Polish cavalry officer. She was British ski champion and competed in three Olympic Games, before retiring in 1972 after missing a bronze medal by 0.3 seconds. For eight years she turned down his proposals of marriage while she concentrated on becoming the world's first female Formula One driver. He gave up waiting after she turned to attempting the world speed-skiing record (she reached 119.3mph), but has not remarried.

HRH Princess Firyal of Jordan, *born* 1945. Married, November 1963, Prince Mohammed of Jordan, younger brother of King Hussein and sometime Crown Prince of the Hashemite Kingdom (two sons), who was dispossessed in favour of his younger brother, Hassan. Erratic Mohammed, who once boarded, at Heathrow, a Royal Jordanian Airlines flight to Amman with a French girl and then ordered the captain to reroute to Salzburg because his companion wanted to get off there, obtained a divorce in 1981 and married the daughter of a former prime minister. For six years Firyal, who lives in two adjoining Belgravia houses between Michael Heseltine and Norman Tebbit, was close to Stavros Niarchos, the Greek shipping tycoon who puts his own worth at £2.5 billion.

FONTEYN, Dame MARGOT, *born* 18 May 1919.
Prima Ballerina Assoluta who married, in 1955, Panamanian politician Robert 'Tito' Arias, Ambassador to the Court of St James

1955–8. While campaigning for the Presidency in 1964, he was shot and paralyzed in an assassination attempt and spent the rest of his life in a wheelchair (he died in November 1989) being tended for by Dame Margot, exhausting all her earnings from a forty-year career. On 30 May 1990, a gala performance of Romeo and Juliet (in which her former partner, Rudolf Nureyev, danced Mercutio) held in Dame Margot's honour raised £250,000 to provide for her – she has been suffering from cancer. She wishes to remain on her cattle ranch 100 miles from Panama City and requested that the fund should eventually benefit students of ballet.

FOOT, PAUL MACKINTOSH, *born* 8 November 1937.
Son of Lord Caradon, former Governor of Jamaica and Cyprus, and nephew of Michael Foot, MP. A close friend of Richard Ingrams (q.v.) and author of the ***Private Eye*** Business News section until joining the ***Daily Mirror*** in 1979, for which he writes a crusading column which has gained him several Journalist of the Year awards. Two sons by his 1962 marriage (dissolved 1970) to Monica Beckinsale and a daughter by his second wife, Rose. Provided refuge in his Hampstead home for Ingrams when his marriage was experiencing strain in the eighties. A keen supporter of Plymouth Argyle football team.

FORBES, BRYAN, *born* 22 July 1926, married Nanette Newman, born 29 May 1939, in 1958 (two daughters).
At their Virginia Waters home, the couple have entertained the Queen and Prince Philip (a particular fan of Nanette's), whom they met through Princess Margaret during her days of friendship with the late Peter Sellers (q.v.), and have been guests at Windsor Castle and Royal Lodge, home of Queen Elizabeth, the Queen Mother. In 1986 sold their two-bedroom Georgian house off the Fulham Road in South Kensington to Peter Palumbo (q.v.) for £425,000, twenty years after buying the property for £12,000. Elder daughter Sara (once engaged to Elton John's

gay manager, John Reid) is married to Eton-educated baronet, Sir John Leon, better known as actor and artist John Standing, and they live in Los Angeles, next to a downtown supermarket. Forbes and Nanette may be found working at The Bookshop in Virginia Water, when not involved in their literary and film commitments. Why has Bryan never received a knighthood? Apparently Her Majesty does not approve.

FORD II, HENRY, *born* 4 September 1917, the grandson of the founder of the Detroit car manufacturers whose first product, the Model T, he said, was available in any colour 'so long as it's black'.
A keen shot, he lived for half the year in Britain, in a Mayfair house next door to the Duke of Marlborough, and Turville Grange, Buckinghamshire, formerly the home of Prince Stanislas Radziwill (q.v.) He had a son, Edsel, and two daughters by his first marriage to Anne McDonnell (dissolved 1963) and then married Italian-born Christina Austin, widow of a Royal Navy submarine officer. Their marriage ended in 1980 after she formed a close friendship with Mme Imelda Marcos, then First Lady of the Philippines, with whom she travelled extensively. His third marriage was in 1980 to divorcée Kathleen DuRoss, who had earlier been the passenger in his car in Santa Barbara when he was arrested for drunk driving. Asked for a comment, he said, 'Never explain, never complain.' When he died in 1987, he left a will which he read out on a twenty-minute video cassette warning his family not to squabble – the bulk of his £250 million fortune went to Kathy. At his St George's, Hanover Square memorial service, the New Dixie Syncopaters played his favourite tune, 'When The Saints Go Marching In'.

FORSYTH, FREDERICK, *born* 1938, educated Haileybury, married actress Carrie Cunningham (two sons) in 1973, the year his first best seller, ***The Day of the Jackal***, was published, and lived in Jesus Pobre, a village

The Fortes

Freddie Forsyth

near Alicante, moving to tax exile in Ireland. In 1980 sold his house in County Wicklow for £238,000 because of kidnap fears and moved to Surrey. In February 1988, after resting for eighteen years, Carrie returned to the stage for seventeen performances, playing the Mother Superior in John Pielmayer's **Agnes of God** (Anne Bancroft's role in the film version). The first night at Camden Town's fringe Etcetera Theatre was attended by the Prince and Princess Michael of Kent, who took the couple out to dinner afterwards. Nine months later Freddie and Carrie informed their friends that they were separating and selling their St John's Wood townhouse. He lives at a 140-acre farm in Hertfordshire, where sons Stuart and Shane spend weekends, and she remains at their

£1.5 million Avenue Road, St John's Wood apartment, close to the boys' day school.

FORTE, Lord CHARLES, *born* 26 November 1908, son of Rocco Giovanni Forte of Casalattico, Italy, who emigrated to Scotland where the young Charles, educated at Alloa Academy and Dumfries College, began his career with a milk bar.

Now Chairman of Trusthouse Forte, with more than 800 hotels around the world and valued on the Stock Exchange in excess of £2.5 billion. Celebrated his eightieth birthday with a banquet at his flagship hotel in Park Lane, London, the Grosvenor House, attended by the Prime Minister and 1,200 guests, who each paid £75 towards a catering trade charity set up by the birthday boy. Mad about fishing and shooting, he has been married since 1943 to Irene Chierico of Venice and has a son, Rocco (q.v.), five daughters and nine grandchildren. His eldest daughter, Olga Polizzi, widow of an Italian marchese, attracted unwelcome publicity after Conservative Minister Norman Lamont, a happily married man, had his eye blacked on the doorstep of her Paddington mews house by her then boyfriend, art dealer Richard Connolly, who arrived unexpectedly and objected to the MP sharing a late-night drink with his lover.

FORTE, The Hon. ROCCO JOHN VINCENT, *born* 22 February 1945.

A fencing champion at Downside and Oxford, he finally married, in 1986, Aliai Ricci (two daughters), daughter of a Roman professor and twenty years his junior, after his father had expressed displeasure at his previous choice of girlfriends, several of whom were not even Catholics – although Bianca Jagger passed on this account, she was unsuitable because she had been divorced. In 1973 he escorted Simone, Countess of Suffolk, who had been divorced not once but twice, and then another divorcée, Valerie Nickerson, and former Miss World, Gina Swainson, was not quite the ticket either. Rocco, who has a £50 million stake in Trust-

house Forte, was forced to withdraw his candidacy for White's, Britain's oldest club (founded 1693) in 1978, although he was supported by former MP Sir Timothy Kitson and the Duke of Marlborough, whose younger brother, Lord Charles Spencer-Churchill, worked for Trusthouse Forte. They were told that the club's more snobbish element had planned to blackball him, had he come up for election.

FOX, ANGELA MURIEL DARITA (née Worthington), *born* 1913.

Actress daughter of playwright Freddie Lonsdale and 'Glitters' Worthington. She married London's leading theatrical agent, Robin Fox (died 1971), who put his recreations in *Who's Who* as, 'Golf and killing Germans', and had numerous affairs, including one for ten years with his secretary, Roz Chatto. Mother of Edward Fox (born 1937), William Fox (born 1939) and Robert Fox (born 1944), all educated at Harrow, their father's old school. Edward has one daughter by his marriage to Tracy Pelissier, stepdaughter of Sir Carol Reed (and who later married 'Dr Finlay's Casebook' star, Bill Simpson) and one daughter by actress Joanna David, with whom he has lived since 1971. A short-service commission in the Coldstream Guards, Willie changed his forename to James as there was already a William Fox in Equity. He made his screen debut, aged ten, in the *Miniver Story*. Engaged in 1962 to Sarah Miles, his co-star in *The Servant* and *Those Magnificent Men in Their Flying Machines*. In 1969 he gave up acting after meeting evangelist Bernie Marks over a breakfast table in Blackpool on Boxing Day. He became a salesman for a telephone serializing company in Sheffield, working by night for a religious sect called the Navigators, marrying fellow disciple, Mary Piper, in 1973 (four sons, one daughter). A decade later he gave up full-time evangelism to return to acting. Robert Fox is a leading impresario who worked for four years for Michael White (q.v.). His 1975 marriage to casting director, Celestia Sporborg (three

The Foxes and mother, Angela

children), daughter of a Hambros Bank director, ended in divorce in 1989. In 1990 he announced plans to marry Natasha Richardson, daughter of Tony Richardson and Vanessa Redgrave, after a four-year romance.

FRASER, Sir HUGH, **second baronet,** *born* 18 December 1936.
Disclaimed title of Lord Fraser of Allander on the death of his father in November 1966, when he inherited the House of Fraser empire which his father, a draper in Sauchiehall Street, Glasgow, had built up, with Harrods as the jewel in the crown. Married in 1962 to Patricia Bowie (three daughters), who left him after four years, he then wed showjumper Aileen Ross in 1972, giving her

a £50,000 horse, but that ended in divorce two years before she was killed in a light aircraft crash. A farmer's daughter, Lynda Taylor, who was expected to become his third wife, died from carbon monoxide poisoning. He once fell in love with a waitress at the Cairngorm ski resort founded by his father, showering the poor girl with flowers, and jilted schoolteacher Annabel Finlay in 1983 after a year's engagement. Desperate to emulate the high lifestyle of Sir Hugh Trevor Dawson (q.v.) who encouraged him to gamble and womanize, he took to the roulette wheels of Mayfair clubs (always backing number 32) and lost an estimated £5 million before giving up in 1981. To pay his losses he had to sell shares and he lost the chairmanship of House of Fraser, in which Lonrho and R.W. 'Tiny' Rowland had built up a 29.9 per cent holding in 1981. Tiny described him as, 'A charming man but a professional loser.' He died in May 1987, aged fifty.

FREEMAN, JOHN, *born* 19 February 1915.
Changed television interviewing techniques with his 'Face to Face' BBC TV series in the late fifties, which included the memorable scene when Gilbert Harding broke down in tears (other subjects were Albert Finney and Adam Faith). Labour MP for Watford 1945–55, Editor of the *New Statesman* 1961–5, he was appointed High Commissioner to India by Harold Wilson in 1965 and was Ambassador to Washington 1969–71, after which he became Chairman of London Weekend Television, which he rescued from disaster, retiring in February 1984. Four times married, he has two sons and a daughter by his third wife, Catherine, a television producer. In Washington he fell in love with South African-born Judith Mitchell, who worked as his wife's social secretary. They married in 1976 (one child). He is now Visiting Professor of International Relations at the University of California, Davis.

FREUD, Sir CLEMENT RAPHAEL, *born* 24 April 1924.
Trained at the Dorchester and the Martinez Hotel in Cannes and began his catering career at the Royal Court Theatre Club, which he owned 1952–63. Grandson of Sigmund (his father, Ernst, was an architect), he married actress Jill Esmond in 1950 (three sons, two daughters) but they have lived separate lives for some years. Liberal MP for the Isle of Ely 1973–83, where he was helped in canvassing by Bunny girls (a close friend of former Playboy chief, Victor Lownes, q.v., Freud was Director and Trustee of the Playboy Club of London). As a restaurant critic, he overstepped the mark in 1986, according to Tim Hart, brother of the Prime Minister's adviser David, and owner of Hambleton Hall. In a magazine review of the hotel restaurant he stated that over-zealous service had ruined his digestion. Hart replied that he

found that mystifying, especially as Freud had taken the waitress, eighteen-year-old Anna Voller, into the rose garden after dinner and that she had handed in her resignation the next day, saying that Freud would set her up in a swish London restaurant. Freud's eldest daughter, Nicola, once posed full-frontal nude across twelve pages of a soft-porn magazine. The younger, Emma, is a television presenter.

FROST, DAVID PARADINE, *born* 7 April 1939.
Twice left at the altar (by singer Diahann Carroll in 1973 and American model, Karen Graham, a year later) after his friend Clay Felker, founder of New York magazine, had given bachelor parties for him, it was third time unlucky for Frost when he fell in love with actress Lynne Frederick, the widow of Peter Sellers (q.v.) from whom she inherited £4 million despite being estranged at the time of his death. Frost and she were divorced in June 1982, seventeen months after their marriage and fifteen weeks after she lost the baby they were expecting. Earlier romances were with actresses Janette Scott, daughter of Thora Hird, and Jenny Logan. But he did marry Lady Carina Fitzalan-Howard, middle daughter of the Seventeenth Duke of Norfolk, Britain's leading lay Catholic, in 1983, a year after her engagement, to property developer, Charles Delevigne, was suddenly called off after just a month. A keen footballer who was once offered professional terms – in one game he scored seven goals with just eight shots – Frostie is now producing a team of his own and has three sons.

GALITZINE, Prince GEORGE, *born* 3 May 1916, second son of Prince Vladimir Galitzine and descended from Tsar Paul I of Russia.
Educated Lancing, St Paul's and Brasenose College, Oxford. Major, Welsh Guards,

married first, 1943, Baroness Anne-Marie von Slatin (two sons), secondly, 1963, leading fashion model Jean Dawnay (one daughter). A fluent Russian speaker he conducts Serenissima tours of Leningrad and Moscow. His elder son, also Prince George, and educated at Harrow, lived for two years with actress Helen Mirren and was one of the founders of the Surrendell commune to which Roddy Llewellyn would invite Princess

Margaret for back-to-the-earth weekends.

GETTY, J(EAN) PAUL, *born* 15 December 1892.

President, Getty Oil Co. from 1947, trustee and founder of the J. Paul Getty Museum, Malibu, California, which he never saw – he moved to England in the fifties, buying Sutton Place, the historic house near Guildford of the late Duke of Sutherland, and had

Paul Getty

a fear of flying caused by a nightmare journey in a Dakota in 1942. Married first, 1923, Jeanette Demont (one son deceased), second, 1926, Allene Ashby, third, 1928, Adolphine Helme (one son), fourth, 1932, Ann Rork (two sons) and fifth, 1939, Louise 'Teddy' Lynch (one son deceased). Left £3 billion when he died in 1976 and his will mentioned eleven women in his life, including Mrs Penelope Kitson, who decorated Sutton Place (£500,000 in oil shares and £800 a month) and was at his bedside in the weeks before his death. His London-based son, J. Paul Getty Jnr, by his fourth wife, was given an honorary knighthood in June 1986 for his charitable donations, totalling more than £100 million, to various British causes, including £50 million to the National Gallery and £3 million to Lord's, which made him a member of the MCC. After spending three years in the London Clinic with phlebitis, a legacy of a sixties heroin addiction, he lives between an apartment overlooking Green Park and Wormsley, a 3,000-acre Buckinghamshire estate which houses his collection of rare books and medieval manuscripts.

GLENCONNER, Third Lord, COLIN CHRISTOPHER PAGET TENNANT, *born* 1 December 1936.
Educated Eton, New College, Oxford. Became Princess Margaret's best friend in 1953 after she had been turned down by the Earl of Dalkeith (later the Duke of Buccleuch, q.v.) as a wife. But marriage to her, he says, was never on and in 1956 he married Lady Anne Coke, eldest daughter of the Fifth Earl of Leicester (two sons, twin daughters, one son deceased). In 1959, having sold a family plantation in Trinidad, bought the 1,400-acre Caribbean island of Mustique for £45,000 and developed it into one of the most exclusive resorts in the world. Eldest son and heir, Charles Tennant, was disinherited from owning Glenn, his 8,000-acre Peeblesshire estate, because of his continuing heroin addiction. Younger son, Henry, contracted Aids and died in January 1990 (his son

Euan will inherit the estate). Youngest son, Christopher, is still recovering from a motorcycle accident in British Honduras in June 1987, which left him in a coma for fourteen weeks. Colin Glenconner sold his last interest in Mustique after hosting a £1 million party to celebrate his sixtieth birthday and is now hoping to develop a property in St Lucia. For many years close to Jill Goldsmith, former sister-in-law of Sir James Goldsmith (q.v.), while Lady Anne counted on the support of Michael Tree, who is married to the Duke of Devonshire's younger sister Lady Anne Cavendish.

Henry (left), and Colin Tennant

GLYN, PRUDENCE, *born* 22 January 1935, former Fashion Editor of *The Times*.
Married 1965 Lord Windlesham (one son, one daughter), former Chairman of the ATV Network and Minister of State for Northern Ireland 1972–3. Made several attempts to gain selection for a Conservative seat, but failed despite husband's backing. When she became engaged, ten years after meeting Windlesham, a friend congratulated her, 'Well Pru, I hear Mr Right has come along

at last.' 'Lord Right, actually,' said Prudence, purring. They were legally separated by the time she died of a brain haemorrhage in September 1986.

GOLD, John, *born* 1933, the son of a Brighton bookmaker (and himself a commission agent until June 1990).
Married model Jan de Souza in May 1971 (one son, one daughter). In 1963 opened Dolly's, a discotheque in Jermyn Street, with Oscar Lerman (husband of author Jackie Collins) and in December 1969 moved sixty yards east down Jermyn Street to the basement premises of the former Society restaurant (haunt of the fifties Princess Margaret set), co-owned by Polish-born Bill Ofner, who became their partner in what became London's most successful and enduring discotheque, where Prince Andrew smooched away his first night after meeting Koo Stark (q.v.). Opened a sister venture in Los Angeles in December 1984, which has been less successful. Tramp, much to Gold's distaste, featured in the famous libel action brought by Andrew Neil (q.v.) against the *Sunday Telegraph* and Peregrine Worsthorne, as the place where the *Sunday Times* Editor met Pamella Bordes.

GOLDSMITH, Lady, Annabel, *born* 11 June 1934, younger daughter of the Eighth Marquess of Londonderry, married, March 1954, Marcus (Mark) Lecky Oswald Hornby Birley (q.v.) (one son, one daughter, and one son deceased).
The marriage was dissolved 1975, eleven years after she started an affair with James Goldsmith (q.v.) and they married in 1978 (two sons, one daughter). A noted beauty and society leader in the fifties and sixties, whose christian name adorns the world's greatest nightclub, she lives at Ormeley Lodge, Ham Common, Richmond, an early eighteenth-century mansion. Close to Princess Alexandra (the nearest neighbour in Richmond Park) and Prince Michael of Kent, for whom she gives birthday parties at Ormeley. Daughter Jemima (born 1974) is one of the leading young British showjumpers and has won numerous events. Brother Alastair, the Ninth Marquess of Londonderry (q.v.), lives in the stable block at Ormeley when visiting London. Lady Annabel's mongrel dog, Copper, known as Superstud for siring most of the litters in the area, is now confined to the four-acre garden after being prosecuted for savaging sweaty joggers passing the Ormeley gates.

GOLDSMITH, Sir James Michael, *born* 26 February 1933, younger son of Major Frank Goldsmith and Marcelle Mouiller.
Left Eton aged sixteen after winning £8,000 at Goodwood races, which he then proceeded to lose to John Aspinall (q.v.) who was running *chemin-de-fer* games up at Oxford University. Father, a former MP, owned the Carlton Hotel in Cannes and two hotels in Paris, where Goldsmith met Bolivian tin heiress Isabel Patino, eloping to Scotland to marry her in 1954. When her father, Antenor, told Jimmy he disapproved of her marrying a Jew, he replied that his family was not happy for him to marry the granddaughter of a Red Indian. She died shortly after giving birth, in May 1954, to their daughter Isabel. His second marriage, to his secretary Ginette Lery (one son, one daughter) was dissolved in September 1978 and she remains at their Paris home. By former *Paris Match* journalist, Laura Boulay de la Meurthe (they met when she interviewed him), he has two children and they live between New York, Paris and his 250,000-acre estate on the Pacific coast of Mexico, where he is building homes for each member of his family. In 1989, launched, with Jacob (now Lord) Rothschild (q.v.) and Kerry Packer (q.v.), Britain's largest ever takeover bid, a £13 billion offer for BAT, which they were forced to abort in 1990.

GORMANSTON, Seventeenth Viscount, Jenico Nicholas Dudley Preston, also Premier Viscount of Ireland, *born* 19 November 1939.
Educated Downside, married, 1974, Eva

Sir James Goldsmith

Antoine Landzianowska (two sons). Artist and leader of the sixties Chelsea set who made his maiden speech in the House of Lords in Gaelic. Spent four days in jail in Rome, and was later given a ten-month suspended sentence for resisting arrest and causing injuries after taking his shirt off in a public place and refusing to give his identity. In November 1984 police stopped a car being driven by Brian Walsh, who has served several jail sentences for drug offences, in the back of which they found Viscountess Gormanston uncon-

scious after attending two late night parties celebrating her husband's forty-fifth birthday. She died an hour later in the Westminster Hospital from effects of an overdose of heroin. Gormanston, who had been in the front passenger seat oblivious of her condition, told the inquest he was unable to say where his wife had obtained the drugs or taken them. He has since sold six of his Lord of the Manor titles to pay for his children's education.

Germaine Greer

GREER, GERMAINE, *born* 29 January 1939. Called the 'Goddess of the Sexual Revolution' following the publication of *The Female Eunuch* in 1970, married building worker Paul de Feu in May 1968 and parted after 'three weeks of drinking and rowing', said the bridegroom who confessed that he had 'seduced her with Guinness'. He was granted a decree nisi in October 1973, a year after he became the first full-frontal nude Cosmo Man in *Cosmopolitan* (he later married black American poet, Maya Angelou). In 1977 Eton-educated journalist James Hughes-Onslow, grandson of an Afghani princess, moved into Greer's Notting Hill, London house and announced, 'She would like me to give her a baby.' Six years her junior, Hughes-Onslow (who once worked on the *Daily Express* William Hickey gossip column) moved out after two years, having failed to help her achieve her ambition. She now says she is bored of sex.

GUINNESS, JONATHAN BRYAN, *born* 16 March 1930, eldest son of Second Lord Moyne and the Hon. Diana Freeman-Mitford (who later married Sir Oswald Mosley).

Merchant banker and former director of family brewery, married first, 1951, Ingrid Wyndham (two sons, one daughter), who then married his cousin, Conservative politician Paul Channon; and second, 1964, Suzanne Lisney (one son, one daughter). Also has two daughters and a son by sixties hippy, Susan Taylor, daughter of a Lancashire butcher, and who served as a masseuse in Cornwall where Jonathan visits one weekend a month and ghosted her 1989 autobiography to help finance his alternative family. Daughter Catherine, by first marriage, married Lord Neidpath, son of the Earl of

Nubar Gulbenkian

Wemyss, in 1983 (one son, one daughter) before divorcing five years later. Daphne, by his second marriage, is married to Spyros Niarchos, second son of Stavros Niarchos (q.v.). Her brother, Sebastian, was sentenced in December 1986 to four months in jail for possessing heroin and cocaine following the death of his cousin, Olivia Channon, six months earlier from a drugs and drink overdose at Oxford.

GULBENKIAN, Nubar Sarkis, *born* Armenia 2 June 1896, the son of Calouste Gulbenkian, the oil entrepreneur known as 'Mr Five Per Cent' for the cut he used to claim in deals between oil producers and consumers.

Educated Harrow, Bonn University and Trinity College, Cambridge, Gulbenkian married first, 1922 (dissolved 1928), Herminia Feijoo, second, 1928 (dissolved 1937), Dore Freeland and third, in 1948, champagne heiress Marie de Ayala, with whom he lives in Arlington House, next door to the Ritz, where he entertained as the Honorary Turkish Counsellor. At lunch he would summon the waiter, tear a £1 note in half and say, giving him one bit, 'If you please me, the other half is for you, if you don't, it's for me.' Wore a different orchid in his buttonhole every day and converted a London taxi, with a Rolls Royce engine, trellis work, coach lamps and registration number NG 1, because, 'I am told it can turn on a sixpence, whatever that is.' He died, in Cannes, in January 1972.

Jonathan Guinness

H*h*

HADEN-GUEST, Anthony, *born* 2 February 1935.

Gordonstoun and Cambridge-educated son of Peter Haden-Guest, Fourth Lord Haden-Guest and Elisabeth Furse, a Russian-born writer and restaurateur. National Service as a rifleman in the Green Jackets. Described by *Private Eye* as 'the gifted magazine writer' and nicknamed 'The Beast' or 'The Uninvited Guest', worked as a cartoonist, photographer and freelance writer for the *Telegraph* weekend magazine, **Queen** magazine and other publications in London before emigrating to New York in 1976 to write for *New York* magazine and, latterly, *Vanity Fair*. Author of several books and regarded as the inspiration for the venal and drunk English journalist Peter Fallon in *The Bonfire of the Vanities* by his old friend Tom Wolfe. His half-brother, Christopher (born 5 February 1948) is heir to the title and is married to actress Jamie Lee Curtis, daughter of Tony Curtis and Janet Leigh. He has never married, falls in love easily and temporarily and is famed for his impecuniosity. Once wrote a feature for Jocelyn Stevens' **Queen** on how to live for a week in London for under £1.

HAHN, Kurt, *born* Berlin 5 June 1886, became British citizen 1938.

Educated Wilhelmgymnasium, Berlin, Christ Church, Oxford and the Universities of Berlin, Heidelberg, Freiburg and Göttingen. Private Secretary to Prince Max von Baden, the last Imperial Chancellor and helped him, in 1920, found Salem co-educational school at Salem Castle. Arrested by the Nazis in March 1933, he was released through the intervention of Ramsay MacDonald in the July and during the following year founded Gordonstoun school with fifteen pupils from Salem, including Prince Philip, to further his belief in strengthening weaknesses and building up an aristocracy of character, not intellect. In 1941 he started Outward Bound to introduce Gordonstoun's methods to a much larger group of young people. He retired from Gordonstoun in 1953. Prince Philip's three sons also went to Gordonstoun, which is in Morayshire. Hahn never married and died in December 1974.

HAIN, Peter, *born* 1950.

As a South African-born engineering student at Imperial College, London, led the Stop the Seventy Tour Committee that disrupted the Springboks rugby football tour in Britain 1969–70. A former Young Liberal, he was selected in October 1985 as the Labour Parliamentary candidate for Putney where, exactly a decade earlier, he had been arrested and charged with stealing £500 from a cashier at Barclay's Bank, close to his Putney home. Hain, who still lives there with his wife, Pat, and two sons, was tried at the Old Bailey in March 1976 where he was

H*h*

acquitted – it transpired that the evidence was entirely circumstantial and the arrest came after three boys, who had joined the chase for the bank robber, saw Hain getting out of his car near the scene of the crime and took the number. In 1987 he published *A Putney Plot*, in which he maintains he was framed by BOSS, the South African secret service.

HAMBRO, Jocelyn Olaf, *born* 7 May 1919. Educated Eton, Trinity College, Cambridge and served with the Coldstream Guards, 1939–45 (losing a leg), joining Hambros Bank Ltd in 1945. Family originally called Levy and hailed from Hamburg, but when ancestor Calver Levy emigrated to Denmark, the officials misheard his name and birthplace and wrote down Hambro. The family moved to London in 1839, retaining Scandinavian banking links. Married, 1942 (she died 1972), Ann Silvia Muir (three sons), in 1976, the Duchess of Roxburghe (she died 1983), widow of 'Bobo', the Ninth Duke, and third, in 1988, Margaret, Countess Fortescue. In 1986 Jocelyn, with his sons Rupert, Rick and James, split from the bank, forming J.O. Hambro & Co., investment bankers. Rupert, born 27 June 1943, in 1970 married Robin Butler (one son, one daughter, both adopted), former wife of Michael Butler, producer of the sixties hippy musical, *Hair*. Rick (born 1946), married in 1973, Charlotte Soames (marriage dissolved 1983. She married Third Earl Peel in 1989) and their daughter Clementine Hambro was a bridesmaid at the 1981 marriage of the Prince of Wales to Lady Diana Spencer.

HAMILTON, James William (Billy) Blackburn, *born* 1930.
Educated at Trinity College, Dublin. Migrated to London in the early fifties where he became a dilettante of the theatre, doing some acting, singing and dancing, and also became a founder member of the Tony Armstrong-Jones set, who congregated at the photographer's Pimlico Road studio. In 1952 he married Irish heiress Joan Murphy (one

son) and they lived at fourteenth-century Church Gate House in Cookham, Berkshire. He remained a lifelong friend of Armstrong-Jones (who, in May 1960, married Princess Margaret) and acted as unofficial public relations officer to several members of the Royal Family, including the Queen Mother and, latterly, Princess Michael of Kent, while his company, Billy Hamilton Associates, advised blue chip clients such as the Cipriani Hotel chain, the Orient Express train, Cartier, Bulgari and Vuitton. In 1986, just after his mother-in-law died leaving more than £3 million, he discovered he was suffering from Motor Neuron disease and he died in July 1988 at the Cipriani Hotel, after the inaugural journey of the Orient Express to Vienna, accompanied by Prince and Princess Michael and the Duchess of Norfolk, as well as his close friend Jim Sherwood, boss of Sea Containers, which owned the Cipriani, and his wife Shirley. He left £1,000 to BBC disc jockey David Jacobs 'in grateful appreciation for many hours of relaxing music.'

HANCOCK, Anthony (Tony), *born* Birmingham 12 May 1924.
Married 1950 (dissolved 1965) Cicely Roumanis, secondly 1965, his publicity agent Freddie Ross. Son of Jack and Lily Hancock, who ran a hotel in Bournemouth, he began his career at the Windmill Theatre in 1946 and toured with the *Gang Show* after being demobilized from the RAF which he joined in 1942. Between 1951 and 1953 he played tutor to Archie Andrews in the BBC radio series 'Educating Archie' before the first of 160 'Hancock's Half Hour' shows, the finest British comedy series ever, was broadcast in 1954, written by Alan Simpson and Ray Galton – it transferred to television 1956–60 and in 1963 moved over to ITV where viewing figures slipped from eight million to five million. All three of his films were unsuccessful. Seven months after the wedding, Freddie was taken to hospital in a coma and in June 1967 she sought leave to present a divorce petition within three years of their marriage, because of his alcoholism,

and moved into the Middlesex home of her estranged husband's literary-agent brother, Roger Hancock, and his wife. Tony began an affair with Joan, the third wife of actor John Le Mesurier. He died in June 1968 of an overdose of barbiturates washed down with a bottle of vodka in a flat in Sydney, where he had gone to make a new television series and a comeback. Freddie moved to America and lives in New York, working for an international film and TV magazine.

HARLECH, PAMELA, **Lady,** *born* 18 December 1934 (née Colin).
Daughter of a Jewish New York lawyer, she took the view that her social future lay in England, became London Editor of *American Vogue* in 1964, met David Ormsby-Gore, Fifth Lord Harlech, at a dinner party and married him (one daughter) in 1969, a year after his wife Sylvia had been killed in a crash near their Oswestry, Shropshire home. Five years later Harlech, former British Ambassador to Washington and close friend of President J. F. Kennedy and his wife Jackie, denied a report in *McCalls* that his wife had been involved with the Earl of Snowdon (q.v.) before their marriage and that this had almost led to a divorce from Princess Margaret. In 1977 she published *Feast Without a Fuss*, a cookbook with, it later transpired, more than 150 recipes purloined from magazines like *Gourmet*. Harlech died in 1985, in a car accident close to the spot where his first wife was killed, and just as he was about to attend the memorial service, Pamela's father, Ralph Colin, died of a heart attack at Claridge's. Member of the Arts Council, Trustee of the V. & A., her appointment as Chairman of the English National Ballet in January led to the dismissal of its Director, Peter Schaufuss, who had supported the candidature of the Marchioness of Douro (q.v.).

HARPER, ALEXANDER (SANDY) JAMES CHRISTOPHER, *born* 16 March 1948.
Polo player, educated at Winchester. Son of Indian Army colonel who lives on the Cowdray estate and played polo with Prince Philip and Lord Cowdray (q.v.) for many years. In 1969 became enamoured of Princess Anne, whom he escorted for a year. In 1972 he married model Peta Seccombe (one son, one daughter) at St Paul's, Knightsbridge (Anne was invited but declined). Marriage dissolved after Peta went off with his polo mentor and best friend, Argentinian professional Juan Jose Diaz Alberdi. In April 1978, married actress Suzy Kendall (one daughter), former wife (1968–72) of Dudley Moore. Works as a commodity broker with interests in Gabon and South America.

Richard Harris

HARRIS, RICHARD, *born* 1 October 1930.
Left Limerick, his birthplace, aged twenty-three with £23 in his pocket. Married in 1957 to the Hon. Elizabeth Rees-Williams

Rex Harrison and Kay Kendall

(three sons), daughter of First Lord Ogmore. Marriage dissolved 1969 (she later married Rex Harrison, q.v. and Peter Aitken). First significant role in *The Sporting Life* opposite Rachel Roberts (later Mrs Rex Harrison). A notorious drinker with fellow actors Peter O'Toole and Richard Burton, he gave up alcohol in 1981. Bought the touring production (props, costume and all) of *Camelot* (he starred in the 1964 film version) which he takes around America when he feels the pinch – it has grossed nearly $100 million. Briefly married to Ann Turkel, the American model-cum-actress he took from David Niven Jnr, who had expected to marry her, but still close to Elizabeth – he bought her a £16,000 Mercedes for her fifty-first birthday in 1988 to replace her battered Renault. Claimed in a 1989 High Court libel action he brought against Express Newspapers that he was on the IRA hit list, which prompted the terrorist organization to issue a prompt denial.

HARRISON, Sir REX CAREY, *born* 5 March 1908 in Huyton, Liverpool and educated at Liverpool College.
Changed his christian name from Reginald when he joined Liverpool Repertory Company in 1924. Best remembered for his portrayal of Professor Higgins in *My Fair Lady*, the musical version of Shaw's *Pygmalion*, which began its run at the Mark Hellinger theatre, Broadway in 1956 before coming to London's West End in 1958, and for which he won the 1964 Oscar for the film version. Married first, 1934, Marjorie Thomas (one son), secondly, 1943, Lili Palmer (one son), thirdly, 1957, Kay Kendall, fourthly Rachel Roberts, fifth the Hon. Elizabeth Harris, sixth Mercia Tinker. Lived for many years in tax exile in Portofino, Italy and New York and returned to Britain to put himself in line for a knighthood, which he finally was given in 1989. A great snob, he was particularly proud that his sister, Sylvia Margaret, married the First Earl of Kilmuir (Conservative politician David Maxwell-Fyfe) and, after his death in 1967, the Ninth

Earl De La Warr.

HARTINGTON, Marquess of, PEREGRINE ANDREW MORNY CAVENDISH, elder son and heir of the Eleventh Duke of Devonshire, *born* 27 April 1944.
Won Amanda Heywood Lonsdale from Lord Antony Rufus-Isaacs, younger son of the Third Marquess of Reading (q.v.), who was also pursuing her, and they married in 1967 (one son, two daughters). Nicknamed 'Stoker' shortly after birth (and not sure why) and Senior Steward of the Jockey Club since December 1988, Hartington has Bolton Abbey and 30,000 acres in Yorkshire, Lismore Castle, with 8,000 acres in Waterford and the majestic Chatsworth to inherit. Will eventually succeed Sir Piers Benough as Her Majesty's Representative for Royal Ascot and lives between Yorkshire and Chiswick. The family's London home was once Burlington House, Piccadilly, now the Royal Academy.

HARTWELL, Lady, PAMELA MARGARET ELIZABETH (née Smith), *born* 1914, younger daughter of the First Earl of Birkenhead (F.E. Smith, the politician who was Solicitor-General, Attorney-General and Lord High Chancellor and Secretary of State for India), married, 1936, the Hon. Michael Berry (two sons, two daughters), second son of First Viscount Camrose.
Her father's favourite child and inseparable companion, who was noted for her precocity of conversation in her early teens, she was also the power behind her husband, who became Lord Hartwell, a life peer, in 1968. At her Cowley Street, Westminster home, *Telegraph* policy was formulated – Hartwell was Chairman and Editor-in-Chief of the *Daily Telegraph* and launched the *Sunday Telegraph* in February 1961, and his Fleet Street office dining room was presided over by a butler. Lady Pamela was particularly scathing about Lord Lambton, whom she accused of 'living off his money'. 'What else does one live off?' he would ask, after penning a vicious profile of her in the *Tatler*.

She made Mark Heathcote Amory take out 'outrageous and untrue' things about her from the Evelyn Waugh letters, which he edited. She died in 1982 and Hartwell lost control of the *Telegraph* (and his butler) to Canadian Conrad Black three years later, as insolvency loomed.

HARTY, (FREDERICK) RUSSELL, *born* 5 September 1934.
Educated Queen Elizabeth's Grammar School, Blackburn and Exeter College, Oxford. A teacher at Giggleswick School, Settle 1958–64 and Lecturer in English Literature, City University of New York, 1964–6. After producing radio programmes, commenced television career in 1969 with 'Aquarius', an arts programme, for LWT before becoming a presenter with LWT from 1972 and with the BBC from 1980. Known as the 'Mr Chips of Chat', his world collapsed in 1987 when a Sunday newspaper exposed that he had paid a twenty-year-old youth for sex. He continued working and in 1988, near the completion of a televised European grand tour, he fell ill with severe hepatitis and died in June, leaving everything to his sister, Sandra Barnes. Rose Cottage, his seventeenth-century Giggleswick home, was bought for an estimated £250,000 by Eddie Shah to use as the setting of the ITV series he produced, 'Capstick's Law'. Harty's friend Jamie McNeill, with whom he shared his last five years, unsuccessfully challenged Russell's £371,000 will.

HASLAM, NICHOLAS PONSONBY, *born* 27 September 1939.
Eton-educated cousin of the Earl of Bessborough. A trendsetter who moved to New York in the early sixties, worked on *Vogue* (pre-Diana Vreeland), gave a famous party in New York in 1964 for the Rolling Stones and Baby Jane Holzer, produced *Show* magazine for Huntington Hartford and ranched in Arizona, 1965–70. After two years in Los Angeles returned to London and started his interior design business. Confidant of both Princess Michael of Kent and the

Princess of Wales (but not Princess Margaret, who inherited his protégé, Roddy Llewellyn, in 1973). His fortieth birthday party at the Hunting Lodge (the Hampshire National Trust home of the late John Fowler) was attended by Sir Cecil Beaton, Lady Diana Cooper, Sir Michael Redgrave and 447 others. A Pekinese lover since the sixties, he lives with Zelda and Zita, both black.

HAYWARD, DOUGLAS, *born* 5 October 1934.
Began as a tailor's apprentice in Regent Street aged fifteen, before joining the Royal Navy for National Service, and was well placed to take advantage of the swinging sixties when, thanks to Bryan Forbes (q.v.) he received an entrée into the film world and became tailor, with his partner, Ukrainian-born Dymitro Major, to Laurence Harvey, Peter Sellers, Michael Caine and Terence Stamp, before striking out on his own. In 1969, took over Danny La Rue's old camping ground, Winston's Club, in Clifford Street, Mayfair, and turned it into Burke's, a membership restaurant, at a cost of £60,000, with the photographer, the Earl of Lichfield (q.v.) as his partner – the venture was nicknamed 'Lord and Tailor'. Married first Diana Smith (marriage dissolved), second, in 1970, journalist Glenys Roberts (one daughter), who had interviewed him for the London *Evening Standard*. Divorced in 1977, she lives in Mount Street, Mayfair, in a flat opposite his tailoring premises. In 1987 former *Daily Express* Editor, Christopher Ward, accused Hayward of stealing his wife, Fanny (the mother of one son, two daughters) and named him in his divorce action. Other women in his life included (for fourteen years) author Marcelle d'Argy Smith, Deputy Editor of *Cosmopolitan*.

HEIMANN, DAVID, *born* South Africa 1936.
A banker, he married, in March 1968, Diana Macleod (two sons and one adopted), daughter of the Rt Hon. Iain Macleod (later Chancellor of the Exchequer) and Baroness Macleod of Borve. Two daughters by his

former wife Josephine, who married, in 1967, Island Records founder Chris Blackwell (q.v.), one of whose groups was Traffic, for whom Miss Francine Heimann, then six, spoke the words on their 1967 hit record 'Hole in my Shoe'. In 1972, bought Hertfordshire House, Coleshill, Buckinghamshire from Laura, Duchess of Marlborough (q.v.) who moved to Blenheim, only to become widowed two months later. She tried to buy her home back, but was refused. In May 1988 the Heimanns gave a £100,000 dance at the house following the marriage of Francine but the marquee floor, which was on three levels, collapsed, plunging some 200 guests into a chasm with their wine and food deposited on top of them. Prince Rupert Loewenstein (q.v.) broke a leg and claims in excess of £150,000 for damages to limbs and *haute couture* ball gowns were submitted to insurers. Quipped the Duke of Marlborough (q.v.): 'David is the only man I know who could give an expensive party and make a profit out of it.'

HESKETH, Third Lord, THOMAS ALEXANDER FERMOR-HESKETH, *born* 28 October 1950.

Educated Ampleforth, from which he ran away in a taxi to London, travelling around on the Circle Line tube until he decided it was time to go back. Made an estimated seven-figure fortune buying and selling a Scottish estate, which financed his Grand Prix motor racing ambitions, starting in 1972 in Formula Three with James Hunt as his driver, operating from the stables of Easton Neston, the eighteenth-century mansion set in 5,000 Northamptonshire acres that he inherited, with the title, at the age of four. In June 1975, after spending £500,000, the combination won the Dutch Grand Prix at Zandvoort but six months later Alexander Hesketh sold up to Frank Williams. A subsequent business

Lord Hesketh

making powerful motorbikes failed. After romancing actress Helen Mirren, and debutantes Jane Leveson and Victoria Warrender (now Lady Reay) he married, in 1977, the Hon. Claire Watson (one son, two daughters), daughter of soap heir Lord Manton, later Senior Steward of the Jockey Club (Hesketh owns Towcester racecourse). He was Lord-in-Waiting (Government Whip), 1986–9.

HILL, GRAHAM, *born* 15 February 1929, married, 1955, Bette Hill (one son, two daughters).
Grand Prix racing driver, 1958–75 who once almost killed the Prince of Wales, whom he was told to follow at Thruxton – Charles put his foot down and vanished only for Hill to take up pursuit and come round a corner to find the Heir to the Throne spinning wildly – Hill missed him by inches. A regular at Annabel's and a gifted and witty after-dinner speaker, he was world champion driver in 1962 and 1968 and runner-up 1963, 1964, 1965. After he died, with five members of his Hill-Embassy team, piloting his Piper Aztec, which crashed, uninsured, in fog three miles short of Elstree on a November night in 1975, 1,300 people, including the Earl of Snowdon, who had turned down the offer of a seat on the fated plane, turned up at his funeral at St Alban's Abbey, Hertfordshire. His son, Damon, is also a racing driver.

HODGE, VICKI ALEXANDRA, *born* 17 October 1946, daughter of Sir John Hodge, second baronet.
Sixties model, married, 1969, Ian Heath, Harrow-educated son of Sir Barrie Heath, Chairman of GKN (marriage dissolved 1980). Involved before, and for most of her marriage, with well-endowed actor John Bindon, whom she took on holiday to Mustique, she effected an introduction to Princess Margaret and then sold the story with informal snaps to the Mirror Group for an estimated £30,000. In 1979 Bindon was charged with the murder of underworld figure John Darke in a Fulham drinking den,

grandiosely called the Ranelagh Yacht Club, but was acquitted at the Old Bailey on the grounds of self-defence. Moved to Barbados, where her brother-in-law John Kidd (a grandson of Lord Beaverbrook) had a family plantation house, Holders. In March 1983 Prince Andrew, whose ship HMS *Invincible* was making a courtesy call to the island, was invited by the Kidds to Holders. There Vicki seduced the naive Prince. She has completed an autobiography which she hopes to publish.

Vicki Hodge and John Bindon

HOHENLOHE-LANGENBURG, Prince
ALFONSO, *born* 1925.
In 1955 married fifteen-year-old Princess Ira von Furstenberg (two sons), niece of Italy's richest man, Fiat chief, Gianni Agnelli (marriage dissolved 1960). Put Marbella on the map after opening the Marbella Club in 1954 on the small estate beside the Mediterranean which his father owned. Married in 1973 (dissolved 1985), former British starlet, Jocelyn 'Jackie' Lane (one daughter) and he has a daughter by German model, Heidi

Balzer. In 1986 he asked Soraya Khashoggi (q.v.) to marry him (she turned him down). Seeking to expand the Marbella Club empire, he was invited in 1979 by Mme Imelda Marcos, wife of the Philippines President, to set up a club on an island near Manila. When it was finished, Mme Marcos expropriated it. Has opened other clubs in Port Antonio, Jamaica and Sharjah, United Arab Emirates, after selling a controlling interest to Syrian-born Mouffak Al Midani, who owned the Dorchester Hotel before the Sultan of Brunei.

HOLDEN, ANTHONY IVAN, *born* 22 May 1947.
Educated at Oundle and Merton College, Oxford. An avid poker player known as 'Golden' and a protégé of Harold Evans who made him Atticus on the **Sunday Times** 1977–9 when he published his first biography of the Heir to the Throne (**Charles, Prince of Wales**) which was so successful that he went into tax exile in America, working as Washington correspondent of the **Observer**. Rejoined Evans on **The Times**, as Features and Assistant Editor 1981–2 and led revolt over sacking of Evans by Rupert Murdoch. Shortly afterwards, at an anniversary party for Hatchards attended by the Queen and Prince Philip, Holden noticed that Murdoch, who was not on the guest list (but whose company controlled Hatchards) had gate-crashed, and rushed over to the Prince, urging him to 'cut' the Australian publisher. Married 1971 (dissolved 1988) musician Amanda Warren (three sons) but left her for American journalist Cindy Blake, whom he met during a spell as Executive Editor of **Today**, 1985–6. To restore his finances, produced an 'intrusive' update of the Charles biography to coincide with the Prince's fortieth birthday, which so offended its subject that Holden was blackballed from Charles's club, the Garrick, when he came up for membership in 1989.

HONEY, ALDINE, *born* 1940.
South African beauty queen who became a top model in London. Wearing Dior, she married, in 1963, fellow South African, Chone Dredzen (two sons). After the marriage was dissolved her escorts included Sir Charles Clore (q.v.) who made her Public Relations Officer for Selfridge's, part of his Sears Holdings empire; sporting baronet Sir William Pigott-Brown (q.v.) and publisher Lord Weidenfeld. From 1975 to 1978 she lived in London with reclusive property tycoon Harry J. Hyams (q.v.) who returned to his Wiltshire manor at weekends to be with his wife, Kay. Now a leading London estate agent, she has never remarried.

HOWARD DE WALDEN, Ninth Lord, JOHN OSMAEL SCOTT-ELLIS, *born* 27 November 1912.
Educated Eton and Magdalene College, Cambridge. Married first, 21 August 1934, Countess Irene Harrach (four daughters), who died 1975 and he married, secondly, Gillian Buckley, former wife of Seventeenth Viscount Mountgarret. Inherited 100 acres of Marylebone, valued at £250 million, and is landlord to many doctors and dentists in Harley Street, Wimpole Street, etc. All four daughters are co-heiresses to the title which dates from 1597 and was given to a son of the Fourth Duke of Norfolk. He gave each daughter twenty-five acres. A member of the Jockey Club and Senior Steward on three occasions, he is England's longest established owner-breeder of racehorses. With apricot colours, he won the 1985 Epsom Derby with Slip Anchor and previously owned the champion miler, Kirs, trained by Henry Cecil (q.v.), both of which are at stud. He has a 2,000-acre estate near Hungerford and in the days of Queen Charlotte's Ball, the first event of The Season, his mother Margherita, Lady Howard de Walden, would have the ceremonial cake, escorted by all the year's debs, presented to her.

HULANICKI, BARBARA, *born* 1938, daughter of a Polish army general.
With husband Stephen FitzSimon, started Biba (the nickname of her sister Biruta) in

Abingdon Road, Kensington in 1964 and is credited with having launched the 'Dolly Bird'. Eight years later they expanded into the Derry and Toms building in Kensington High Street (famous for its roof gardens), but within five years the business had collapsed. The couple, with their son Witold, went to Brazil, where they started a fashion business, but in 1986 Barbara took a ten-week crash course in photography at the London Polytechnic and began a new career. The couple now live in Florida and Witold is in the movie business after studying film-making at university in New York. In 1990 Barbara published **Disgrace**, a steamy semi-autobiographical novel.

Barbara Hulanicki

HUNT, JAMES SIMON WALLIS, *born* 29 August 1947.
Educated Wellington College, one of four sons of the former senior partner of the Hedderwick, Hunt stockbroking firm. After

starting as Lord Hesketh's driver, became the world champion in 1976 in the last Grand Prix race of the season in Japan, beating Niki Lauda who had continued racing after suffering horrific burns in a crash earlier in the season. Married first, 1974, model Susan Miller after meeting on a beach in Marbella, the Costa del Sol resort that became their tax exile home. Within a year they planned to separate but Hunt, who offered his wife $10,000 and a plane ticket as a settlement, took Suzy to Gstaad where she met Richard Burton (they married, after she obtained a Haitian divorce in August 1976). Finally legally divorced in England, Hunt married, in 1983, Sarah Lomax (two sons), daughter of the first woman racehorse trainer to win a race at Royal Ascot. His bride gave him two budgerigars, which eventually led to the end of their marriage six years later. He became a fanatic, breeding and showing birds (last count 380) spending four hours every day with them, in an aviary in the garden of his Wimbledon house.

HUSTON, JOHN, *born* Nevada, Missouri, 5 August 1906.
Amateur boxer, Mexican cavalry officer, painter in Paris, he made his first film, **The Maltese Falcon** (in which his father, Walter Huston, made a fleeting appearance) in 1941. Grandson of Irish immigrants who settled in Canada, Huston returned to Ireland, buying a 100-acre estate in Galway and became an Irish citizen in 1964, riding to hounds with the Galway Blazers (which formed the backdrop of his unusual 1963 film, **The List of Adrian Messenger**). Married first Dorothy Harvey, second Lesley Black, third Evelyn Keyes, one adopted son, fourth Enrica Soma (one son, two daughters), who died 1969, and fifth, in 1972, Celeste Shane (dissolved 1975). Also a son Danny, born 1962, by Zoe Sallis. Once Miss Keyes found him at a party with a blonde on his knee and pulling her off, pointed at ballerina 'Ricki' Soma, saying, 'I'm his wife, Ricki is his mistress and you're superfluous.' Daughter Anjelica, involved for twelve years with Jack Nicholson, co-starred

with him in *Prizzi's Honour*, directed by her father, and won an Oscar as Best Supporting Actress. Lived the last part of his life at Las Caletas, a group of white houses on a lonely, unspoilt bay twenty-five miles south of Puerto Vallarta with his fifth wife's former maid, Maricela, a Mexican. He suffered from emphysema, which he caught after smoking when recovering from double pneumonia and died in Newport, Rhode Island in August 1987 while working on the film *Mr North*, which his son Danny was directing and in which Anjelica starred. When Nicholson saw him in beatific state in his open casket before burial he remarked, 'Boy, the person who made John up must have been a fan!'

HYAMS, HARRY JACK, *born* 1928.
A property developer who perplexed the City by building the thirty-four-storey Centre Point skyscraper at the junction of Tottenham Court Road and Charing Cross Road in 1964, only to see it remain empty for more than a decade. His Oldham estates company, formed in 1959 with £50,000, was sold for £531 million in 1987 (he owned

Harry Hyams

thirty per cent). A keen shot and fisherman, he bought the 450-acre Ramsbury Manor, Berkshire estate, with its beautiful Caroline house, from the late Lord Rootes for £300,000 in 1965, where he lives in squir-archal style with his wife Kay (no children). His box at Epsom is next to the Royal box. For three years, until 1978, he was involved with South African-born former model, Aldine Honey (q.v.), but returned to his wife after a 'marry me or' ultimatum. In 1968 he bought *Shemara*, the 850-ton yacht formerly owned by Sir Bernard Docker (q.v.) but she has remained unused in a Southampton marina after a dispute with the Vosper ship-yard over repairs. During his philandering years, he would begin an affair with the irre-sistible line, 'You must have my child.'

His Exalted Highness Eighth Nizam of Hyderabad, MUKARRAM JAH, MIR BARKAT ALI KHAN BAHADUR, FATEH JUNG, *born* 1933.
The most senior of the Saluted Princes of India (twenty-one guns) who, in 1967, suc-ceeded his grandfather, often referred to as the world's richest man, inheriting a fabled collection of jewels and 200 raddled con-cubines. Educated at Harrow and Cambridge, and was Senior Cadet at the Royal Military Academy, Sandhurst. In March 1960 married Turkish student Esra Birgin (one son, one daughter) at Kensington Register Office (marriage dissolved). In the seventies he bought a one-million-acre cattle and sheep station 600 miles north-east of Perth, Western Australia, and married local lass Helen Simmons (two sons), giving her the title Princess Helen Ayesha (Radiant One). They separated in 1987 and she died of Aids two years later. Often to be seen driving one of his tractors, the Nizam is known locally as Mr Jah. He has a house in Perth and a Lear Jet on call. The Nizam, whose mother was the daughter of the last Caliph of Turkey, is now involved with Turkish beauty queen Manolya Onur. Prin-cess Esra lives in Campden Hill, Kensington and is the best friend of Princess Michael of Kent.

I*i*

INGLEBY-MACKENZIE, Colin David, *born* 1935.

Educated Eton, an insurance broker and son of surgeon Vice-Admiral Sir Alexander Ingleby-Mackenzie. A left-handed batsman, he was Captain of Hampshire County Cricket Club, leading them to their first county championship in 1961 – he retired four seasons later. In April 1963 he was cleared by a jury at Abingdon Quarter Sessions of driving a car while unfit through drink after admitting that he had imbibed nine whiskies, three glasses of wine and one brandy during a cricket dinner. He was arrested for jumping a red traffic light and mounting a kerb while overtaking another car. In January 1975 he married Mrs Susan Stormonth-Darling (one daughter), daughter of racehorse-owning solicitor Raymond Clifford-Turner. By her previous marriage she had four children aged between seventeen and six.

INGRAMS, Richard Reid, *born* 19 August 1937.

Educated at Shrewsbury and University College, Oxford. National Service as a

Richard Ingrams

private in the Royal Army Service Corps after failing to gain a commission when he told the interview board that he played the cello, not football. Joined **Private Eye**, founded by fellow Old Salopians, in 1962, becoming its second Editor, after Christopher Booker, the following year. Married, 1962, Mary Morgan (one son, one daughter, one son deceased), a **Private Eye** secretary from Anglo-Irish hunting stock. When sued for criminal libel in 1976 by Sir James Goldsmith (q.v.), he went to Bow Street Magistrates Court preparing to be sent to prison, having had a haircut and wearing a new brown corduroy jacket. Asked what he feared about jail, he replied, 'Being visited by Lord Longford'. In the event he escaped and the massive Goldsmith-Eye litigation made the Organ more popular than ever. Gave up editorship in 1986 to concentrate on writing books, while retaining his annual salary estimated (with pension contributions) at £45,000, and an office car. Has a cottage on Romney Marsh near Rye, where he spends increasing periods, while Mary Ingrams remains at their Aldworth, Berkshire home. There have been several separations but no hint (she is a staunch Catholic) of a divorce. His maternal grandfather was Queen Victoria's Balmoral physician. In 1990 his daughter, Jubby, married David Ford, son of the Queen's former Assistant Private Secretary, Sir Edward, and former lover of Margaux Hemingway.

IVANOVIC, IVAN (VANE) STEVAN, *born* 9 June 1913.
Educated Westminster, Peterhouse, Cambridge. Married, 1939, June Fisher (died 1970), daughter of the Canon of Colchester (two sons, one daughter). Yugoslav shipping heir, who was a quadruple Blue at university and hurdled in the 1936 Berlin Olympics, he has been Consul-General for Monaco in London since 1967. An aqualung spearfisherman for four months a year at his homes in Majorca and Tortola, he lives in London by Regent's Park, running every morning at 6.30a.m. to the Royal Automobile Club in

Pall Mall, where he has a turkish bath and massage and a two hour sleep before his chauffeur wakes him up at 10.30a.m. with his clothes and a goat's-milk yoghurt.

IVEAGH, Third Earl of, ARTHUR FRANCIS BENJAMIN GUINNESS, *born* 20 May 1937.
Educated Eton, Trinity College, Cambridge and the University of Grenoble. Married, 1963 (dissolved 1984), Miranda Smiley (two sons, two daughters). Former Chairman of Guinness PLC and President since 1986. Known as Ben, denied during the Guinness trial, when cross-examined by QC for sacked Guinness Chief Executive Ernest Saunders, that he had a drink problem. In 1966 he took out Irish citizenship. In May 1984 the contents of Elveden Hall, Norfolk, a former family home set in 23,000 acres, were sold for £5,750,000. His younger sister Lady Henrietta Guinness (born 19 August 1942) threw herself from a 250-foot high aqueduct in Spoleto, Italy in May 1978, three months after marrying former waiter Luigi Marinori, the father of her seven-month-old daughter, Sara. She had suffered from depression following a crash in France in 1963, when she was engaged unofficially to Chelsea adventurer Michael Beeby, who was driving the car, a drophead Aston Martin DB4.

J*j*

JACKSON, GLENDA, *born* 9 May 1936.
A bricklayer's daughter, she worked on the laxatives counter of Boots, Birkenhead after West Kirby County Grammar School for Girls, before going to RADA and starting in rep. in 1957. Married actor Roy Hodges (one son) 1958, and fell in love with lighting designer Andy Phillips on her 1975 world tour of Ibsen's **Hedda Gabler**. The marriage was dissolved in 1976 and the affair ended five years later. Won Oscars for **Women in**

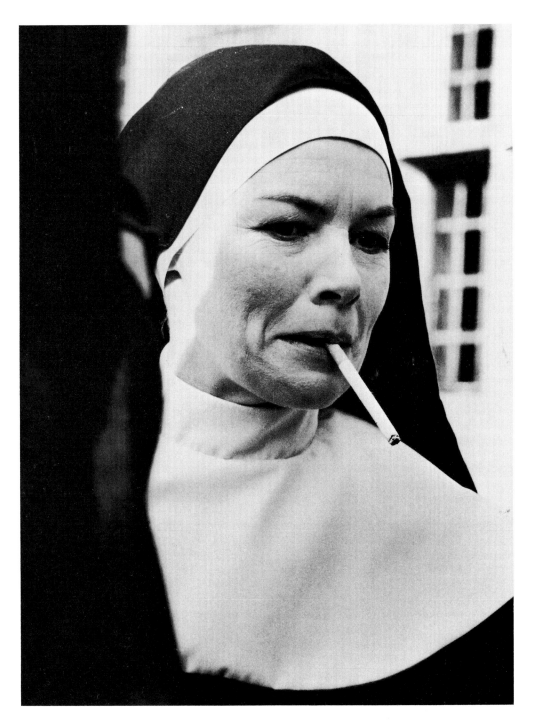

Glenda Jackson

Love (1971) and *A Touch of Class* (1974). Her ex-husband said if she ever went into politics, she would become Prime Minister (she served on the Equity Council 1972–3) and in March 1990 she was selected as the Labour Parliamentary candidate for the marginal Conservative-held seat (2,221 majority) of Hampstead and Highgate and says she will give up acting if elected.

JAGGER, MICK, *born* 1943.
Educated Dartford Grammar School, London School of Economics. Helped form the Rolling Stones in 1962 as a small blues combo, playing upstairs at a Soho pub. The group's first society date was the Hastings Caves coming-out-dance of the Hon. Roxana 'Bunty' Lampson, younger daughter of First Lord Killearn, July 1963, for a fee of £20. Married St Tropez, May 1971, Bianca Perex Morena de Macias (one daughter, Jade), with the Earl of Lichfield (q.v.) as best man. Divorced 1972. He has another daughter, Karis, by Marsha Hunt, and a daughter, Elizabeth Scarlett, and son, James, by his fourteen-year romance with Texan model Jerry Hall, one of five daughters in Mesquite, Texas, to a truck-driver father and librarian mother. Jade achieved early notoriety by being expelled from St Mary's Calne, a top boarding school, and being involved with Josh Astor, natural son of Lord Kagan (q.v.) and adopted son of the Hon. Michael Langhorne Astor, who subsequently pleaded guilty in 1988 to drug charges. Homes include a château in France (with four resident gardeners), a villa in Mustique. Bianca, known as 'The Nicaraguan Firecracker', moved to America, where she became part of Andy Warhol's entourage but objected to references to her amorous nature in his posthumously published diaries and sued for libel in Britain in 1989. Top model Jerry, who ran off briefly with racehorse owner Robert Sangster in 1983, says Mick likes her *au nature* and does not encourage a daily bath.

Lieutenant-General His Highness the Thirty-Ninth Maharajah of Jaipur, RAJA RAJINDRA SHRI MAHARAJADHIRAJA SAWAI SIR MAN SINGHJI BAHADUR, *born* 21 August 1911.
The second son of the Thakur of Isarda, he was adopted at the age of ten by the Maharaja of Jaipur, whom a year later he succeeded. Educated at Mayo College, Ajmer and Royal Military Academy, Woolwich, and known as 'Jai'. In 1924 he married the sister of the late Air-Vice-Marshal Sir Umed Singh, Maharaja of Jodhpur (two sons). Secondly, in 1932, the daughter (one son, one daughter) of the late Sir Sumer Singh, Maharaja of Jodhpur and, thirdly, in 1940, Ayesha Gayatri Devi (one son), sister of the Maharaja of Cooch Behar, having four sons and a daughter by these marriages. Ruler of three million people in Rajasthan, where the fabled pink City Palace, one of five he owned, has 500 rooms. A fanatical polo player, he bought an estate, King's Beeches, near Ascot to play at the Guards Polo Club, Smith's Lawn every summer, becoming among the closest friends, with his wife Ayesha, of the Queen and Prince Philip. In 1986 he was appointed India's first Ambassador to Spain. He died of a heart attack in June 1970, playing polo at Cirencester. In 1975 the Maharanee, an Opposition MP, was jailed by the Government of Mrs Indira Gandhi, accused of hoarding more than £7 million in gold and jewels – she was never charged and eventually freed.

JAY, The Hon. PETER, *born* 7 February 1937.
Educated Winchester, Christ Church College, Oxford. Midshipman and Sub-Lieutenant, RNVR 1956–7. Economics Editor of *The Times* whose column was once queried by a sub-editor, saying he was not able to understand it. 'You are not meant to,' replied Jay. 'It has been written for three people.' Married, 1961 (dissolved 1986), Margaret Callaghan (one son, two daughters) and appointed Ambassador to Washington in 1977 when her father, James Callaghan, was Prime Minister. While in Washington,

Mick Jagger and Marianne Faithfull, 1967

she fell in love with Carl Bernstein, husband of scriptwriter Nora Ephron, and the reporter who helped break the Watergate scandal for the *Washington Post*. Jay had an affair with his children's nanny, Jane Tustian, and is the father of her son Nicholas, born 1981. He married Emma Thornton (two sons), a furniture designer, in 1986 when he joined publisher Robert Maxwell as Chief-of-Staff, resigning in December 1989 to become Economics Editor of the BBC.

JELLICOE, Second Earl, GEORGE PATRICK JOHN RUSHWORTH *born* 4 April 1918.
Son of Admiral of the Fleet Earl Jellicoe and godson of King George V. Educated Winchester and Trinity College, Cambridge. Married first, 1944 (dissolved 1966), Patricia O'Kane (two sons, two daughters), secondly Mrs Philippa Bridge (née Dunne), one son, two daughters. Lord Privy Seal and Leader of the House of Lords 1970–3, he resigned in the wake of the callgirl scandal involving Lord Lambton (q.v.) when he admitted paying for the services of a prostitute after his name came up by chance during a Scotland Yard inquiry into Soho strip club king, James Humphreys. In 1956 Jellicoe, First Secretary at the Embassy in Washington and Brussels, gave up his Foreign Office career because his first wife would not give him a divorce and he was involved with Mrs Bridge. He has been Chairman of Booker Tate since 1988 (and a director of Tate and Lyle since 1974).

JENKINS, SIMON DAVID, *born* 10 June 1943.
Son of a Welsh Congregationalist Minister, educated Mill Hill school and St John's College, Oxford. Started journalistic career on *Country Life*, 1965, before becoming News Editor of *The Times Literary Supplement*. Made Editor of the London *Evening Standard* in 1976 by his mentor, former *Evening Standard* Editor Charles Wintour (q.v.) but quit after two less than successful years. In 1978 married actress Gayle Hunnicutt (one son), former wife of actor and director David Hemmings, who had pre-

viously been escorted by the Marquess of Douro (q.v.). Appointed Editor of *The Times* in March 1990 drawing the headline in the *Evening Standard*, 'Dallas star's husband to edit *The Times*.' The only full-time journalist on the Calcutt committee which, in June 1990, recommended tough, new privacy laws and a strict code of conduct by newspapers. Once laid siege to by an amorous Fleet Street harpie, Jenkins finally submitted, telling her, 'Oh, all right, Mary. Just this once.'

JERMYN, Earl, FREDERICK WILLIAM JOHN AUGUSTUS HERVEY, *born* 15 September 1954 (succeeded father as Seventh Marquess of Bristol, 1985).
Educated Harrow and went into tax exile in 1979 in Monaco, living between Monte Carlo and Manhattan until announcing his engagement, in May 1984, to Miss Francesca Fisher, twenty, whose father, Douglas, had owned various restaurants in Knightsbridge and Chelsea in the fifties and sixties and had retired to Marbella to become a property consultant. Previously described as either 'exotic' or 'confirmed bachelor', John Jermyn asked newspapers to desist and took legal action over reports that his fiancée was a divorcée, having married American musician Phillip Jones at Westminster register office in 1983 – in July 1984 Francesca had obtained a nullity in Nevada. The wedding, at Ickworth, the family seat, was boycotted by the bridegroom's father, the Sixth Marquess of Bristol (q.v.) and after less than two years of marriage, Francesca ran off with Brazilian playboy Roberto Shorto after meeting him on a yachting holiday in Greek waters. The marriage was dissolved in 1987. In June 1988 Bristol was arrested smuggling cocaine. He was sentenced to one year in jail and released in April 1989. In the September he was fined £3,000 by Bury St Edmunds magistrates court for possessing cocaine at Ickworth and lost his driving licence for refusing to give a sample after passing a breathalyzer test. In February 1990 he rented a house in Double Bay, Sydney for six months but was deported

from Australia in June for failing to obtain a permit needed by visitors with a criminal record. He is alleged to have told the authorities, 'I don't know what you're worried about – most of you are descended from criminals anyway.'

JOEL, HARRY, (JIM), *born* 4 September 1894. Doyen of the Turf (racing colours: black, scarlet cap), owner and breeder of Royal Palace, the Epsom Derby winner 1967. Son of South African diamond magnate Jack Barnato Joel, who won every English Classic race, including the Derby twice, he was educated at Malvern and served 1914–18 with the Fifteenth Hussars. Inherited Sefton Lodge, Newmarket as training stables and Childwick Bury, St Albans as a home and stud (selling the house to film producer Stanley Kubrick in 1977). Paid a record £30,000 in 1946 to Viscount Astor for his 2,000 Guineas winner, Court Martial. In 1986 he sold all his in-foal mares and three-year-old fillies for more than £4 million. At the age of ninety-two he finally won the Grand National, with Maori Venture, which he says was the greatest thrill of his racing life. Never married.

His Majesty King Hussein of Jordan, *born* 14 November 1935.
Educated Harrow, trained Royal Military Academy, Sandhurst. Married first, April 1955 (dissolved 1957), Sharifa Dina Abdul Hamid (one daughter), secondly, 1961 (dissolved 1972), Toni Avil Gardiner of Ipswich (two sons, twin daughters), thirdly Alia Toukan (one son, one daughter, one adopted daughter), fourthly, in June 1978, Elizabeth Halaby (two sons, two daughters). The Hashemite Monarch bore an uncanny resemblance to a leading, well-endowed libidinous character in a *roman-à-clef* written by Viviane Ventura (q.v.). His second wife was the daughter of an English colonel who ran the royal mews in Amman and he met his fourth wife, to whom he gave the name Noor, when she turned up in Amman in blue jeans to work for Royal Jordanian Airlines. Her

father Najeeb, was the Syrian born President of Pan Am, and her mother, Doris, a Swede. They married after a whirlwind romance. They have homes in Vienna, the Canary Islands, Washington, London and Ascot, where the King bought Buckhurst Park for £4.2 million, the former home of Arts Council Chairman Peter Palumbo (q.v.). He has given, rent free, his other local residence, Castlewood, which was used by his children, to the Duke and Duchess of York until their new house at Sunninghill is built. The Queen has allowed him to expand seventy-acre Buckhurst into the adjoining Crown Estates for 'security reasons'. Financially supported by America, Saudi Arabia and, briefly, Brunei, Hussein now rules over a virtually bankrupt country and exile in one of his foreign homes is becoming an increasing probability.

King Hussein of Jordan

JOSEPH, Sir MAXWELL, *born* 1910.
Built up the Grand Metropolitan group from a modest hotel operation to an international business including Watney, Mann brewery, the Inter-Continental Hotels and the Liggett drink and tobacco combine in America with 130,000 employees. Refused to work more than an eight-hour day, five days a week and would spend the weekends out of telephonic contact. In 1932 married Sybil Nedas, sister-

in-law of property magnate Lord (Harold) Samuel. They separated but did not divorce until 1981, when he married Eileen (one son, one daughter), a gifted interior decorator, who had shared his life for twenty years and had changed her surname to Joseph by deed poll. Joseph had the finest private stamp collection in Britain, apart from that of the Queen, but sold it for £1.04 million because HM would not swap with him. He died in September 1982 leaving £16 million to his widow and £200,000 to her personal assistant, Judith Bowen.

JUNOR, Sir JOHN, *born* 15 January 1919.
Educated Glasgow University, married, 1942, Pamela Mary Welsh (one son, one daughter). After serving in the Second World War as a Lieutenant in the RNVR, he was the unsuccessful Labour candidate for Kincardine and West Aberdeen, 1945; East Edinburgh 1948, and Dundee West, 1951. Describes the most frightening experience of his life as when, training in Canada and on his first solo night flight, he lost all sense of direction. With fuel running out, he finally saw the wing-tip lights of another plane and followed it, landing safely – and has been following the wing-tip lights of great Fleet Street proprietors ever since – Lord Beaverbrook, for whom he was Editor of the *Sunday Express* (1954–86) and, following his resignation in 1989 from writing his famous Current Affairs column, which put Auchtermuchty, his personal Brigadoon, on the map, moved to Viscount Rothermere's *Mail on Sunday*. After Lord Matthews took over Beaverbrook Newspapers, Junor summoned Richard Ingrams (q.v.) to an urgent lunch promising to reveal hot news. 'Richard,' said Junor as Ingrams sat down in the Terrazza Est., 'Victor Matthews is not a Jew.' Separated for several years from Lady Junor, he lives in a house in a wood near Dorking and plays golf nearby at Walton Heath. He is devoted to his author daughter Penny and her children, visiting them on his way home every evening. Claims he was persecuted by the City of London Police for several weeks after an altercation in Fleet Street over which he made an official complaint, with mysterious unmarked cars following him down the A3 and trying to force him into ditches. Mystery never solved.

K*k*

KAGAN, Lord, JOSEPH, (life peer created 1976), *born* 6 June 1915.
Educated High School, Kaunas, Lithuania, Leeds University. Married, 1943, Margaret Stromas (two sons, one daughter). Invented Gannex, which his close friend Harold Wilson, the Prime Minister who ennobled him, helped publicize internationally by wearing on an official visit to Moscow. An early admirer of Mrs Marcia Williams, later Lady Falkender (q.v.), who was Wilson's private and political secretary. When Kagan began an affair with Judy Innes, then Fashion Editor of the *Daily Mail*, he told her inconsolable husband, *Daily Telegraph* journalist John Moynihan, 'Let me introduce you to Marcia.' With Judy, who later married the late Hon. Michael Langhorne Astor, younger brother of Third Viscount Astor, he had a son Joshua (see Mick Jagger), born November 1966, who was adopted by Astor. In 1980, Kagan, who claims he has never accepted any allowance for his frequent appearances in the House of Lords, was jailed after being extradited from France for theft and false accounting associated with his Yorkshire textiles business. He has fled abroad with his secretary Angela Radford, who had been one of his mistresses.

KASTNER, ELLIOTT, *born* 17 January 1933.
Educated University of Miami and Columbia, joining the MCA agency in 1957, becoming senior agent in the motion picture and literary department and when MCA took over Universal Studios in 1964, he continued with the company as an executive

producing films, claiming to have financed and produced more than fifty in twenty-five years. Famed for spawning litigation – author Alistair Maclean sued for $100,000 over the film Kastner made of his novel, **Where Eagles Dare**, and at the 1986 Cannes Film Festival, was sent sprawling in the Mougin de Mougins restaurant by Peter Holm, then married to Joan Collins, after she claimed she had been knocked over by Kastner – the feud went back seven years over a claim by Jackie Collins that Kastner owed her money. In 1988 Kastner declared himself bankrupt in Britain rather than pay Moses Rothman, owner of the rights of the major Charlie Chaplin films, who had sued for an outstanding debt going back a decade and totalling £500,000. Married, 1960, Carolyn Hughes. By Tessa Kennedy (former wife of the late Dominic Elwes, q.v.) he has one son, one daughter and, despite reports to the contrary, his first marriage has never been dissolved, and therefore, has never married Tessa, a close friend of Queen Noor of Jordan, whose houses she decorates.

KAUSOV, Sergei Danyelovich, *born* 1942. First wife, Natalya (one daughter), marriage dissolved 1978. Married second, in Moscow, 1 August 1978 (dissolved 1980), Christina Onassis. Former Paris Director of the tanker division of Sovfracht, a department of the Soviet Ministry of the Maritime Fleet. Gave his bride a golden cocker spaniel, which she named Uri after the hero in **Dr Zhivago**, her favourite film. He moved to her Avenue Foch, Paris apartment after their attempts to set up home in Moscow palled, but she became bored of him, telling her friends he was 'not chic'. As a divorce settlement, Kausov was given two tankers valued at $7.5 million and moved to Arlington House, Piccadilly, a block of flats overlooking Green Park, setting up his shipping business with an office also in Greece. He later bought an apartment in Basil Street, Knightsbridge, near Harrods, and moved his business headquarters to Switzerland. In London he became a member of leading clubs, like Annabel's and Aspinall's and in July 1989 he paid £2 million for the Mustique villa of Lord Glenconner, set in twenty acres, with three guest houses on stilts. For much of the eighties he escorted Andrea Leveque, twenty years his junior, whose family own a large dairy business in Massachusetts.

KEATING, Geoffrey, *born* 1914. Son of an Irish MP at Westminster who began his career as a photographer in Fleet Street working for the **Daily Sketch** (merged, 1971, with the **Daily Mail**). In 1939 he was appointed public relations officer to the British Expeditionary Force in France, later moving to the Middle East to become chief war photographer to Field Marshal Viscount Montgomery and was wounded several times, winning the MC at Tobruk. After the Second World War he joined British Petroleum, working first in Persia and then London, and was the company's 'Mr Fixit' until his retirement in 1974. In 1966, married Susan Shafto (one daughter), former wife of John Dashwood (younger brother of Sir Francis, q.v.) and daughter of Countess Howe by her first marriage. Famed for knowing everyone in London, Keating attempted to resolve the titanic battle between **Private Eye** and his friend Sir James Goldsmith (q.v.). He died in 1981.

KEAYS, Sarah, *born* 1948. A colonel's daughter with political ambitions, who became the secretary and mistress of Cecil Parkinson, MP for Hertsmere since 1983, (previously Enfield West, and Hertfordshire South). She gave birth to their daughter, Flora, on New Year's Eve, 1983, three months after he resigned as Secretary of State for Trade and Industry after her affair and pregnancy were revealed during the Conservative Party Conference. Miss Keays had been keen to become an MP but had experienced difficulty getting on the candidate list. In July 1988 Flora underwent a brain operation to remove a brain tumour and has since suffered from epilepsy. Mr Parkinson, who has three daughters by his 1957 marriage to Ann Jarvis, has never seen Flora, but increased his maintenance payments for her to £10,000 a year in 1988. Claiming that Mr Parkinson was the 'only man' she had ever loved, Miss Keays said in 1986 that she doubted she would ever marry and lives in a stone-built cottage close to the Marksbury, Wiltshire home of her father, Colonel Hastings Keays.

Sarah Keays and friend

KEITH OF CASTLEACRE, Lord,
KENNETH ALEXANDER, (life peer), *born* 30 August 1916.
Norfolk landowner, married first, 1946 (dissolved 1958), Lady Ariel Baird (one son, one daughter), secondly, 1962 (dissolved 1972), Mrs Nancy Hayward, thirdly, 1973, Mrs Marie Hanbury. Educated at Rugby, trained as a chartered accountant, served with Welsh Guards (Colonel, 1945) in North Africa, Italy, France and Germany. Vice-Chairman of British European Airways 1964–71, British Airways, 1971–2, Chairman Hill, Samuel Group 1970–80, Chairman and Chief Executive Rolls Royce Ltd 1972–80, Chairman of Beecham Group 1986–7. Once complained of having to travel economy class to Hong Kong among crowded, chattering Chinese on his lifelong British Airways free pass, because all first and business-class seats were sold, only for the BA executive to reply that the Chinese had complained as well because, at 6ft 4ins tall, he took up too much room! His daughter, Camilla, was married to Sir Rupert Mackeson (q.v.).

KENWRIGHT, BILL, *born* 1946.
Turned impresario in 1970 after achieving national celebrity status as Gordon Clegg in 'Coronation Street', Britain's number one rated series. His first success was *The Miracle Worker*, starring Pat Phoenix, but then lost £400,000 on a West End revival of *West Side Story* – which he made back on *Joseph and the Amazing Technicolour Dreamcoat*, which toured Britain for eight years in the eighties. In April 1978, after a short romance, he married New Zealand-born actress Anouska Hempel (who later married Sir Mark Weinberg, q.v.) and they divorced in March 1980. His previous loves included Shirley Anne Field and, after his divorce, actress Heather Wright, Miss World Mary Stavin and Koo Stark (q.v.).

KERMAN, ISIDORE, *born* 13 March 1905.
London's most fashionable pre-war and post-war solicitor, specializing in divorce. Married, in 1943, Blanche Rowe (two sons). A director of Pergamon when Robert Maxwell's company received a 1969 takeover bid from American computer company Leasco, whose President, Saul Steinberg, they sued for the return of £9 million in respect

Michael White, Koo Stark and Bill Kenwright

of 22 million shares purchased, leading to a Department of Trade and Industry Inquiry. Family company controls Scott's, the Mount Street restaurant, and other restaurants, which included the Mirabelle, sold to George Walker (*see* Milford Haven, Marquess of) in 1989. Also Chairman of Fontwell and Plumpton racecourses. He keeps his race-horses and prizewinning beef herd at his 700-acre Edenbridge, Kent farm, called Kybo after advice given to him in letters to school from his mother: 'Keep Your Bowels Open.'

KESWICK, HENRY NEVILLE LINDSAY, *born* 29 September 1938.
Educated Eton, the great-grandson of the Dumfries trader who married into the Jardine family, co-founders of Jardine, Matheson, Hong Kong's major trading concern, which became the first company into Japan in 1886 and had its origins in the Chinese opium

trade. Ran the company in Hong Kong between 1972 and 1975 and is reputed to have made a £15 million fortune in that period, while local investors experienced heavy losses gambling on the Hang Seng index. In June 1975 bought the *Spectator*, losing £50,000 a year until selling the publication to Algy Cluff (q.v.) in 1981. Seemingly a lifelong bachelor, he was rumoured to have become engaged in 1980 to Sabrina Guinness, a former fancy of the Prince of Wales, who summered at his Scottish estate, but eventually married, in 1985, the Hon. Tessa Fraser, former wife of Lord Reay and younger daughter of the Seventeenth Lord Lovat. Nicknamed 'Scotch Egg' and once weighing seventeen stone (he is 6ft 3ins tall), he is now a trimmer thirteen and a half stone. His youngest brother Simon (Sammy), born 20 May 1942, took over the chairmanship of Jardine, Matheson in 1983, handing it back to

Henry in 1989. Their sister Teresa, a barrister, retreated into a Norfolk nunnery, the closed Order of Carmelites in 1983.

KHASHOGGI, ADNAN, *born* 25 July 1935. Married first, 1961 (dissolved 1974), Sandra Jarvis-Daley (four sons, one daughter) secondly, 1978, 'Countess' Laura Biancolini (one son). Son of the physician to King Ibn Saud of Saudi Arabia, Khashoggi became the 'Mr Fixit' between the desert kingdom and arms suppliers and defence contractors such as Lockheed, who admitted paying him £50 million. At a Senate hearing, he was accused of taking the money as a bribe, to which he replied, 'In my country, we call it commission.' Formed Triad Corporation with his two younger brothers and when his first wife, who became a Muslim and was named Soraya, sued in 1979 in California for half his fortune, it was estimated at $2 billion. In the end she settled for an estimated $10 million. In the eighties his outgoings on two private jets; the world's largest private yacht, *Nabila*, named after his daughter; an estate outside Marbella and a penthouse in Olympic Towers, Fifth Avenue, were put at $500,000 a week. In 1989 Khashoggi was arrested in Switzerland and spent three months in jail before being extradited to New York to face charges of helping President Ferdinand Marcos and his wife Imelda obscure the origin of more than $150 million used to purchase various properties in New York. They were acquitted in July 1990. He was allowed bail so long as he resided in Manhattan and wore an electric tag so that local police could keep track of him. The trial began in March 1990 and, if found guilty, he faced up to ten years in jail. The *Nabila* was seized by the Sultan of Brunei over a $50 million unpaid loan and sold, for £30 million in 1988 to Donald Trump, who renamed her the *Trump Princess*.

KIDD, JANET GLADYS (née Aitken), *born* 9 July 1908, only daughter of First Lord Beaverbrook.
Married first, December 1927 (dissolved 1934), Ian Douglas Campbell (one daughter), Eleventh Duke of Argyll, second, March 1935, the Hon. William Drogo Montagu (one son), third, July 1942, Thomas Edward Dealtry Kidd (one son, one daughter). Claimed in her autobiography that the Duke took her to Paris on honeymoon and made her watch a couple making love in a bordello to learn all about it, and then stole her tiara to pay gambling debts. By her third husband she is the mother of Harrow-educated Johnny Kidd, the showjumper and polo player who, aged sixteen, painfully thin and 6ft 5ins tall, went to see his grandfather for advice about a career and was told, 'Why don't you try the circus?' Claimed that her elder brother, Sir Max Aitken, had never fought, as credited, in the Battle of Britain, because he was 'too tired' after the Battle of France. Her nephew, Maxwell, the Third Lord Beaverbrook, produced research that his father had flown for the first ten days and had shot down at least one German plane. Known as 'Boadicea' for her carriage-driving exploits, she died in 1988.

Adnan Khashoggi and lawyers

KILBRACKEN, Third Lord, JOHN RAYMOND GODLEY, *born* 17 October 1920. Voluble Irish peer, educated Eton and Balliol College, Oxford, served as pilot in the Fleet Air Arm, 1940–6. Married first, 1943 (dissolved 1949), Penelope Reyne (one son and one son deceased), secondly, 1981, Susan Hazlewood (one son), who was thirty-six years his junior – they separated in July 1987 citing the generation gap. Reporter for the *Daily Mirror* 1947–9, *Sunday Express* 1949–52 and contributor to the London *Evening Standard* of articles from Killegar, his home in Cavan, Ireland. Joined the Liberal Parliamentary Party in 1960 and transferred six years later to Labour, becoming President of the British-Kurdish Friendship Society (he covered the 1966 uprising for the *Evening Standard*), and the Parliamentary group concerned with Aids issues. 'I am still interested in the opposite sex,' he said, announcing his separation in 1986.

KILLEARN, Lady, JACQUELINE (née Castellani), widow of First Lord Killearn, *born* 1916.
Daughter of the Italian doctor, Marchese Aldo Castellani, who discovered the cure for malaria and was the personal physician to ex-King Umberto of Italy in exile in Portugal. She married diplomat Sir Miles Lampson (one son, two daughters) as his second wife in 1934, when he was fifty-four. During the Second World War he was first High Commissioner and then Ambassador to Egypt, being ennobled in 1943 after sending British troops to quell a rebellious King Farouk, who wanted to side with the Germans. Noted for pinching boyfriends from her daughters (Killearn died in 1964). Son Victor, married to MP's daughter Melita Morgan-Giles, paid £1.5 million for Little Sodbury Manor, Gloucestershire, in 1990; elder daughter, Jacquetta, married Lord Eliot, later the Earl of St Germans (q.v.) and younger daughter, Roxana, has six children by her marriage to Ian Ross, co-founder of Radio Caroline, the first pirate radio station.

KIMBERLEY, Fourth Earl of, JOHN WODEHOUSE, *born* 12 May 1924, educated Eton, Cambridge, served Grenadier Guards 1942–5.
Married first, 1945 (dissolved 1949), Diana Legh, second, 1949 (dissolved 1952), Carmel Dunnett (one son), third, 1953 (dissolved 1961), Mrs Cynthia Westendarp (two sons), fourth, 1961 (dissolved 1965), Margaret Simons (one son), fifth, 1970 (dissolved 1982), Mrs Gillian Raw, sixth, 1982, Sarah Jane Consett. Inherited Wymondham Hall, with 4,250 Norfolk acres, when he succeeded his father in 1941 and sold it for £250,000 in 1958 to pay off divorce proceedings, moving to Mayfair, where he became a public relations consultant, working for American film producer Sam Bronston (*Fall of the Roman Empire*, *El Cid*, etc) and W. & A. Gilbey, for whom he launched Smirnoff Vodka. Went into tax exile in Jamaica in 1963 with Indian beauty 'Tiger' Cowley, estranged wife of Earl Cowley, returning five years later when Cowley died of a heart attack in bed with a Bayswater prostitute. Moved to Cornwall, where he owned a large part of the back streets of Falmouth, and declared himself an alcoholic, becoming Vice-President of the World Council on Alcoholism and Chairman of the National Council on Alcoholism until 1985, when he went back to 'gentle' drinking. Lives in Cricklade, frequent attender of the House of Lords, where he was former Liberal spokesman on aviation and aerospace, leaving the party in 1979 to join the Conservatives.

KING OF WARTNABY, Lord, JOHN LEONARD (life peer), *born* 29 August 1916.
Started work in Dusfold, Surrey aged fifteen in a small engineering business, and bought a derelict mining village in Yorkshire aged twenty-eight where, in 1945, he founded Ferrybridge Industries and Whitehouse Industries, which became Pollard Ball and Roller Bearing Co., Ltd from which he made his fortune, buying the 2,000-acre Wartnaby estate near Melton Mowbray in the late fifties to become Master of the Duke of Rutland's

Foxhounds 1958–72. Married first, 1941, Lorna Sykes (three sons, one daughter) who died after a hysterectomy operation in 1969. The following year he married his longtime companion, the Hon. Isabel Monckton, daughter of the Eighth Viscount Galway, joining Babcock International, of which he became Chairman in 1978, and became Chairman of British Airways in 1981 prior to privatization, successfully turning the company around – 1989–90 profits were £345 million and his annual salary rose by 200 per cent to £515,818. Called 'King John' by his many friends, who include the Prince of Wales (with whom King hunts) and ex-President Jimmy Carter.

KLUGE, Patricia (née Rose), *born* September 1948.

Born Baghdad where her father, Edmund Rose, worked in the office of a British insurance firm and whose wife, Sylvia, was an Iraqi with a Scots mother. Came to London in 1965 after her father had returned to Britain, leaving her mother, and in 1973 married Russell Gay, thirty-two years her senior, in Hampstead. He published ***Knave***, a soft-porn magazine, and in it, under full-frontal nude pictures of voluptuous 5ft 9ins tall Patricia, there appeared a column dispensing sex advice. They divorced in 1976, after she had turned to running a sandwich bar in Leicester Square, and she moved to New York where she met Yolanda Kluge, second wife of John Kluge, the 5ft 4ins tall head of the Metromedia chain of independent radio and television stations. Kluge divorced Yolanda, converted to Roman Catholicism and married Patricia in St Patrick's Cathedral, New York in 1981, with Cardinal Terence Cook officiating. They adopted a son, John Kluge Jnr, who is now seven. Kluge

Patricia Kluge (right), husband and stepdaughter

Herbert Kretzmer and companion

(thirty-four years older than Pat) bought Metromedia from the shareholders for $750 million and sold part of it to Rupert Murdoch for $2.4 billion. The couple moved to Albemarle, a 10,000-acre estate in Charlottesville, Virginia on which they spent $30 million rebuilding an eighteenth-century house. The house-warming was attended by ex-King Constantine of Greece and Queen Anne-Marie and Lord Grade, among 120 others. In 1988 their gamekeeper, Irish baronet Sir Richard Musgrave, was convicted of killing 400 hawks and other federally protected birds, which were threatening pheasant shooting on the estate. In 1989 the Kluges paid £7 million for Mar Lodge and 77,000 acres close to Balmoral. In April 1990 Kluge announced he was separating from his wife and seeking a divorce that would give her the income from a $1 billion trust. He moved to a small estate next to Albemarle. Pat's father died in Sussex in July 1989 and she flew his remains in her Falcon 50 jet to be buried in the crypt of the chapel at Albemarle.

KRETZMER, HERBERT, *born* South Africa, 5 October 1925.
Educated Kroonstad High School, Rhodes University, Grahamstown. Entered journalism 1946, from 1951 to 1954 feature writer and columnist for the *Daily Sketch* (merged 1971 with the *Daily Mail*), theatre critic *Daily Express* 1962–78, television critic *Daily Mail* 1979–87. Contributed weekly songs to 'That Was The Week That Was', the BBC programme that launched David Frost (q.v.), and 'Not So Much A Programme..'. Wrote lyrics for 'Goodness Gracious Me' (for Peter Sellers and Sophia Loren) and 'Yesterday When I Was Young'. Gold record for 'She' (Charles Aznavour) 1974. Retired from daily journalism after writing lyrics for *Les Misérables*, with worldwide royalties estimated at £500,000 a year. Married first, 1961 (dissolved 1988), Elizabeth Wilson (one son, one daughter), secondly, 1988, Sybil Sever. Takes a weekly turkish steam bath at the Royal Automobile Club with his close friend from the sixties, actor Terence Stamp.

L*l*

LACEY, ROBERT, *born* 1944.
Peripatetic author and biographer (Raleigh and Essex) who moves to where his new project is – he learnt Arabic and went with his wife, Sandi, (two sons, one daughter) to Saudi Arabia to research *The Kingdom*. They spent two years in Detroit while he researched and wrote *Ford*, about the car family, which was ill-received by Henry Ford II (q.v.), and is now in Miami, Florida playing polo and writing about the Mafia. His first best seller, in 1977, was *Majesty*, (250,000 hardback copies sold) which revealed the inner workings of the Royal Family, with help from Prince Philip.

LA FRENAIS, IAN, *born* 7 January 1937.
Educated Dame Allan's School, Northumberland. Married, 1984, Doris Vartan (one stepdaughter). Formed Witzend Productions with partner (Richard) Dick Clement, born 5 September 1937, married first, (dissolved 1981), Jennifer Sheppard (three sons, one daughter), second, 1982, Nancy Campbell (one adopted daughter). Co-writers of hit television series 'Whatever Happened to the Likely Lads?', 'Porridge', 'Going Straight', 'Auf Wiedersehen Pet', and many films. Their new series, 'Freddie and Max', will star Anne Bancroft, who won an Oscar for *The Graduate*. The duo moved to Los Angeles in 1975 with plans to write a musical based on the lives of Laurel and Hardy, but instead stayed, buying homes in Beverly Hills, and turned 'Porridge' into a local series called 'On The Rocks', which was aborted when the studio wanted to put the prison in Hawaii because seeing waving palm trees through the bars would be less depressing.

LAKER, Sir FREDERICK ALFRED, *born* 6 August 1922.
Educated Simon Langton School, Canter-

L*l*

Freddie Laker

bury. Knighted, 1978, for his services to the British travel industry after founding the cut-price Skytrain Air Passenger Service to the United States. Chairman and Managing Director of Laker Airways Ltd., from 1966 until it was forced out of business on 5 February 1982, leaving debts of £280 million. He brought a legal action in America under their anti-trust laws, claiming $1.75 billion from British Airways and other airlines which had conspired to force him out of business and in 1985 he accepted £6 million for himself and £35 million for creditors of his airline. Backed by 'Tiny' Rowland of Lonrho, Laker is now living in the Bahamas, running Lonrho's fleet of thirty-eight small aircraft. In 1985 he married his fourth wife, Jacqueline Harvey, a former Eastern Airlines stewardess. He has a son, Freddie Jnr, born in 1978 to his third wife, and who goes to school in Miami.

LAMBTON, ANTONY CLAUD FREDERICK, Fifth Earl of Durham (disclaimed 1970), *born* 10 July 1922.
Known as Tony but allowed by Mr Speaker Lloyd to continue sitting in Parliament using his courtesy title, which made his son and heir, the Hon. Edward Richard Lambton (born 19 October 1961), take another courtesy title, that of Lord Durham. Married, 10 August 1942, Belinda Blew-Jones of Westward Ho! Devon (one son, five daughters). Conservative MP for the Berwick-on-Tweed Division of Northumberland 1951–73, Parliamentary Under-Secretary of State at the Ministry of Defence from 1970 to May 1973, when it was revealed that he had been consorting with callgirls and was photographed by a Rupert Murdoch newspaper in bed in Maida Vale with two prostitutes, one white, one black, smoking marijuana, while his official car and chauffeur waited outside. After giving a tearful interview to old friend Ludovic Kennedy, he resigned from Parliament and eventually went into exile with his mistress Claire Ward, former wife of the Earl of Dudley's brother Peter and mother of actresses Rachel and Tracy (who married

the Marquess of Worcester). They live, attended by liveried servants, at Villa Cetinale near Siena. Aqua-diving fanatic Belinda ('Bindy'), who formed an attachment in the fifties to artist Lucian Freud, lives in equally grand style on the Lambton estates in Durham and Northumberland and is known to summon a maid with the bell-pull if her book should fall from her bed while reading. In the early sixties Lambton was close to Lady Antonia Fraser and has now become, like her, an acclaimed author, writing, in 1989, an abrasive biography of the Mountbattens, whom he despised.

LANGAN, PETER DANIEL, *born* 13 May 1941.
Son of Dan Langan, Chairman of Texaco, Ireland, who played rugby football full-back for Ireland against Wales in Cardiff in 1933. Educated National School, Clarecastle and Castleknock, Dublin. Worked as a porter in Findlater's store, Dublin, then as a petrol pump attendant for Regent Oil, Sunderland. Married, 1971, Susan Blake-Davies. Was walking down Devonshire Street, Marylebone in 1966 when he found a woman in tears on the pavement. On inquiry she told him she owned a restaurant, her chef had just walked out and they had full bookings for lunch. He told her he could cook and became chef at Odin's, eventually buying the business. In 1976 he bought the old Coq d'Or in Stratton Street, Mayfair and turned it into Langan's Brasserie where, as it became more successful (Princess Margaret was an early customer), he became more eccentric, re-treating into alcoholism and patronage of Shepherd's Market prostitutes. Bored with London, he moved to Los Angeles in an attempt to start a restaurant there, but lost an estimated $500,000 by failing to complete on various properties, and blamed Michael Caine, his 24.5 per cent partner in London, for not bringing in backers. Back in Britain in 1988 he learned that his wife had a lover, Roger Fleming, then forty-nine and a BBC telegraphist. On 20 October he took her to dinner in Colchester to discuss separation and divorce, and, returning to their country

home, set fire to some petrol in their bedroom at three a.m. His wife and their sheepdog, Megan, jumped from the first floor (Mrs Langan broke an ankle) and Langan was blown out from the window. He was taken to Colchester Hospital with first and second degree burns and never regained consciousness, dying of kidney failure six weeks later. In his will he left Susan £300,000, his former mistress, Beth Coventry (sister of London *Evening Standard* restaurant critic Fay Maschler)

Peter Langan

£110,000, and the rest, to come from his fifty-one per cent share in Langan's, to London Lighthouse, an Aids charity. During his life, Langan had always been very scathing about homosexuality. On his forty-ninth birthday, there was a wake for 450 people at Langan's Brasserie, as per instructions in his will.

LEIGH, VIVIEN, *born* Darjeeling 5 November 1913.

Married first, 1932 (dissolved 1940), solicitor Leigh Holman (one daughter), second, 1940 (dissolved 1960), Laurence Olivier. Educated Roehampton, trained France and Academy (later Royal) of Dramatic Art, London. Became international star after David O. Selznick cast her in **Gone With The Wind**, for which she won the Oscar. Cuckolded Olivier with Peter Finch during filming in Ceylon in 1953, an affair which Larry tolerated until it finally became too public. They even met in a civilized manner to discuss the situation and one night Vivien burst in saying, 'Which one of you is coming to bed with me?' She called him 'Larry Boy' and he called her 'Puss'. Her last film was **The Roman Spring of Mrs Stone**, which introduced Warren Beatty to the screen. Canadian-born actor John 'Jack' Merivale, who was fifteen years younger, lived with her for seven years until her death from tuberculosis in 1967 (he subsequently moved in with actress Dinah Sheridan, former wife of Sir John Davis, q.v. and married her four years before he died in 1990).

LERNER, ALAN JAY, *born* New York City 31 August 1918.

Educated Bedales, Choate and Harvard, married first Ruth Boyd, second Marion Bell, third Nancy Olson, fourth Micheline de Borgo, fifth Karen Gundersen, sixth Sandra Payne, seventh Nina Bushkin (all dissolved), three sons, one daughter; eight, 1981, Liz Robertson. Playwright and lyricist of **Brigadoon**, **An American in Paris**, **Paint Your Wagon**, **My Fair Lady**, **Camelot** and **Gigi**. Met his eighth wife, thirty-six years his junior and the daughter of an Essex policeman, when she joined, as Eliza, the cast of the touring company of **My Fair Lady**, prior to a West End run. A lifetime chain-smoker, he gave up in 1985 and died of lung cancer in

New York in 1986. His most famous songs were performed at his memorial service in September 1986 in St Paul's Church, Covent Garden, on what would have been his sixty-eighth birthday. Most of his fortune went to pay the United States Internal Revenue Service and his widow commented, 'The one thing Alan left me was a taste for champagne.'

LEVER OF MANCHESTER, Lord HAROLD, (life peer), *born* 15 January 1914.
Educated Manchester Grammar School, Manchester University, called to the Bar 1935. Married first, 1939 (dissolved), Ethel Samuel. Second, 1945 (she died 1948), Betty 'Billy' Woolfe (one daughter), thirdly, 1962, Diane Bashi (three daughters), former wife of Selim Zilkha (q.v.). In 1961 Bashi had inherited £2 million on the death of her father, a Lebanese businessman. For a dozen years, after the death of his second wife, Lever lived with Rixi Markus, the bridge champion and author. In 1968, when Prime Minister Harold Wilson limited Britons travelling abroad to taking just £50, Lever, then Financial Secretary to The Treasury, was seen by Alan Clore (q.v.) at the Palace Hotel, Gstaad, occupying a £100-a-day suite and playing backgammon for stakes in the thousands. Mr Clore reported the matter to me and when I telephoned Lever at the hotel, he admitted everything adding, 'My wife is a very rich woman and I am just enjoying her hospitality.' Her wealth also extended to buying a spacious Belgravia apartment occupying one whole floor of an Eaton Square house. Lever is on the board of several European banks.

LEWISHAM, Viscount, WILLIAM LEGGE, *born* 23 September 1949.
Eldest son of the Ninth Earl of Dartmouth. Educated Eton, Christ Church, Oxford, Harvard Business School. A chartered accountant with political ambitions, he contested Leigh, Lancashire in February 1974, Stockport South in October 1974. In 1975 he went to Abu Dhabi to work for accountants

Whinney, Murray and then moved to New York to work for Macmillan publishers (later bought by Robert Maxwell, q.v.), and bought a holiday house in Montego Bay, Jamaica. Among his girlfriends have been property millionairess Mrs Davina Phillips (once escorted by Prince Michael of Kent), and Vanessa Hedley, who left him for multi-millionaire financier 'Black' Jack Dellal. In September 1983 he became engaged to Houston heiress Pamela Franzheim, twenty-five, but the marriage in Jamaica with 250 guests was called off at the eleventh hour. She claimed that he was mean and had given her, as a birthday present, one of his company's own books. He returned to London in 1985 and invested £250,000 in Officescape, a Kensington design company, which went into liquidation in 1988. He sued his two partners for £630,000 and won an out-of-court settlement in January 1990. While his Bayswater house was being renovated he moved in with former model, Lucinda Murray, but she turned down his proposal of marriage in 1987. Given to falling in love easily – on the train down from the Earl of Lichfield's wedding reception in 1975, he was introduced to actress Fiona Lewis and became so besotted that he forgot to get off at Watford, the stop for his country home. Following her off the train at Euston, he watched, moist-eyed, as she was met by her steady boyfriend.

LICHFIELD, Fifth Earl of, THOMAS PATRICK JOHN ANSON, *born* 25 April 1939.
Educated Harrow, trained Royal Military Academy, Sandhurst, Lieutenant with the Grenadier Guards 1959–62. Intemperate father Viscount (Bill) Anson died in March 1958, eleven months before his grandfather, the Fourth Earl, thus occasioning double death duties which resulted in the sale of much of the Staffordshire estate (now 6,000 acres) surrounding Shugborough, where Patrick Lichfield lives in a spacious apartment in the National Trust mansion. He used to dine in silence with his grandfather, who would write on a pad beside his plate. The

night he died, Patrick looked at the pad for inspiration and found, 'Butler farted, fish cold.' Became a professional photographer in 1963 after Dimitri Kasterine took him on as his assistant. Not modest about mentioning his relationship with the Monarch (his mother was the Queen Mother's niece). Blossomed during the swinging sixties, forming Patrick Lichfield Studios in Campden Hill, Kensington. After romances with Britt Ekland, Alexandra Bastedo and Princess Margaret (who said, 'We are kissing cousins') married, in 1975, (dissolved 1986) Lady Leonora Grosvenor (one son, two daughters), daughter of the Fifth Duke of Westminster. At the Chester Cathedral wedding, the best man, the Hon. Brian Alexander (see Earl Alexander of Tunis), who had complained that Patrick had stolen his girlfriend, fainted as he was about to hand over the ring. Bought gatehouse to Princess Margaret's property, *Les Jolies Eaux*, in Mustique, before building his own villa nearby. Separated after one of the scantily clad models used on his Unipart calendar shoot sold her kiss 'n' tell memoirs to one of the rags. Now involved with Mrs Jennifer Emery, divorcée daughter of Sir Hugh Wontner.

Lord Lichfield and friend

LINDSAY, Patrick, *born* 14 November 1948.
Younger son of the Twenty-eighth Earl of Crawford, educated Eton and Magdalen College, Oxford, served with Scots Guards in Malaya. Married, 16 December 1955, Lady Annabel Yorke (three sons, one daughter), eldest daughter of the Ninth Earl of Hardwicke. Joined Christie's in 1952 and became the Senior Picture director. He was also a substantial shareholder and, from the early sixties, conducted every major Old Master and English sale held by the auction house, creating a world record of £7.5 million for Mantegna's *Adoration of the Magi* in 1985. A collector of vintage cars and planes, he was well known for his daredevil exploits in them and in June 1984 he marked the seventy-fifth anniversary of the first Cross Channel flight by piloting a reproduction of the original Louis Bleriot aircraft, and he crossed the Himalayas in a 1930 Phantom Two Rolls. He lived at Folly Farm and died of cancer in January 1986. He left £5,401,387 and a priceless collection of cars and planes, which his sons hire out for films and drive in races.

LINDSAY-HOGG, Michael Edward, *born* 5 May 1940.
Son of Irish-American actress Geraldine Fitzgerald and heir to baronetcy of father, Sir Edward Lindsay-Hogg. Educated Christ Church, Oxford, became a TV and film director in Dublin where he was spotted by Elkan Allan, who made him director, at the age of twenty-five, of ITV's 'Ready, Steady, Go!' pop programme. Married in 1965 (dissolved 1971), Lucy Davies (*see* Earl of

Snowdon), daughter of Irish clothing manufacturer Donald Davies. Liked to romance that Orson Welles, who was a friend of his mother's, was his real father (at one stage Michael resembled the young Welles). Director of West End plays such as *Whose Life Is It Anyway?* and *The Millionairess*, he lived for eight years, until 1977, with Jean Marsh, the actress who conceived 'Upstairs Downstairs'. In 1984 he began an affair with Nona Gordon, then wife of fine arts dealer, Martin Summers (who later divorced). In February 1985, having been searched at Heathrow, she was fined £1,000 for trying to take nearly three grammes of cocaine out of the country. Michael is now based in Dublin.

LINLEY, Viscount, DAVID ALBERT CHARLES ARMSTRONG-JONES, *born* 3 November 1961. Educated Bedales. Only son of the Earl of Snowdon and Princess Margaret, who married in 1960 and divorced in 1978. As his mother once said, 'My children aren't Royal, they just happen to have the Queen as their aunt.' Artistic and mechanically-minded like his father, who gave him for his twenty-fourth birthday, the Aston Martin DB 5 drophead that he had bought from Peter Sellers (q.v.) for £3,000 (now worth £60,000). Linley was banned from driving three times between September 1987 and October 1989 for speeding, and resorted to bicycling to his New King's Road, Fulham shop, where he designs and sells furniture, including a £75,000 custom-built twelve-foot bed for Elton John (with whom he shares John Reid as a manager). Also partner, with the Earl of Lichfield (q.v.), in Deal's, a hamburger and fast food restaurant in Chelsea Harbour. A five year romance with fashion PR Susannah Constantine became more off than on in 1989, although they still see each other frequently. Won £35,000 in a 1990 libel action against *Today* which admitted printing an invented story about him behaving badly in a pub next to Chelsea Harbour.

LIVANOS, GEORGE STAVROS, *born* 1935, educated St Paul's, Concorde, New Hampshire.

Only son of Stavros and Arietta Livanos and younger brother of Eugenie, who married Stavros Niarchos (q.v.), and Tina, who married first Aristotle Onassis, second, the Marquess of Blandford and third, Stavros Niarchos. In November 1966 married Lita, fifteen-year-old daughter of Greek tobacco tycoon Stamati Voivoda and Stassa Voivoda (one son, four daughters). Officially resident in St Moritz, with homes in Grosvenor Square, London, Manhattan, Greece and the private Greek island of Coronis. In 1965 George was fined £25 and disqualified from driving for three months after crashing his £10,000 blood-red Ferrari into a line of stationary cars waiting to drive into Cranbourne House, Ascot, where John Aspinall (q.v.) was giving a gaming party. His passenger, the Hon. Lavinia Woodhouse, daughter of Lord Terrington, was unhurt. When his niece, Christina Onassis, died in November 1988, George and Lita offered to have her daughter, Athina, but Thierry Roussel claimed the couple were trying to 'kidnap' the little girl and flew her to a secret destination in case any attempt to take her away was made.

Lord Linley

LIVERPOOL, Fifth Earl of, EDWARD
PETER BERTRAM SAVILE FOLJAMBE, *born*
posthumously 14 November 1944.
Educated Shrewsbury and University for
Foreigners, Perugia. Joint Chairman and
Managing Director of Melbourns Brewery.
Succeeded great-uncle in 1969, married, in
1970, Lady Juliana Noel, eldest daughter of
the Earl of Gainsborough, after whom Juliana's mobile discotheque was named by brothers Tom and Oliver Baughan, whose first
engagement as disc jockeys had been at her
1967 coming-out dance – it is now a public
company.

LLEWELLYN, Sir HENRY MORTON
(HARRY), **third baronet.** *Born* 18 July 1911.
Married, 1944, the Hon. Christine Saumarez
(two sons, one daughter). Captain of the
British Olympic Showjumping team that
won the gold medal at the 1952 Helsinki
Olympic Games – when Llewellyn, riding
Foxhunter, had a faultless final round after
earlier disasters. 'One clear round and you've
never heard the end of it,' he likes to joke.
His grandfather, Sir David, was given the
title by Lloyd George and owned the largest
coal mines in South Wales, which were
nationalized without recompense at the outbreak of war. A close friend of Prince Philip,
Llewellyn (who succeeded to the title on the
death of his bachelor brother, Sir Rhys, in
1978, having been knighted the previous
year) had been President of Whitbread,
Wales since 1972, the year before his younger
son, Roddy, began a seven-year relationship
with Princess Margaret, seventeen years his
senior. Then out of work, Roddy joined the
Surrendell commune started by artist Sarah
Ponsonby, a cousin of the Earl of Bessborough, and to which the Princess paid several
weekend visits. Details of his relationship
with Princess Margaret surfaced in a Sunday
newspaper when Roddy's elder brother, Dai,
sold the story for an estimated £30,000,
including details about his brother's troubled
sexuality. For good measure Dai sold versions
of the same story again in 1980 to a Fleet
Street newspaper 'to clear my debts', he

explained in a letter to Sir Harry, after fleeing
to Israel. On 15 August 1954 'Tini' Llewellyn, driving her two sons from Wales to a
seaside holiday in Dorset, crashed head-on
outside Salisbury into a lorry after crossing
into its path, severely injuring herself and the
boys, who still bear the scars.

LLOYD WEBBER, ANDREW, *born* 22
March 1948.
Educated Westminster, joined up with lyricist Tim Rice (q.v.) after being discovered
by impresario David Land, who paid them
£20 a week. In 1968 they came up with *Joseph and the Amazing Technicolour Dreamcoat, Jesus Christ Superstar* 1970, *Evita*
1976, at which point the collaboration was
ended. Further successes included *Cats* 1981,
Song and Dance 1982, *Starlight Express*
1984, *The Phantom of the Opera* 1986,
Aspects of Love 1989, and at one time Lloyd
Webber had four productions in both London's West End and on Broadway. Married
first, 1971 (dissolved 1983), Sarah Hugill (one
son, one daughter), known as 'The Vole' and
second, 1984, Sarah Brightman, the former
Hot Gossip dancer. In February 1990 he took
his Really Useful Group private in a £77.4
million deal, losing his £20,000 a year Royal
production assistant Prince Edward, who left
with his boss Biddy Hayward. Formerly
Lloyd Webber's secretary, she wanted to
form her own production company con-
centrating on theatre while he was opting for
films (*Evita* and *Phantom of the Opera*.) Her
pay-off was estimated at £350,000. In April
1990, five months after buying number
eleven Eaton Square (once the home of Mrs
Soraya Khashoggi), Lloyd Webber put the
ten bedroom property back on the market
for £11 million, saying he had never really
felt comfortable in it. His country home,
Sydmonton Court, adjoins the 2,230-acre
Watership Down estate, which he bought in
1989 for £5 million. There is also a villa near
the lighthouse on Cap Ferrat in the South
of France. On 3 July 1990, Lloyd Webber
announced that 'sadly' his marriage to Sarah
Brightman was over and that he was now

involved with Madeline 'Gurtie' Gurdon, twenty-eight, a three-day eventer and lady jockey.

LONDONDERRY, Ninth Marquess of,

ALEXANDER CHARLES ROBERT VANE-TEMPEST-STEWART, *born* 7 September 1937.
Educated Eton. Known as Alistair, married first, 1955 (dissolved 1971), Nicolette Harrison (one son, two daughters), second, 1972 Doreen Wells (two sons). Inherited eighteenth-century Wynyard Park, Billingham-on-Tees and 6,000 surrounding acres, built by an ancestor with the profits from coal mining. With his beautiful wife Nicolette, was the focus of artistic London in the sixties (he sponsored pianist John Ogden and gave parties for Benny Goodman). In 1971, after hearing evidence of blood tests from two doctors, a divorce court ruled that

the Londonderry heir, Viscount Castlereagh, born 23 October 1969, was not the son of the Marquess and had no claim to the title. The following year Lady Londonderry married singer and composer Georgie Fame (real name Clive Powell), with whom she had been involved for four years, and the couple had a second son in 1973. In 1972 Londonderry married Doreen Wells, a principal of the Royal Ballet and daughter of a Walthamstow cabinet maker. Their son, Frederick Aubrey Vane-Tempest-Stewart, born 6 September 1972, became Viscount Castlereagh. With her career fading, 'Dor' turned to 'Professor' Ron Thatcher, also known as 'Dr Death', to be taught Aikido, a Japanese philosophy and martial art. Alistair moved out of their Barnes, London home in 1984 to the stable block of his sister, Lady Annabel Goldsmith. Dor made a brief come-

Andrew Lloyd Webber, wives and children

back in the London West End musical, *On Your Toes*, and started divorce proceedings, on the grounds of two years' separation, in 1989. In January 1987 Londonderry sold Wynyard to former miner, John Hall, the Northumbrian who pioneered the £200 million Metrocentre shopping complex on Tyneside. He lives in part of the seventy-room mansion, the rest of which is a conference and leisure centre. Alistair has bought a home near Shaftesbury, a few miles from where his first wife and Fame live.

LONGFORD, Seventh Earl of, FRANCIS AUNGIER PAKENHAM, *born* 5 December 1905. Educated Eton, New College, Oxford. Married, 3 November 1931, Elizabeth Harman (four sons, three daughters, and one daughter deceased). Lecturer in Politics at Christ Church, Oxford, enlisted in 1939, Lieutenant, Oxford and Buckinghamshire Light Infantry, resigned on account of ill health 1940. Heir to his brother (who died 1961), he was created Lord Pakenham of Cowley on 12 October 1945, and became lord-in-waiting to King George VI, Chancellor of the Duchy of Lancaster 1947–8, Minister of Civil Aviation 1948–51, First Lord of the Admiralty 1948–51. Returned as Lord Privy Seal and Leader of the House of Lords in the Wilson Government, 1964–8. Best remembered for his 100,000-word Longford Commission investigating pornography, published in 1972, which earned him the Fleet Street sobriquet, 'Lord Porn', during which he fearlessly interviewed prostitutes and pimps, Soho strip clubs and made a tour of Copenhagen porn shops and live sex shows with Gyles Brandreth and Peregrine Worsthorne (q.v.) – it became a best seller with 120,000 copies printed. In the eighties he attracted opprobrium for his campaign to have Moors murderer, Myra Hindley, released on parole and appeared a soft touch for other controversial criminals seeking the termination of their sentences. Wife Elizabeth is the much-acclaimed biographer, as is eldest daughter Lady Antonia, with youngest daughter, Lady Rachel, also an accomplished

writer and author. Eldest son and heir does not use his courtesy title of Lord Silchester, calling himself Thomas Pakenham. Sussex neighbours have become used to seeing Frank Longford jogging around their lanes in long, baggy pants.

LOVAT, Seventeenth Lord, SIMON CHRISTOPHER JOHN FRASER, Twenty-fourth Chief of the Clan Fraser, *born* 9 July 1911. Married, 1938, Rosamond Delves Broughton (four sons, two daughters). Educated Ampleforth and Magdalen College, Oxford. Known as 'Shimi', served in the Second World War as Lieutenant Colonel, Brigade Commandos, and distinguished himself on D-Day, by marching without a weapon at the head of his commandos until wounded at Amfreville (he was portrayed by Peter Lawford in the film, *The Longest Day*). Inherited 190,000 acres around Beauly, Invernesshire, which had been in the family for 500 years. Handed over the estate and Beaufort Castle, its principal residence, to his eldest son, the Hon. Simon Augustine Fraser, Master of Lovat, who, in June 1990 sold the 30,000-acre Braulen Deer Forest and eleven miles of the Beauly River for £15 million to Landmatch, a timeshare company. Lovat's younger brother was the Hon. Hugh Charles Patrick Joseph Fraser (born 23 January 1918), who married Lady Antonia Pakenham (three sons, three daughters), eldest daughter of the Seventh Earl of Longford, on 25 September 1956 (dissolved 1977). He was MP for Stafford and Stone from 1950, and Secretary of State for Air 1962–4. She left him to marry Harold Pinter, managing to retain the family house in Campden Hill Square, Kensington. He died in 1984.

LOEWENSTEIN-WERTHEIM-FREUDENBERG, Prince RUPERT ZU, *born* 1932.
A direct descendant of George III, whose family were accorded the Bavarian title of Prince in 1812. Educated Oxford, married, 18 July 1957, Josephine Clare Lowry-Corry (one son, one daughter). A City banker with

Leopold Joseph who became financial adviser to Mick Jagger (q.v.) and the Rolling Stones after their muddled affairs in the sixties led them almost to bankruptcy. His West End office above the Embassy Club is guarded by an iron gate, double doors with four separate locks and a phalanx of assistants and secretaries. A giver of noisy parties that have attracted the police (in 1969 the Princess, known as 'Not Tonight Josephine', said her Kensington neighbours might have cause for annoyance as a party, attended by the Stones and Princess Margaret, had three bands and finished at 6.30a.m.), he broke his leg when the marquee collapsed at David Heimann's wedding reception for his daughter Francine (q.v.). His coming-out dance for his daughter, Dora, in 1986 at Osterley Park cost an estimated £250,000. In 1987 he bought eighteenth-century Petersham Lodge, set in three acres beside the Thames at Richmond, for £2 million, only to discover that it was riddled with dry rot. He had to rebuild at a cost of £1 million.

LOWNES, VICTOR, *born* 17 April 1928.
Educated Elementary and Junior High School, Miami, New Mexico Military Institute, University of Chicago. Married first, 22 September 1946 (dissolved 1955), Judith (one son, one daughter), secondly, 23 June 1984, Marilyn Cole, the 1972 Playmate of the Year. Joined *Playboy* magazine in 1955 as special projects director, became President, Playboy Club New York in 1963 and, on 1 July 1966, opened the London Playboy Club in Park Lane. Founder of the Great American Disaster, London's first hamburger joint in the Fulham Road. To emulate his old friend, Hugh M. Hefner, founder of Playboy, he bought Stocks, a forty-two-room former girls' school near Tring, as his 'mansion' for romps and weekend parties. Became head of Playboy International and, in 1977, was Britain's highest paid executive with a salary of £247,000. In July 1979 he gave a twenty-five-hour party at Stocks to celebrate twenty-five years of Playboy centrefolds. In June 1980 he invited 500 friends to Stocks to cel-ebrate his mother's seventy-fifth birthday. In April 1981, a week after fracturing his skull while out riding, he was dismissed from Playboy after the gaming licence of its Park Lane club was threatened. He bought Wedgie's, a King's Road club that was the Club Del'Aretusa in the sixties, renamed it Stocks, and turned his country mansion into a club. After marrying longtime love Marilyn, who used to work in a Portsmouth Co-Op and was Britain's first centrefold, he sold both and bought No. 1 West Halkin Street, the former home of Bernie Cornfeld (q.v.). He applied £1,500 of gold leaf to the spearheads of his railings in 1989 and received a curt letter from the Grosvenor Estates, his landlords, which was referred in June 1990 to the Secretary of State for the Environment.

Victor Lownes and Marilyn

LOWSON, Sir DENYS COLQUHOUN FLOWERDEW, first baronet, *born* 22 January 1906.
Educated Winchester and Christ Church,

Oxford. Married, 17 July 1936, the Hon. Patricia Macpherson (one son, two daughters). Elected Lord Mayor of London for the Festival of Britain Year 1950–1, during which he spent £50,000 of his own money (equivalent to £1 million today) entertaining at the Mansion House and Guildhall. His elder daughter, Gay, married the Fifteenth Earl of Kinnoull and his younger, Melanie, married Charles Black, whose family publishes *Who's Who*. Sir Denys lived in great style in Sussex, where one large room of his house was devoted to an enormous, complex electric train set with which he would play for hours. In 1973 it was revealed that he had furtively bought control of the National Group, the country's third largest unit trust group, from publicly owned trusts which he controlled and resold six months later for personal profit. A Department of Trade and Industry inquiry began and he repaid £3 million. In 1975 he paid £28,000 for two suites on the **QE 2**, making a world tour. On his return he died in the September three hours after summonses concerning a £5 million share deal were issued against him. He was succeeded by his son Ian, born 4 September 1944 and educated at Eton, McGill University and Duke University.

LUARD, Nicholas, *born* 1938.
Educated Winchester and Cambridge, served with the Coldstream Guards. Met Peter Cook (q.v.) in the Footlights at university, secured a First Class degree in English and opened, in 1961, in Greek Street, Soho, London's satirical nightclub, the Establishment, (with Cook) where Lenny Bruce made his last infamous appearance in Britain before being banned from the country in April 1963 by the Home Office, and Frankie Howerd made a comeback in 1962. A former part-owner of **Private Eye**, where his wife, Elizabeth Longmore (married 1963), worked as a part-time secretary. He sold his share of the club in 1963 for £40,000 to Lebanese-born Raymond Nash, an associate of the notorious slum landlord Peter Rachman. Nash turned it into a gambling joint while Dudley Moore played jazz in the basement. Luard has written fifteen novels, thrillers and travel books, including, in 1989, **Gondar**, a 628-page saga described as '**King Solomon's Mines** with sex'. He settled on a thirty-acre estate on the remote west coast of the Isle of Mull in 1987, after taking a residential seaman's navigational course.

LUCAN, Seventh Earl of, Richard John Bingham, *born* 18 December 1934.
Educated Eton, Lieutenant with the Coldstream Guards. Married, November 1963, Veronica Duncan (one son, two daughters). Nicknamed 'Lucky' after winning £30,000 playing *chemin-de-fer*, after which he retired from working in a City bank. A house player (making up the numbers on the *chemin-de-fer* table) for his close friend, John Aspinall (q.v.) at the Clermont, and a man of habit. Had luncheon every day at the Mirabelle in Curzon Street with a group of friends, including stockbroker Stephen Raphael, racing figure Charles Benson (q.v.) and Dominic Elwes (q.v.) and dinner nightly at the Clermont. It was said he ate cold lamb cutlets for lunch, hot cutlets for dinner. At weekends he played golf at Sunningdale. In 1972 he separated from his wife and started a costly court action, which he lost, to gain custody of their children. In November 1974 the children's nanny, Sandra Rivett, was bludgeoned to death in the basement of the family house in Lower Belgrave Street. A few minutes later, Lady Lucan ran screaming from the house to the pub opposite, saying that her husband had murdered the nanny and had tried to kill her. He was seen once more, later that night, by Susan Maxwell-Scott, the wife of his friend Ian Maxwell-Scott, and a cousin of the Duke of Norfolk. Lucan explained, as he had in telephone calls to his mother and brother-in-law, William Shand-Kydd (q.v.) that he had been passing the house and seen a man in the basement who had then run away. His final words were that he was going to 'lie-doggo' for a bit. His car was found the next morning in Newhaven and he has never been seen again,

but his family and son and heir, Lord Bingham (born 21 September 1967), have made no attempt to declare him dead. Two books in recent years claim he could not have been the murderer and the police still believe that he is alive. John Aspinall says that Lucan, like a gentleman, 'fell on his sword'.

LYCETT GREEN, RUPERT WILLIAM, *born* 24 October 1938.

Educated Eton and served as Second Lieutenant, Royal Armoured Corps. Married, 24 May 1963, Candida Rose Betjeman (two sons, three daughters), only daughter of Poet Laureate Sir John Betjeman (see Lady Elizabeth Cavendish) and the Hon. Penelope Chetwode. After patronizing Eric Vincent, a popular tailor in Sackville Street (and later 10 Savile Row), Rupert started his own tailoring and menswear design business, Blade's, in a shop at the Old Burlington Street entrance to Albany. An athlete of Corinthian quality, Lycett Green has tackled many tests, including marathons and triathlons, while his wife Candida, a longtime contributor to ***Private Eye***, has published books on gardens. The couple live in harmony in Wiltshire.

LYONS, Sir (ISADORE) JACK, *born* 1 February 1916.

Educated Leeds Grammar School. Married, 1943, Roslyn Mary Rosenbaum (two sons, two daughters). Philanthropist and fund raiser for the arts, he made his fortune at United Drapery Stores, where his brother, Bernard, was Chairman, has been Chairman of J.E. London Properties since 1986, and faced eight charges at Southwark Crown Court when the Guinness Trial opened in February 1990 and, it was claimed in court, shared £6.5 million with former stockbroker Anthony 'The Animal' Parnes, paid illegally,

Lord and Lady Lucan, 1974

it was alleged, by the brewery after its successful takeover of Distillers. Lyons pleaded not guilty. On bail of £500,000, told the court that his personal intervention, with his old friend Mrs Margaret Thatcher, had led to the bid not being referred to the Monopolies and Mergers Commission and that his £3.3 million 'success fee' was justified. In 1987 he was attacked by his daughter-in-law, Alison, during divorce proceedings from his son David. The couple, who had moved to Canada, had a son and a daughter and Alison called Sir Jack a 'social climber'. When he was knighted in 1973, Roslyn gave a party and was heard to proclaim, 'The House of Lords next!'

M*m*

McALPINE OF WEST GREEN, Lord,
ROBERT ALISTAIR (life peer), *born* 14 May 1942.
Educated Stowe, and joined family construction business (Sir Robert McAlpine and Sons) in 1958. Married first 1964, (dissolved 1979), Sarah Baron (two daughters), secondly, 1980, Romilly Hobbs (one daughter). After his family sold The Dorchester Hotel for £8 million, he helped diversify their business, buying the Inter-Continental Hotel in Sydney and becoming the major property developer in Perth, Western Australia, where his home is the Bishop's House. Treasurer of the Conservative Party 1975–90, he was known at school (where he gained only three 'O' levels because of dyslexia) as 'Roly Poly' because of his weight. He slimmed down considerably after a seven-hour, six-valve heart bypass operation in November 1987. A gourmet, he was noted for giving five hour lunches, catered by Albert Roux of Le Gavroche, at West Green House, his Hampshire National Trust home, which was bombed by the IRA in June 1990, a month after he had moved

out, selling its contents for more than £1 million. After one long lunch at Le Gavroche, he arranged for a Conservative Party colleague to meet him there for cocktails at 6p.m. As time went on, he was presented with a menu and asked what he would like for dinner. His answer: 'The same again.' He owns a large part of Broome, an old pearling station on the remote north-west coast of Australia, where he started the Pearl Coast Zoo and Aviary, to protect endangered species.

McGOWAN, CATHY, *born* 1944. Married 1969 (divorced 1988) Hywel Bennett (one daughter).
Became known as the Queen of the Mods in the sixties when she presented the seminal ITV pop programme 'Ready, Steady, Go!' In 1979 she was granted a decree nisi on the uncontested grounds that she and Hywel had lived apart for two years but never sought an absolute decree. Hard-drinking Hywel, who had moved, with his stuffed badger, to the Wandsworth house of Tessa Dahl, returned home to live under the same roof as Cathy to give security to their daughter, Emma. On 16 August 1986, Hywel, star of the 'Shelley' television series, gave up drinking. Two years later, he and Cathy, who had resumed her television career, gained a 'quickie' divorce. Hywel moved the stuffed badger to his mother's house in Wales. Close to Cathy since she interviewed him in January 1989 has been Michael Ball, the lead in *Aspects of Love* first in London's West End and later on Broadway where, after the first night, production assistant Prince Edward, who had been named as a close friend of the bachelor Ball, stated, 'I am not gay.'

McNALLY, PATRICK 'PADDY', *born* 1937, educated Stonyhurst College.
Married, 1968, heiress Anne Downing (two sons), who died of cancer in 1980. Former reporter for *Autosport* magazine, he graduated into racing sponsorship with Marlboro, who backed the McLaren team in their championship years, and now is associated, from

an office beside Geneva airport, with Bernie Ecclestone, President of the Formula One Constructors Association, which runs the worldwide Grand Prix racing circuit. For four years until she met Prince Andrew in 1985, he was involved with Sarah Ferguson, whom he met first when she was skiing in Verbier, where he has a spacious chalet known as The Castle, with her previous boy-friend, Kim Smith-Bingham. Sarah became close to his sons, Sean and Rollo (and still sends them birthday and Christmas cards) and parted from Paddy in October 1985 after giving him an ultimatum at the Italian Grand Prix: 'Marry me or else.' With his family, including his parents and brother, he had a front-row seat at her July 1986 wedding. His next girlfriend, Becky Few Brown, became the Marchioness of Blandford with Paddy as best man at the February 1990 wedding, and for the last three years he has been involved with three-day eventer Lucinda McAlpine, twenty-seven years his junior, niece of former Conservative Party Treasurer Lord McAlpine (q.v.). In 1988 McNally paid in excess of £1 million for Sevenhampton Place, Gloucestershire, once owned by the late James Bond author, Ian Fleming. Bland-ford's sister, Lady Henrietta Gelber, was commissioned to do the interior decoration.

MACKESON, second baronet, Sir RUPERT HENRY, born 16 November 1941.
Educated at Harrow and Trinity College, Dublin, Captain, Royal Horse Guards. Married, 1968 (dissolved 1972), the Hon. Camilla Keith, daughter of Lord Keith of Castleacre (q.v.). Son of senior Conservative backbencher who was MP for Hythe and Folkestone 1945–59 and Secretary for Over-seas Trade 1952–3 and given a baronetcy in 1954. Sir Rupert's wife arrived at the High Court divorce hearing wearing dark glasses after he had attacked her, badly bruising her face. In 1977 he fled Britain, leaving an esti-mated £100,000 in debts after running Master Classes, a cultural-tour firm which collapsed. He surfaced in Rhodesia, where he worked as a teacher – in 1979 local police

failed to deport him when a British Airways pilot refused to allow him aboard after a scuffle. In April 1980 he was again arrested in Salisbury and held on the grounds that he was a prohibited immigrant, and was flown to Gatwick, escorted by two police officers. He was remanded on £15,000 bail and faced a total of nineteen charges under the theft act. In 1981 he escaped prosecution when two judges ruled that he had been extradited illegally. In 1985 he was working under an assumed name selling advertising space in fourteen publications for the Diplomatic and Consular Year Book Ltd., and in November 1989 he was awarded just one penny libel damages in the High Court after he sued nineteen partners in a firm of solicitors over a letter sent to him at his firm, which was not marked confidential and was read to his subordinates, accusing him of using 'grossly defamatory words'.

MALLINSON, third baronet, Sir (WILLIAM) PAUL, born 6 July 1909.
Educated Westminster and Christ Church, Oxford. Married first, 22 January 1940 (dis-solved 1967), Eila Guy (one son, two daugh-ters), secondly, 15 February 1968, Dr Margaret Gorrill. Consultant psychiatrist to St George's Hospital, Hyde Park Corner and Chairman of William Mallinson and Sons, the timber merchants. When his son William (born 8 October 1942) joined the firm, Sir Paul said he would drive him to the East End offices but lost the way as he had not been there for some years. In 1966 he stunned his wife by telling her he had been having an affair for twenty years with a former pupil and colleague, whom he subsequently married. He used to take tea every Tuesday with Queen Elizabeth, the Queen Mother and Princess Margaret at Clarence House where, unofficially, he was able to give psy-chiatric advice. He died in March 1989 and was succeeded by his son, who had conquered alcoholism in the early eighties.

MANCROFT, Second Lord, STORMONT MANCROFT SAMUEL, born 27 July 1914.

Educated Winchester, Christ Church, Oxford, called to the Bar, 1938. Married, 1951, Mrs Diana Elizabeth Quarry (one son, two daughters), daughter of Lieutenant-Colonel Horace Lloyd. Lord-in-waiting to the Queen 1952–4, Minister without Portfolio 1957–8. Chairman, Horserace Totalisator Board 1972–6, Chairman, British Greyhound Racing Board 1977–85. Renowned as one of the best after-dinner speakers in Britain, he resigned as a director of Norwich Union in 1963 as a result of Arab pressure on the company not to deal with Jewish interests. His elder stepdaughter, Venetia, married multi-millionaire Viscount Wimborne (q.v.), the younger, Miranda, was the wife of Peter Sellers (q.v.), his own elder daughter, Victoria, married Prince Nicholas of Prussia (brother of the Marchioness of Douro, q.v.), and his son Benjamin, known as 'Beano' (born 16 May 1957) became a heroin addict after being treated for severe injuries following a near-fatal car crash in 1975. Seven years later he was caught after stealing a £5,000 brooch from Miranda, which he sold for £1,300 to pay debts to a drug dealer. His family took the decision to prosecute and the magistrate agreed he should be sent to a clinic in America for treatment. He is now completely recovered and speaks on drug-related subjects in the House of Lords. In 1989 he had to give up as Joint-Master of the Vale of White Horse Hunt when creditors, claiming debts of £21,000, sought judgement against him. Stormont Mancroft died in 1987 on a fourteen-day cruise of the Greek islands, recuperating from a stroke. His manservant was Raymond Gurton, whom he inherited from Peter Sellers (q.v.) and who had previously 'done' for Cecil Beaton.

MARLBOROUGH, Tenth Duke of, JOHN ALBERT EDWARD WILLIAM SPENCER-CHURCHILL, *born* 18 September 1897.

Educated Eton, Lieutenant-Colonel, Life Guards. Married first the Hon. Alexandra Cadogan (two sons, three daughters), secondly, 1972, Laura Canfield. Known as

'Bert' and a notorious snob, whose mother was the New York heiress Consuelo Vanderbilt, married by the Ninth Duke solely to restore his fortunes and pay for Blenheim. Bert lived in some style at Blenheim and once, when his cousin, Randolph Churchill, came to stay the night while researching a book, spoke not a word when the latter was announced and persisted in watching the television which was showing the 'Black and White Minstrel Show'. When Randolph reproached him on his manners and lack of hospitality, he rang the bell, and on the arrival of his butler said, 'Mr Churchill wishes to leave.' Famous for his put-down of Sir Charles Clore (q.v.) and when his granddaughter, Serena Russell, brought an American called Santangelo, who was considered unsuitable, to stay at Blenheim for Royal Ascot, all he said on introduction was, 'Santangelo? Used to have a footman called that.' The man left and the engagement ended. He died in 1972, shortly after inveigling Laura Canfield to marry him and leave her treasured house.

MARLBOROUGH, Eleventh Duke of, JOHN GEORGE VANDERBILT HENRY SPENCER-CHURCHILL, *born* 13 April 1926.

Educated Eton, Captain, Life Guards. Married first, 1952 (dissolved 1960), Susan Hornby (one son, one daughter), second, 1961 (dissolved 1971), Mrs Athina Onassis, thirdly, 1972, Rosita Douglas (one son). Known universally as 'Sunny' from the days when he bore the courtesy title, Earl of Sunderland, and nicknamed 'Sunbun' by his stepdaughter Christina Onassis (q.v.). Lives the winters at Lee Place, Charlbury, the summers at Blenheim, surrounded by 11,500 acres. Worked briefly for Stavros Livanos in the shipping business during second marriage, and spends a holiday every summer on Coronis, the private island of George Livanos, his former brother-in-law. His heir James, Marquess of Blandford (born 24 November 1955) was educated at Harrow and, briefly, the Royal Agricultural College, Cirencester. A heroin addict, he spent Christmas and New Year 1985 in Pentonville jail after breaking a probation order, and in November 1986 received a two-year suspended sentence for possessing cocaine, while his supplier was jailed for ten years. After six months at Farm Place, Ockley, his seventh attempt at a cure, he has remained free of drugs and in 1988 his father bought him an 850-acre farm at Wooton Down on the edge of the Blenheim estate and a £1.2 million house, which is being refurbished, with the addition of a tennis court and swimming pool. In February 1990 Blandford married kindergarten teacher Becky Few Brown and his best man, Paddy McNally (q.v.) gave him a Range Rover as a wedding present.

Jamie Blandford (left) with his father, the Duke of Marlborough

MARNHAM, PATRICK, *born* 1942, educated at Downside and Oxford.
Elder son of Sir Ralph Marnham, Sergeant Surgeon to the Queen 1967–71. Immensely secretive freelance writer and author who started the Grovel column in *Private Eye* in 1966 and was believed by his closest colleagues to have several mistresses and children. His addition to a *Private Eye* item about the disappearance of the Earl of Lucan (q.v.), alleging that Sir James Goldsmith (q.v.) had helped smuggle the fugitive peer out of the country led to nearly 100 writs from the financier who also sued Marnham and Richard Ingrams (q.v.) for criminal libel. Chosen as the official biographer of the satirical organ, he published *The Private Eye Story* in 1982, which led to a rift with Ingrams, who disputed certain references to himself. In 1987 he wrote *Trail of Havoc*, his account of the Lucan mystery, half of which is devoted to perpetuating his vendetta against Goldsmith. He now lives in Paris where he writes for the *Independent*.

MASCHLER, THOMAS MICHAEL, *born* 16 August 1933, educated Leighton Park School.
Married, 1970 (dissolved 1987), Fay Coventry (one son, two daughters). Secondly, 1988, Regina Frederick. Production assistant André Deutsch, 1955, Editor MacGibbon & Kee 1956–8, Fiction Editor Penguin Books 1958–60, Editorial Director Jonathan Cape 1960, Managing Director 1966, Chairman 1970. Famed for his parsimony, offering authors coffee and a sandwich in his office rather than taking them out to lunch, and for serving plonk at dinners superbly cooked by his wife Fay, the restaurant critic, at their Hampstead home. Reputed to have bowled over Meryl Streep when she made *The French Lieutenant's Woman*, on which he was Associate Producer. For some years Fay was involved with architect Nathan Silver (now living with Maria Aitken) and they were in the throes of a divorce on the grounds of two years' separation when Jonathan Cape was sold to American publishing billionaire Si Newhouse – Maschler collected £6.5 million for his thirty-six per cent shareholding. Fay began legal action after being offered a £100,000 settlement. In 1987 Tom paid an estimated £1.1 million for the Hampstead home of Dame Peggy Ashcroft and is renovating a property in the South of France.

MASSIMO, Prince STEFANO, *born* 10 January 1955.

Educated Gordonstoun, he was the tug-of-love child of Prince Vittorio Massimo and English actress Dawn Addams, who separated when he was four, after Vittorio accused Addams of not behaving like a princess because she appeared in a film wearing a black negligée. At one stage of the seven-year custody battle the Italian judge ordered both parents to be seen by a psychiatrist. They divorced finally in 1971. Stefano became a photographer in London but incurred the wrath of his father in 1973 when he married seventeen-year-old Atalanta Foxwell (two sons, one daughter), daughter of film director Ivan Foxwell and his wife Lady Edith. From his palazzo in Rome, Prince Vittorio said: 'I am worth about £2.8 million but not a penny will go to my son – my only child – after this marriage.' Prince Stefano replied: 'When my father was twenty-one he ran away with a Danish girl and his father put Mussolini on his trail. He was chased to the border but got away and married her in a Danish register office.' Dawn, who starred opposite Charlie Chaplin in *A King in New York*, married James White in 1974, and died of cancer in 1985.

MATTHEWS, Lord, VICTOR COLLIN (life peer), *born* 5 December 1919.

Educated Highbury, served RNVR 1939–45. Married, 1942, Joyce Pilbeam (one son). Islington-born, he went into the building business and worked his way up Trollope and Colls, becoming contracts manager for ten years before branching out on his own with a couple of Brixton building companies. Taken over in 1965 by Trafalgar House, headed by Sir Nigel Broackes, he became Group Managing Director in 1968 after successfully bidding for his old company. Trafalgar took over Beaverbrook Newspapers from Sir Max Aitken (q.v.) in 1977 and when he was ennobled three years later, Matthews was dubbed 'Lord Whelks' by *Private Eye* because of his humble background, while his son, Ian, became 'The Honourable Winkle'.

When the company, floated as Fleet Holdings, was taken over in 1985, Matthews cashed in his stake for £8 million, sold his 220-acre Enfield, north London farm and went into tax exile in Jersey. He put his string of racehorses in the care of Ian (who, in 1984, married Mrs Helen Cooke) to train at Newmarket. In 1988 Ian won twenty-one races worth £69,541 and quit at the end of the following year to join his father in Jersey, where he had bought a bakery business.

MAXWELL, (IAN) ROBERT, *born* Jan Ludwig Hoch 10 June 1923.

Married, 1945, heiress Elisabeth Meynard (three sons, four daughters, and one son, one daughter deceased). Personally decorated by Viscount Montgomery on the field after being awarded the Military Cross in 1945 for single-handedly attacking a nest of German machine gunners holding up his regiment's advance. Assumed various names, including Du Maurier after a brand of cigarette, until given 'Robert Maxwell' by fellow soldiers. Met his wife, a translator, in Paris when he arrived with the liberation. After the Second World War he helped the Germans set up their printing businesses and, settling in England, started making his fortune in the same field. The Maxwells' eldest son went into a coma in 1961 after a road accident and died seven years later. All seven children went to university at Oxford, on the outskirts of which Maxwell leases, from the council, spacious Headington Hill Hall, which he calls the country's most expensive council house. In 1964 he became Labour MP for Buckingham, losing the seat in 1970, after he lost control of Pergamon, his company in which the American firm Leasco had bought a thirty-eight per cent stake, later to sue for £15.8 million for 'the depression and virtual destruction of the value of their shareholdings through fraud and deceit'. A Department of Trade and Industry report later found that Maxwell 'was not a fit and proper person to control a public company'. He made another fortune from printing and, in 1984, bought Mirror Group Newspapers for £90 million, from which he has expanded across the world. His own newspaper states that his fortune is now in excess of £1 billion. Once trim, he is now panda-proportioned, weighing around twenty stone. Is known to eat in the back of his Rolls on the way to lunch, and on the way back. Champagne and caviar are his staple food and drink.

MEADE, RICHARD JOHN HANNAY, *born* 4 December 1938.
Educated Lancing, Magdalene College, Cambridge. Son of the owner of a preparatory school who bred Connemara ponies, he married, 1977, Angela Farquhar (two sons, one daughter and one son deceased). Known as 'Tiddles', she had been his girlfriend for seven years. Winner of two team and one individual Olympic gold medals in the three-day event, in 1958 and 1972. Winner, Badminton 1970 and 1982. A one time favourite to marry Princess Anne (she wanted to, he did not), he worked as an investment banker and property broker and was sponsored by builders George Wimpey 1979–85, retiring in 1986 after a quarter of a century of competitions. He became President of the British Equestrian Federation in 1989 – the Princess Royal is head of the International Equestrian Federation and still feels she should have married him.

MEINERTZHAGEN, DANIEL, *born* 2 March 1920.
Educated Eton and New College, Oxford, served in the 1939–45 War in the RAFVR (Wing Commander). Married, 1949, Dido Pretty (two sons). Joined Lazard Brothers 1936, Managing Director 1954, Deputy Chairman 1971, Chairman 1973–80. Chairman Royal Insurance 1974–85. Not to be confused with his elder son, Daniel Meinertzhagen (born 1943, educated Eton and New College, Oxford) who lost £25,000 playing *chemin-de-fer* after coming down from Oxford, where he was Captain of Boxing, and put an advertisement in **The Times**: 'Young man, Eton and Oxford, obtained Blue but failed degree having sought pleasure

too exclusively now intends to work hard and seeks employment where high IQ and wide acquaintanceship can be fully utilized.' Instead of the City, he began work for John Aspinall (q.v.) at the Clermont. In October 1970 he married Amanda Lumb, niece of Lord Hanson. After Aspinall sold the club to the Playboy organization, and Dan lost an estimated £200,000 there, he founded Figurehead, a hairdressers in Pont Street, Belgravia, with Dominic Elwes (q.v.), the Marquess of Northampton and Blue Star garages heir John Deen. In 1977 he separated from his wife after estimates of his annual entertaining bill were put at £30,000 and when Aspinall returned to casino owning, Dan was taken on as a manager. In 1988 he was paid off by the new owners of Aspinall's Curzon Casino and went into business with his old boss, running a betting operation. For some years he has lived in the spacious Chelsea house of heiress Hilly Pilkington, a divorcée, and spends one night a week in a poker school with players including Anthony Holden (q.v.). He is often to be found dieting – in 1973, for a £10,000 bet with the Hon. Michael Pearson (q.v., and whose family owns Lazards) as to who could lose more weight, he shed five stone, beating his opponent by 5lbs.

MELCHETT, Third Lord, JULIAN EDWARD ALFRED MOND, *born* 9 January 1925.
Educated Eton. Married, 26 April 1947, Sonia Graham (one son, two daughters). Grandson of Sir Alfred Mond, who founded Imperial Chemical Industries, he started in the City with a small merchant bank, becoming Managing Director of Hill, Samuel. In 1966 Richard Marsh, then Minister of Power, persuaded him to accept the post of Chairman of British Steel Corporation, responsible for the transfer of the steel industry to public ownership. An indefatigable party-goer and giver, with his wife Sonia, at their large house in Tite Street, Chelsea. He died in June 1973, aged forty-eight, as he sunbathed in the grounds of his holiday home in Majorca. His Socialist son Peter (educated at Eton and

Pembroke College, Cambridge) turned the family's Norfolk estate into a cooperative and served in the Governments of Harold Wilson and James Callaghan, latterly as a Minister of State for Northern Ireland from 1976–9. Sonia was escorted for a year by Italian journalist Count Paolo Filo della Torre and expected to marry the Hon. Sir Hugh Fraser, following his divorce from Lady Antonia. But in July 1984, four months after Fraser's death, she married author Andrew Sinclair, seven years her junior.

MELLY, (ALAN) GEORGE (HEYWOOD), *born* 17 August 1926.
Married first, 1955 (dissolved 1962), Victoria Vaughan (one daughter), secondly, 1963, Diana Dawson (one son). Educated Stowe, Able Seaman with the Royal Navy 1944–7. Sang with Mick Mulligan's Jazz Band 1949–61, has been with John Chilton's Feetwarmers since 1974. Between 1956 and 1971 he wrote the Flook stripcartoon for the *Daily Mail*, drawn by Wally Fawkes (Trog). Author of autobiographies *Owning Up*, *Scouse Mouse*, and *Rum, Bum and Concertina*. Accused by Peregrine Worsthorne of having seduced him at school with 'incredible dispatch on the art-room sofa one afternoon', a fact brought up by the famous libel action brought against Worsthorne by *Sunday Times* Editor, Andrew Neil (q.v.). Melly claims *he* was seduced, pointing out in evidence that Worsthorne was the senior by almost three years.

MENUHIN, Sir YEHUDI, *born* 22 April 1916, adopted British nationality 1985, taking an honorary knighthood awarded to him in 1965.
In 1987 the Queen appointed him a member of the Order of Merit, restricted to twenty-four holders at a time. Violinist and conductor, educated by private tutors, married first, 1938 (dissolved), Nola Ruby Nicholas, secondly, 1947, Diana Gould (two sons). Made his debut with orchestra, San Francisco aged seven, in Paris, aged ten, in New York, eleven, Berlin, thirteen. During the 1939–45 War he performed 500 concerts for US and Allied armed forces and benefit concerts for the Red Cross. Lived for twenty-four years, until July 1984, in a beautiful Highgate, London house, from which he moved into a stuccoed early-nineteenth-century house in Belgravia, costing £1 million. In 1987 he sued the surveyors for £197,850 damages, having overpaid due to excessive valuation – he had been quoted £124,000 to install a lift and add a conservatory and received a bill for £438,000. Guests are greeted by an Epstein bust of himself, completed in 1945. His piano is one of the three Bechsteins belonging to his late mother-in-law Lady Harcourt, who was Evelyn Stuart, the pianist. In 1963 he founded the Yehudi Menuhin School of Music at Stoke d'Abernon, Surrey, for musically talented children. He is a fitness fanatic, eating yoghurt and fruit and lying on the floor for fifteen minutes a day after standing on his head.

METCALFE, DAVID PATRICK, *born* 8 July 1927.
Educated Eton, where, because of his early physical development (his height later reached 6ft 5ins) he was excused wearing shorts. Son of Major Edward Dudley 'Fruity' Metcalfe, who was Equerry and best man to the Duke of Windsor when he married Mrs Bessie Wallis Warfield on 3 June 1937 at the Château de Cande, Monts. Married first, 1957 (dissolved 1964), Alexandra Bovcun (two sons, two daughters), widow of film chief Sir Alexander Korda. Secondly, 1968 (dissolved 1978), Countess Anne de Chauvigny de Blot (one son). Thirdly, 1979, Sally Howe (one daughter). Known as 'Metters' and a pillar of transatlantic society, he is a director of a leading firm of Lloyd's insurance brokers. His first wife, who was left Korda's fortune, committed suicide in 1966 after a leading London surgeon had broken off his three-week engagement to her.

George Melly

MILES, SARAH, *born* 9 September 1941, educated Roedean and Royal Academy of Dramatic Art.

Made film debut in 1963 in **Term of Trial**, followed by **The Servant**, in which she co-starred with Dirk Bogarde and James Fox (q.v.). She became engaged to the latter during filming of **Those Magnificent Men in Their Flying Machines**. Married first, 1967 (dissolved 1976), as his second wife, Robert Bolt (one son), the playwright who won Oscars for his screenplays of **Dr Zhivago** (1965) and **A Man For All Seasons**. In 1973 in Gila Bend, Arizona, where she was filming **The Man Who Loved Cat Dancing** with Burt Reynolds and Lee J. Cobb, her business manager David Whiting, twenty-six, who was infatuated with her, committed suicide in the TraveLodge motel in which they were all staying. In evidence at the inquest she told of a fight in her room prior to his death, when he threw her to the ground 'three or four times' and threatened to kill her. Whiting, she said, was 'half-mad'. She was divorced in 1975 on the grounds of two years' separation but in 1988, after returning to England following seven lean years in California, she remarried Bolt, who was partly paralyzed following a stroke. They had got together to help their son, Thomas, be cured of heroin addiction. In 1989 they sold Sussex House, Chiswick for £800,000 and moved to a small estate in Sussex, bought for £1 million.

MILFORD HAVEN, Fourth Earl of, GEORGE IVAR LOUIS MOUNTBATTEN, *born* 6 June 1961.

The son of David Milford Haven, who was best man to his first cousin, Prince Philip, in 1947 and died in 1970 at Liverpool Street station waiting for a train. Educated Gordonstoun, the Fourth Earl had to give up his ambition to join the Royal Marines, of which his great-uncle, Earl Mountbatten, was Colonel Commandant, after failing Maths 'O' level four times. Worked as a diver in Queensland, Australia before joining a drilling company owned by Exxon oil in Tulsa, Oklahoma in 1982. Learned to fly a helicopter, buying his own, and started a polo team, which was sponsored by leisure company, Brent Walker. In 1989 he married Sarah Walker (one daughter), the divorcée daughter of former Billingsgate fish porter George Walker, who started the £135 million leisure company with the earnings of his sixties heavyweight-boxing brother, Billy 'The Blond Bomber' Walker. In 1990 Sarah paid £11 million for the half share in Moyns Park, a fifty-two-room house and estate in Birdbrook, Essex, which was inherited by her husband's younger brother, Lord Ivar Mountbatten.

MILLS, JOHN, *born* Poland, 31 December 1911.

Reputed to have served in the Belgian army and to have been an amateur boxing champion, he became one of several Poles who opened clubs in London during the Second World War. In 1941 founded Les Ambassadeurs and the Milroy at 5 Hamilton Place (in those days, the continuation of Park Lane into Piccadilly), which became the favourite club (members included Prince Philip and, later, Prince Charles) of Princess Margaret and her set in the early fifties, dancing to the band of Harry Roy and Paul Adam. Married first, 1935 (dissolved 1979), Kitty Aptaker (one son, one daughter), secondly, 1980, Diana Iles (who had changed her surname to Mills by deed poll). In 1961 opened London's first gaming casino (with the Earl of Kimberley, q.v., doing the PR) on the first floor of the ornate building, once owned by the Rothschild family. The club lost three-quarters of its extensive garden when the new Park Lane was created in 1963 and the following year Mills paid £357,000 for New York's most famous restaurant and nightclub, El Morocco, selling the business after five years. When Mills, who lived in the South of France, where he kept his yacht, died in 1982, his son Robert discovered that part of the building, which had a twenty-two-year lease, had been sold to the Grand Metropolitan group of Sir Max Joseph (q.v.)

without his, Robert's, knowledge. Les Ambassadeurs now operates out of the basement area that used to be the Garrison nightclub.

MONCKTON, The Hon. ROSAMOND MARY, *born* 26 October 1953, only daughter of Second Viscount Monckton of Brenchley, a former Major-General in the Rhine Army whose father, Walter, was legal adviser to King Edward VII during the Abdication crisis and later a Cabinet Minister.

Known as Rosa, she started the first British post-war branch of Tiffany's in Bond Street in 1986, a decade after she began working at Cartier, from where she moved to Asprey's. During her three years at Cartier she enlivened business by cajoling London hotel porters to feed her the names of potential clients and left after a personality clash with cigar-smoking Nathalie Hocq, who inherited the empire after her father Robert was run over in Paris in December 1979. Rosa's great-aunt was the Hon. Mabel Strickland, owner of the *Times of Malta*.

MONTAGU, (ALEXANDER) VICTOR EDWARD PAULET, *born* 22 May 1906.

Educated Eton, Trinity College, Cambridge. Married first, 1934 (dissolved 1958), Rosemary Peto (two sons, four daughters), secondly, 1962 (annulled 1965), Lady Anne Cavendish, daughter of the Ninth Duke of Devonshire. As Viscount Hinchingbrooke was Conservative MP for South Dorset 1941–62, after which he succeeded his father as Tenth Earl of Sandwich. On 24 July 1964 he disclaimed his peerages for life in the hope of getting back into Parliament. In 1967 Conservative Central Office took his name off the candidates list and by 1974, when he failed to be selected as prospective candidate for West Dorset, he had been rejected for twenty-five seats. In 1984 he moved out of Mapperton, his Elizabethan, Dorset manor house, offering it for rent at £5,000 a year. 'I have been crippled by Mrs Thatcher's taxation,' he announced, estimating the cost of running the house at £20,000 a year.

MONTAGU OF BEAULIEU, Third Lord, EDWARD JOHN BARRINGTON DOUGLAS-SCOTT-MONTAGU, *born* 20 October 1926.

Educated Ridley College, St Catharine's, Ontario, Eton, New College, Oxford. Married first, 1959 (dissolved 1974), Belinda Crossley (one son, one daughter), second, 1974, Fiona Herbert (one son). Inherited title and the 8,000-acre Beaulieu estate, including the Beaulieu river, on the death of his father (grandson of the second son of the Fifth Duke of Buccleuch) in 1920. Founded the Montagu Motor Museum in 1952 (now the National Motor Museum) and Beaulieu is now Britain's leading stately home attraction. Chairman of the Historic Buildings and Monuments Commission since 1963 and fond of giving fancy-dress parties. Once linked as an eligible proposition for Princess Margaret, he was annoyed in the sixties when she and the Earl of Snowdon passed by his table at the Club Del'Aretusa, the restaurant of the decade, without acknowledgement. He threw the bread basket at the back of Snowdon, uttering the words, 'You're no better than I am.'

MONTGOMERY OF ALAMEIN, First Viscount, BERNARD LAW, *born* 17 November 1887.

Educated at St Paul's School and Royal Military Academy, Sandhurst. Married, 27 July 1927, Elizabeth Hobart (one son), widow of Captain Oswald Armitage Carver (she died 19 October 1937). Served in First World War, was severely wounded and awarded the DSO. In 1939 was Colonel Commanding, Eighth Division. General 1942, Field Marshal 1944, Commander-in-Chief British Forces of Occupation in Germany 1946–8. Bought a derelict water mill and oast houses on the River Wey near Alton in 1947, which he rebuilt, naming it Islington Mill, with New Zealand wood and Tasmanian oak – the timber was given to him after he had complained on a visit to the Antipodes that he could not find materials in post-war Britain. In 1959, to the annoyance of Prime Minister

Lord Montagu and wife, Fiona

Harold Macmillan, he made a one-man peace mission to Soviet leader Nikita Kruschev in Moscow and annoyed President Eisenhower by declaring on a television programme that the President should have stayed out of politics. Ike labelled him a 'chattering magpie'. In 1967, complaining of being short of funds, he started doing the Pools – Littlewoods personally sent one of their representatives to explain how to fill out the coupon after he complained he could not understand the system. He was delighted in 1970 when his only son, David Bernard Montgomery (born 18 August 1928) married, as his second wife, the daughter of one of his old comrades, Lieutenant General Sir Frederick 'Boy' Browning, and Daphne du Maurier (q.v.). David's first marriage, 1953, to Mary Connell – one son, one daughter – was dissolved in 1968. 'Monty' died in 1976 and in 1989 his son put Islington Mill on the market for £600,000.

MOORE, DUDLEY STUART JOHN, *born* 19 April 1935, educated County High School, Dagenham, Guildhall School of Music and Drama, Magdalen College, Oxford.
Married first, 1958 (dissolved 1971), Suzy Kendall, secondly, 1975 (dissolved 1980), Tuesday Weld (one son), thirdly, 1988, Brogan Lane. Suzy has made him guardian of her only child, daughter Elodie Harper, born 1979. Infuriated his former collaborator Peter Cook ('Dud 'n' Pete', 'Not Only...But Also', 'Goodbye Again') by becoming a Hollywood sex symbol in the film *10* with Julie Andrews and Bo Derek. Cook pointed out that Dud had a club foot and was of restricted stature (5ft 2ins). For twenty years in psychiatric analysis, he lives in Malibu and has two restaurants in the Los Angeles area. In June 1990 he collected his Master of Arts and Bachelor of Music degrees at Oxford, thirty years after he had obtained them, and made his debut in a series of commercials extolling the virtues of Tesco's fresh produce, for a fee which will eventually be £1 million.

MORLEY, SHERIDAN ROBERT, *born* 5 December 1941.
Educated Sizewell Hall, Suffolk, Merton College, Oxford. Son of Robert Morley, and grandson of Gladys Cooper, he married, 1965, Margaret Gudejko (one son, two daughters) whom he met when she was sharing a room at the University of Hawaii with Bette Midler. A prolific author, journalist and broadcaster, including editing the diaries of Noel Coward (godfather to Sheridan's son Hugo) and writing the musical *Noel and Gertie*. On the appointment of a new editor, resigned from *Punch* as drama critic 1989, after fourteen years, to work for the *International Herald Tribune*. In 1988 he left his wife midway through writing a book with her celebrating the joys of old age, to live in a flat just behind Madame Tussaud's belonging to video producer Ruth Leon, who was a friend of his at Oxford thirty years before. Morley stated that she spent half the year in London and the other six months in New York with her husband, and he would be seeking a divorce.

MORRISON, BRYAN ANTHONY, *born* 14 August 1942.
Married, 1972, Greta Van Rantwyk (one son, one daughter). Former manager of groups who became a music publisher associated with Pink Floyd, Elton John, the Bee Gees and Wham! In 1972 he gave evidence in an Old Bailey trial of three brothers who were paid £250 to beat up the road manager of the Bee Gees. In 1974 saw his first game of polo and became a fanatic, taking lessons and eventually sponsoring his own team, becoming a two-handicap player and close to Major Ronald Ferguson (q.v.) through whom he became friendly with the Prince of Wales. In 1986 he bought a disused Berkshire racecourse and exercise grounds which, with his partner Norman Lobel, a construction millionaire, he has developed, at a cost of £3 million, into the 240-acre Royal County of Berkshire Polo Club. There are sixty-five playing members, several with their own teams, who have paid an entrance fee of

125

£20,000 and an annual subscription of £3,500. He bought the Holyport mansion of Colonel William Henry Gerard Leigh, former Colonel Commanding the Household Cavalry and Silver-Stick-in-Waiting to the Queen.

Bryan Morrison

MORRISON, The Hon. CHARLOTTE ANNE, *born* 16 April 1955, only daughter of the Ninth Viscount Galway and Lady Teresa Fox-Strangways, in turn the only daughter of the Seventh Earl of Ilchester.
Married, 1983 (dissolved 1987), Guy Martin James Morrison (one son). When their engagement was announced, a former girl-friend of St James's art dealer Morrison, an heiress member of the Cayzer shipping family, sent him a telegram which read: 'Congratulations for finding someone richer, fatter and uglier than me.' From her father, who died in 1971, Charlotte inherited Serlby Hall, Bawtry and Bishopsfield House,

Bawtry and 3,000 acres straddling the Nottinghamshire-Yorkshire border. The Earl of Ilchester, whose two sons were killed in accidents, left Charlotte his 15,000-acre Melbury estate near Sherborne, Dorset. When her mother died in September 1989, she left £40,030,307 and Charlotte moved from her sixteenth-century house in Abbotsbury, Dorset to Melbury, which is noted for its foxes. Legend has it that when a male heir to the Ilchester family dies, the foxes gather at night in front of the house and howl. That, eerily, was how Ilchester first knew of the deaths of his sons.

MORTIMER, JOHN CLIFFORD, *born* 21 April 1923.
Educated Harrow, Brasenose College, Oxford, called to the Bar, 1948. Married first, 1949 (dissolved 1972), Penelope Fletcher (one son, one daughter), second, 1972, Penelope Gollop (two daughters). A better known playwright than advocate (he failed to save *Private Eye* from £14,000 damages and £50,000 costs when the satirical magazine was sued by Desmond Wilcox for libel after

John Mortimer

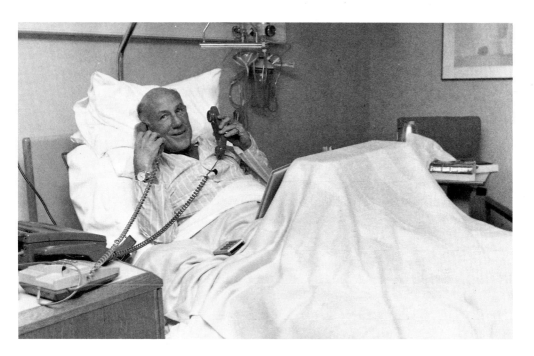

Stirling Moss

he was alleged to have committed plagiarism). His play, *A Voyage Round My Father*, about his blind father who was a barrister, was made into a film, starring Lord Olivier. Since introducing Rumpole in 1977 ('Rumpole of the Bailey'), there have been seven further televised offerings. First wife, the writer Penelope Mortimer, used love letters addressed to him, which she found in a drawer, to devastating effect when writing *The Pumpkin Eater*, which was later filmed – the letters were quoted verbatim as an episode in the book.

MOSS, STIRLING, *born* 17 September 1929. Educated Haileybury. Married first, 1957 (dissolved 1960), Kathleen Moison, secondly, 1964 (dissolved 1968), Elaine Barbarino (one daughter), thirdly, 1980, Susan Paine (one son), whom he had known since she was five. Ten times British National Champion driver, the only Englishman to win the Mille Miglia, 1955, he competed in 494 races, rallies, sprints and endurance runs, winning 222. Driving the green Vanwall VW10, he was runner-up by one point to Michael Hawthorne in the 1958 World Championships and retired after a serious accident at Goodwood in 1962. Lives in a gadget-packed Mayfair mews house (the dining table is lowered into the floor below for washing-up) with 240 electrical circuits. Immortalized by the police catch phrase when stopping speeding drivers, 'Who do you think you are then, Stirling Moss?' In June 1990 he sued a motorist for damages after breaking his hip when he was crashed into, doing 20mph on his 80cc motorbike near his home. He was in plaster for twelve weeks following the accident in the March.

MOYNIHAN, Third Lord, ANTHONY PATRICK ANDREW CAIRNES BERKELEY, *born* 2 February 1936. Educated Stowe, Second Lieutenant, Coldstream Guards. Married first, 1955 (dissolved 1965), Ann Herbert, secondly, 1958 (dissolved 1967), Shirin Quereshi (one daughter), thirdly, 1968 (dissolved 1979), Luthgarda Maria Fernandez (three daughters), fourthly, 1981, Editha Ruben (one son deceased). Grandson of a famous surgeon who was ennobled in 1919, he was known in the fifties for his bongo playing and early marriage, in secret, to an actress and one-time nude model. Chased by creditors, he spent four years touring Far-East nightclubs accompanying his second wife on the bongo drums. In 1969 he fled to Spain before police were able to serve a warrant for his arrest on charges of fraudulent trading, false pretences, fraud against a gaming casino and deception. Extradition was sought from Spain but he disappeared, surfacing a year later in the Philippines, where he is immune from extradition. He has been running massage parlours, but suffered in the clean-up following the election of President Cory Aquino. In 1988 it was revealed in court in Miami that he was the 'supergrass' behind the arrest in Majorca of Oxford-educated Howard Marks, charged with supervising a worldwide drug smuggling operation. Heir to the title is his half-brother Colin Moynihan, a cox who is a former Oxford rowing Blue, world gold medallist and Olympic silver medallist and an MP for Lewisham East since 1983. In 1987 he was appointed Minister of Sport and because of his restricted height he is known as 'The Miniature for Shorts'.

MURRAY THREIPLAND, Stuart Wyndham, *born* 1948.

Educated Eton. Married first, 11 October 1972 (dissolved), Belinda Mary 'Min' Musker (three sons, including twins, one daughter), former wife of John Aspinall (q.v.). Secondly, 1984, Claire Pelly, ex-wife of the Earl of Pembroke (q.v.). Known as 'Tertius' and heir to a Cardiff property fortune, he joined F. Pratt Engineering Corporation in 1974, becoming a director in 1977 and Chief Executive in 1980. Profits nose-dived from £1.35 million in 1975 to a six-month loss of £171,000 in 1981 and he was dismissed. He bought Trafalgar, a mansion formerly owned by the Eleventh Duke of Leeds and

subsequently his brother-in-law, Viscount Chandos, and in 1977 he ended a two-year relationship with Jessica 'Nobbles' Mancroft, younger daughter of the Second Lord Mancroft (q.v.), to begin an affair with the wife of film director Henry Herbert, the Fifteenth Earl of Pembroke, his best friend who lived nearby at Wilton House, set in 14,000 acres. In July 1980 the affair was discovered and Lady Pembroke moved to a house on the estate. She was divorced the following year. In 1990 Trafalgar, built for the descendants of Admiral Horatio Nelson, was put on the market, with twenty acres, at the asking price of £3.5 million.

N*n*

NEIL, Andrew Ferguson, *born* 21 May 1949. Educated Paisley Grammar School and University of Glasgow. Joined ***The Economist*** in 1973 after a year in the Conservative Party Research Department, working as reporter in Ulster, Lobby correspondent, Labour correspondent and, between 1979 and 1982, American correspondent, before becoming UK Editor. Appointed Editor of the ***Sunday Times*** in 1983 after impressing Rupert Murdoch, much to the shock of that newspaper's staff, few of whom had ever heard of him. Since then most have gone, to be replaced by Neil's own appointments as he moves towards his ambition of publishing a 200 page newspaper – it is estimated already to be making £1 million a week profit, swallowed up by the losses of Sky Television, which began broadcasting by satellite on 5 February 1989, and is estimated to be losing £100 million a year. Neil was made Executive Chairman of Sky in 1988 and left in January 1990 after Murdoch predicted it would make a profit in 1993. A chance meeting in Tramp, the Jermyn Street nightclub, in March 1988 with Pamella Bordes led to the High Court in January 1990, when

Andrew Neil

he brought a libel action against Peregrine Worsthorne, former Editor of the *Sunday Telegraph*, who had written in the newspaper that Neil had brought the *Sunday Times* into disrepute with his five-month association with Miss Bordes, who had been exposed in another Murdoch publication, the *News of the World*, as a £500- a-night prostitute. Neil's QC told the court that it was 'quite a serious affair, but not the love story of the century'. The jury awarded Neil £1,000 and costs, which both sides claimed as a victory. He remains unmarried.

NEVILL, Lord, RUPERT CHARLES MONTACUTE, *born* 29 January 1923, younger son of the Fourth Marquess of Abergavenny and heir presumptive to that title.
Educated Eton, Captain, Life Guards in 1939–45 War, ending as ADSC to Lieutenant-General Sir Brian Horrocks. Married, 22 April 1944, Lady Ann Wallop (two sons, two daughters), eldest daughter of the Ninth Earl of Portsmouth. Known because of their diminutive stature (passed on to all their children) as 'The Tiny People'. Lord Rupert, a stockbroker, was appointed Treasurer to Prince Philip in 1970 and Private Secretary from 1975, and with his wife 'Mickey' was among the closest friends of the Queen, Prince Philip and Princess Margaret. Became heir after the Marquess of Abergavenny's son Harry, Earl of Lewes, a page-of-honour to the Queen, died of leukaemia aged seventeen. President of the British Olympic Association from 1977, he died in July 1982 leaving £1,770,989. His elder son, Guy Nevill (born 29 March 1945 and married to Lady Beatrix

Lambton, second daughter of Viscount Lambton) became heir to the marquessate.

NEWPORT, Viscount, RICHARD THOMAS ORLANDO BRIDGEMAN, *born* 3 October 1947 (became Seventh Earl of Bradford in 1981). Educated Harrow and Trinity College, Cambridge. Married, 1979, Joanne Miller (three sons). A seventies entrepreneur who studied cooking and opened a series of restaurants in Central London, now just owner of Porters in Covent Garden. Inherited Weston Park, Shropshire, built in 1671 and where Disraeli, who gave the house a stuffed parrot, was a frequent visitor, with 1,000 acres of parkland and a further 12,500 acres, mostly tenanted farmland, including the village of Weston-under-Lizard. His wife Jo is the daughter of Mayfair commission agent (bookmaker) Benjamin 'Benno' Miller, a familiar figure on the racecourse. Richard is the author of two books, *My Private Parts and the Stuffed*

Parrot (1984) and *The Eccentric Cookbook* (1985). Weston, opened to the public, attracted 170,000 visitors in 1989 and the couple live in a farmhouse on the estate.

NIARCHOS, STAVROS SPYROS, *born* 3 July 1909.
Educated University of Athens. Married first, 1939 (dissolved 1947), Melpomene Capparis, secondly, 1947 (dissolved 1965), Eugenie Livanos (three sons, one daughter), thirdly, 1965 (dissolved 1967), Charlotte Ford (one daughter), daughter of Henry Ford II (q.v.), fourthly, 1971, the Marchioness of Blandford (Athina Livanos). Joined family grain and shipping business, starting own independent shipping concern in 1939. Joined Royal Hellenic Navy Volunteer Reserve in 1941, serving on a destroyer engaged on North Atlantic convoy work (mentioned in despatches). Demobilized with rank of Lieutenant-Commander and returned to shipping busi-

Stavros Niarchos, sons and daughter

ness, pioneering the supertanker. Niarchos group now controls 5.75 million tons of shipping. Wanted to marry Tina Livanos but his rival, Aristotle Onassis (q.v.) made first play, so he wed the elder sister. In May 1970 Eugenie was found dead in her bedroom on the private Niarchos island, Spetsopoula. After taking twenty-five Seconal sleeping tablets, she wrote Stavros in red pencil, in English: 'For the first time in all our life together I have begged you to help me. I have implored you. The error is mine. But sometimes one must forgive and forget. Twenty-six is an unlucky number. It is the double of 12.10b of whisky.' Niarchos, who had found his wife unconscious, tried to revive her by shaking and slapping her. The public prosecutor recommended that he be charged with causing bodily injuries which led to his wife's death, but the judges in the Athens High Court ruled that she had merely taken her own life. She had remained married during Niarchos' affair with Charlotte Ford, but when she became pregnant Niarchos divorced her in Mexico (not recognized in Greece), and married Charlotte in Mexico, where they were later divorced. When he finally married Tina, she, too, was taking pills and drinking too much and she died in their Paris apartment on 10 October 1974 of a lung oedema. For some years Niarchos was close to Princess Firyal of Jordan (q.v.) but in 1990 said he would never marry again. He puts his fortune in excess of £3 billion and spends much of the time on his yacht *Atlantis*, which is his business centre. In January 1990 he almost lost his right eye when he stumbled into a television aerial in his Fifth Avenue, Manhattan apartment.

NICKERSON, Sir JOSEPH, *born* 19 April 1914.
Educated De Aston Grammar School, Market Rasen. Married Eugenie (two sons, two daughters). The eldest of seven children of a prosperous coal merchant and farmer, he developed a special interest in plant breeding, which he called 'the Cinderella of sciences', and founded Rothwell Plant Breeders, which

became Britain's largest independent research station, producing many high-yielding world varieties of barley and wheat. The Nickerson Group of Companies went on to operate in more than sixty countries. He came to prominence in 1952 when he shot, with five other guns, the largest partridge bag in a day on his Lincolnshire estate, 1,059 $\frac{1}{2}$ brace. Nickerson, knighted in 1983, liked to compare himself with the Second Marquess of Ripon, who died in 1923 having killed a total of 187,763 birds in his last twenty-four seasons. Sir Joseph's total for a similar period was 188,172, an average of 7,841 a year. His motto should have been 'If it flies, it dies.' In 1984 Nickerson's close friend, Viscount Whitelaw, then Deputy Prime Minister and Leader of the House of Lords, accidentally winged him in the arm during a grouse shoot on his 17,000-acre Wemmergill Moor estate in County Durham. He died on 3 March 1990 in the United States and left £11,764,447 and a 120-page will in which one of the bequests was a lifetime's supply of pillows to the Prince and Princess of Wales.

NIVEN, (JAMES) DAVID (GRAHAM), *born* 1 March 1910, educated Stowe and Royal Military Academy, Sandhurst.
Married first, 21 September 1940, Primula Rollo (two sons) who died 1946, secondly Hjordis Tersmeden (two adopted daughters). Commissioned, Highland Light Infantry 1929, served in Malta, resigned commission 1932 and roamed Canada, America, West Indies and Cuba until 1935, working variously as a journalist, whisky salesman, pony-racing promoter and laundry delivery man. Arrived in California, becoming an extra in Hollywood and gaining the casting description: 'English Type No. 2008'. First starring role, 1938, in *Bachelor Mother* with Ginger Rogers. Returned to England at outbreak of 1939–45 War and was commissioned into the Rifle Brigade, later Phantom Reconnaissance Regiment, serving in Normandy, Belgium, Holland and Germany. Returned to Hollywood to become international star,

beginning with *Wuthering Heights* co-starring with Merle Oberon and Laurence Olivier. His wife, Primula, granddaughter of Twelfth Lord Rollo, died falling down cellar steps at a Hollywood party on 21 May 1946. His elder son, David Niven Jnr, became a Hollywood film producer, making his father's last film, *Ménage a Trois*. The younger, Jamie Niven, is an investment banker in New York and married to former debutante Fernanda Wetherill (two daughters). They inherited half their father's £20 million estate when he died from Motor Neurone disease in 1983, leaving his St Jean-Cap Ferrat house, where he often entertained close friends Prince Rainier and Princess Grace, to his widow, Hjordis.

NORFOLK, Seventeenth Duke of, MILES FRANCIS STAPLETON FITZALAN HOWARD, also Premier Duke and Earl of England, *born* 21 July 1915.
Educated Ampleforth and Christ Church, Oxford. Married, 4 July 1949, Anne Constable Maxwell (two sons, three daughters). Earl Marshal and Hereditary Marshal of England, responsible for organizing State occasions. Second Lieutenant, Grenadier Guards 1937, served 1939–45 War in France, North Africa, Sicily, Italy (despatches, MC). Appointed Head of British Military Mission to Russian Forces in Germany 1957, became Major-General 1963, retired 1967, succeeded cousin 1975. Lives modestly in Henley although he owns Arundel Castle, Sussex and Carlton Towers, Goole, Yorkshire, which has 365 windows. Britain's senior Catholic layman, his wife devotes herself to the charity she founded in 1984, Help the Hospices and has raised more than £3 million from the sale of Christmas cards of her paintings. Known as 'The Mighty Miles', Norfolk was none too happy when his middle daughter Lady Carina (*see* David Frost) went off to live in Barbados with Trinidadian-born Noel Charles, who ran the island's nightclub, Alexandra's. The Duke objected not to Noel's colour but to the fact that he was a divorced man – his former wife was a

Scandinavian blonde called Alexandra. When they became engaged (said Charles at the time: 'She proposed, I accepted') the Norfolks flew to the Caribbean to inform Carina that she was on her own. The affair ended a year later, at which time she accused the *Daily Mail* gossip columnist of ruining her life for revealing the relationship.

NORMANTON, Sixth Earl of, SHAUN JAMES CHRISTIAN WELBORE ELLIS AGAR.
Educated Eton, Captain in the Blues and Royals (formerly the Royal Horse Guards). Married, 1970, Victoria Beard (one son, two daughters). Left army in 1972 to manage his 6,000-acre Hampshire estate, Somerley, near Ringwood, and became a powerboat racer with his brother-in-law, boat designer and manufacturer James Beard, who died of leukaemia in 1982. Hosts shooting days, dinners (£150 per person per night) and weekend parties at his sixteen-bedroom mansion and says, 'Everything is for rent!' Also for hire, as a model, is his wife Vickie, who was used frequently by the photographer Earl of Lichfield (q.v.) in his Burberry campaign, which featured only aristocrats – Shaun occasionally modelled.

NORTHAMPTON, Seventh Marquess of, SPENCER DOUGLAS DAVID COMPTON, *born* 2 April 1946.
Educated Eton. Married first, 1967 (dissolved 1973), Henriette Bentinck (one son, one daughter), secondly, 1974 (dissolved 1977), Annette Smallwood, thirdly, 1977 (dissolved 1983), Rosemary Hancock (one daughter), former wife of the Hon. Lionel 'Bun' Dawson-Damer, fourthly, 1985 (dissolved 1988), Ellen 'Fritzi' Erdhardt, former wife of the Hon. Michael Pearson (q.v.). Known as the 'Mystic Marquess' for his belief in spiritualism and the supernatural (he was once told from the other side that one of his Old Masters had been painted over an earlier work. When he had it X-rayed, this was found to be true). Inherited Castle Ashby in Northamptonshire and Compton Wynyates, Warwickshire, Britain's finest example of

David Niven

Tudor architecture with 25,000 acres, and a London estate in Islington. His father 'Bim', who died in 1978, married three times after being sued in 1913 for breach of promise by actress Daisy Markham. He settled for £50,000, equivalent to £2 million today. 'Spenny' Northampton says that he has been 'told' he will marry five times. He nabbed Fritzi, who became known as 'Lady Fourthampton', from Viscount Cowdray's heir after they met through a mutual interest in spiritualism. In 1990 it was revealed that Northampton was the anonymous vendor of the 'Sevso Treasure' which Sotheby's, New York, were asked to auction. The magnificent hoard of Roman silver, comprising fourteen massive pieces (dishes, wine jugs, bowls and buckets), is valued in excess of £40 million, but is the subject of court action in the United States from Lebanon and Yugoslavia, both claiming that the silver was illegally smuggled out of their countries. Spenny, who wants the money to ensure the future of his two homes, sold Mantegna's *Adoration of the Magi* through Christie's in 1988 for £8.1 million. A believer in Buddhism, he says, 'In my next life I may return as a beggar.'

NORTHUMBERLAND, Eleventh Duke of, HENRY ALAN WALTER RICHARD PERCY, *born* 1 July 1953.

A godson of the Queen, he was educated Eton and Christ Church, Oxford. Descended from Harry 'Hotspur' Percy, the fourteenth-century soldier-statesman who fell at the Battle of Shrewsbury in July 1403, he inherited, on his father's death in October 1988, the fortress Alnwick Castle, Northumberland, with 100,000 acres and Syon House, Isleworth, Middlesex with 200 acres landscaped by Lancelot 'Capability' Brown. The latter is the only private stately home in the Greater London area, dating from its origins as a fifteenth-century nunnery. Harry Northumberland, who has suffered from ME (myalgic encephalomyelitis), the chronic fatigue syndrome, for fourteen years, is a film buff who has amassed an impressive library

of thirties and forties movies. He lives during the week on the top floor of Syon House, where there are also apartments for his two sisters, and which is open to the public. A bachelor, but not confirmed, he says he has thoughts of marriage one day. He has two younger brothers. In September 1987 the family greeted with some amusement the widely reported claim by Dave Stewart, founder of the Eurythmics, that he was the real Duke of Northumberland.

NUTTALL, Sir NICHOLAS KEITH LILLINGTON, **third baronet,** *born* 21 September 1933.

Educated Eton and Royal Military Academy, Sandhurst, Major, Royal Horse Guards. Married first, 1960 (dissolved 1971), Rosemary York (one son, one daughter), secondly, 1971 (dissolved 1975), Julia Beresford, thirdly, 1975 (dissolved 1983), Miranda Quarry (three daughters), fourth, 1983, Eugenie McWeeny. Raised eyebrows in the Household Cavalry when he became the third brother officer to marry Julia. Her first husband was Captain Darel Carey (married 1959, one son), who resigned his commission on medical grounds shortly before his ex-wife married Captain Lord Patrick Beresford on 26 November 1964 (he later became an SAS Major). They had a son and daughter and he divorced her in 1971 on the grounds of her adultery with Sir Nicholas. Heir to an engineering fortune, ginger-haired Nuttall sold his 1,086-acre Leicestershire estate in 1977 to go into tax exile in Switzerland and the South of France with his third wife Miranda, formerly married to Peter Sellers (q.v.). When they moved to Lyford Cay, Nassau, Nuttall fell for the charms of a local beauty, hotel receptionist's daughter, Eugenie 'Jeannie' McWeeny, known, parodying the fifties song, as, 'Jeannie with the light brown skin'.

O₀

OGILVY, the Hon. Sir ANGUS JAMES BRUCE, *born* 14 September 1928, younger son of the Twelfth Earl of Airlie.

Educated Eton, Trinity College, Oxford, Lieutenant, Scots Guards 1946–8. Married, 24 April 1963, Princess Alexandra of Kent (one son, one daughter), and bought, for £300,000 a grace-and-favour Richmond Park residence, Thatched House Lodge, after turning down the offer of another royal house in the middle of Hyde Park because it was too exposed. A protégé of the fifties financier Harley Drayton who had, among his portfolio of companies, a small African mining concern called Lonrho. In 1961 Drayton commissioned Angus to find an energetic figure to build up the company, and on a trip to Rhodesia he met a farmer and businessman called Roland Rowland, known because of his extreme height as 'Tiny'. Because of a glowing report from Ogilvy, Drayton duly elevated Rowland, even then a controversial figure. In 1969 Ogilvy was summoned to see the Secretary to the Cabinet, Sir Burke Trend, who advised him to resign from Lonrho, which could become involved with sanctions-busting following Rhodesia's Unilateral Declaration of Independence. In 1973 he did resign after a boardroom row involving overseas payments to former Conservative Colonial Secretary Duncan Sandys – payments labelled in the Commons by Prime Minister Edward Heath as 'the unacceptable face of capitalism'. Ogilvy recounts how he then received a call from a former colleague informing him that his family 'would be destroyed'. Following a Department of Trade and Industry report three years later which 'severely' censured Ogilvy, he resigned from the sixteen boards to which he belonged – but only Rank and the property giant MEPC refused to accept his resignation. In October 1989 Ogilvy and Princess Alexandra were stunned to learn that their daughter Marina, then twenty-three, and her lover, Paul Mowatt, had sold their story, for an estimated £50,000, to *Today* newspaper. In it they announced that she was pregnant and made allegations that her parents had tried to trick her into an abortion and had cut her off, claims which were denied. In January the couple married but Angus and Alexandra were not present when their daughter gave birth, by caesarian section, to a daughter in May 1990.

OLDFIELD, BRUCE, *born* 14 July 1950, educated Ripon Grammar School, Ravensbourne College of Art, and St Martin's School of Art.

Son of a Jamaican boxer and Betty Eileen Oldfield, a packer in an electric light bulb factory, he was a Dr Barnardo's boy who was fostered for eighteen months by a woman called Violet Masters in the County Durham village of Hett. His first collection, when he was twenty-three, was shown in New York and he opened his first Knightsbridge showroom in 1977 with a loan of £1,000. The Princess of Wales became a customer in 1982 and other customers included Princess Grace of Monaco, Joan Collins, Marie Helvin, Charlotte Rampling and Bianca Jagger, paying up to £2,000 for *couture* clothes. When Alan Bond's (q.v.) daughter, Susanne, married in 1986, Bruce was flown over to make the wedding dress, the bridesmaids' clothes and Mrs Eileen Bond's outfit – at a cost of £75,000. He was made an OBE in the Queen's June 1990 Birthday Honours List. He says that it is unlikely that he will ever marry.

ONASSIS, CHRISTINA, *born* 11 December 1950.

Educated Headington Girls' School, Oxford, St George's, Switzerland. Married first, 1971 (dissolved 1972), Joseph Bolker, secondly, 1975 (dissolved 1977), Alexander Andreadis, thirdly, 1978 (dissolved 1980), Sergei Danyelovich Kausov (q.v.), fourthly, 1984 (dissolved 1987), Thierry Roussel (one daughter). Inherited £500 million on the

135

Bruce Oldfield and clients

death of her father Aristotle Socrates Onassis, in March 1975, as well as his apartment at 88 Avenue Foch, Paris, an apartment in Olympic Towers, New York and the island of Skorpios. Worked 1976–9 for her own shipping company, Olympic Maritime, through which she met her third husband, Sergei Kausov, described by the press as a 'balding, one-eyed, gold-toothed KGB agent'. Attempted to commit suicide over a lost lover in her Mayfair, London, mews house in August 1974, which led to the death of her mother, Tina, two months later. After a later attempt in 1980, she was prescribed antidepressants and began popping pills which led to dangerous swings in her weight – she ballooned at one stage to fifteen stone, before taking appetite depressants. Travelled in her own Falcon 50 jet and gave her fourth husband nearly £60 million during their marriage, eventually divorcing him when his mistress, Swedish model Gaby Landhage, gave birth to a second child, a daughter – her first, a son, was born five months after Christina's daughter, Athina. Christina died in the rented house of her Argentinian friends, Alberto and Marina Dodero, outside Buenos Aires, in November 1988. The cause was a lung oedema, which also killed her mother. Her body weight was 76kg (167lbs). In May 1990 Thierry Roussel finally married Gaby Landhage, with whom he had been involved for seventeen years, thus uniting his three children. Athina will receive her mother's fortune on her eighteenth birthday in January 2003. In the meantime, a trust gives her an annual income of $4.25 million. Christina is buried in the chapel on Skorpios alongside her father, brother Alexander (who was killed piloting a plane that crashed in January 1973) and her aunt.

Christina Onassis and Thierry Roussel wedding

O'NEILL, TERRY, *born* 30 July 1938, educated Ilford until the age of thirteen and a half. Married first, 1963 (dissolved 1980), Vera Day (one son, one daughter) secondly, 1982 (dissolved 1987), Faye Dunaway (one son). Former Fleet Street lensman (***Daily Sketch***)

who left to become one of the glamour photographers of the eighties. He described his attempt to transfer into the movie business during his fraught marriage to Oscar winner Faye Dunaway – he was executive producer of ***Mommie Dearest*** when she portrayed Joan Crawford – as, 'the worst experience of my life'. He wasted four years setting up the screen version of Tom Kempinski's tragic play ***Duet For One***, in which he planned to direct Faye – he met her in 1977 when she was married to rock musician Peter Wolf, who learned of their affair when his answering machine inadvertently recorded an

Tony O'Reilly

intimate conversation in his Manhattan apartment. Wolf pronounced himself 'humiliated'. Terry's February 1988 portraits of the Duchess of York in a flying jacket made her, temporarily, into a sex symbol. From his side of the lens, Terry said, 'She's not just a good-looking woman, she's sensational. One of the six most beautiful in the world.' Worked from the South Kensington, London studio he bought from Royal portrait painter Bryan Organ until moving to Maida Vale in 1990. For the last year he has been involved with model agent Laraine Ashton, who has a son (born 1987) by award-winning war photographer, Don McCullin.

O'REILLY, Dr Anthony John Francis, (Tony O'Reilly), *born* 7 May 1936.
Educated at Belvedere College, Dublin and University College, Dublin. Married, 1962, Susan Cameron (three sons, three daughters, of whom two sons and one daughter are triplets). Known as 'Lover Boy', in 1955 he won the first of twenty-nine caps playing rugby football for Ireland and gained ten caps with the British Lions in-between. At the age of thirty-four he was a surprise recall for Ireland against England at Twickenham, turning up for training in a chauffeur-driven limousine (he was Managing Director of Heinz UK). Towards the end of the game, which England won, O'Reilly dived for the ball and was kicked unconscious, which led to one Irish supporter yelling, 'And kick his bloody chauffeur as well while you're at it.' After making his name with the Irish Dairy Board, marketing Kerrygold butter, in 1961, he moved to the Irish Sugar Company in 1966 and joined Heinz in 1969, becoming President and chief executive officer in 1973 with headquarters in Pittsburgh. He was made Chairman in 1987, earning £1.4

million a year, and is also Chairman of his own company in Ireland, the Fitzwilton group, which owns the Independent Newspapers chain. There was no mention in the Irish Press when, in the summer of 1988, his Australian-born wife, a talented musician, left him and their eighteenth-century County Kildare mansion, Castlemartin, to live in London.

OSBORNE, JOHN (JAMES), *born* 12 December 1929, educated Belmont College, Devon.
Married first, 1951 (dissolved 1957), Pamela Lane, secondly, 1957 (dissolved 1963), Mary Ure, thirdly, 1963 (dissolved 1968), Penelope Douglass (one daughter), former wife of Professor Roger Gilliatt, who was the Earl of Snowdon's best man in 1960, fourthly, 1968 (dissolved 1977), Jill Bennett and fifthly, 1978, Helen Dawson. Started as an actor, making his first stage appearance in 1948 at the Lyceum, Sheffield in *No Room at the Inn*. Toured, playing in seasons in Ilfracombe, Bridgwater, Camberwell, Kidderminster and Derby and a Royal Court season with the English Stage Company, appearing in *Death of Satan*, *Cards of Identity*, *Good Woman of Setzuan* and *The Making of Moo*. His first play, *Look Back in Anger*, was produced in 1956, followed by *The Entertainer* in 1957. His take-off of gossip columnists, *The World of Paul Slickey* (William Hickey was the *Daily Express* gossip, Paul Tanfield the *Daily Mail*'s) was produced in 1959. Annual income from his works estimated in excess of £300,000. In 1981 he mounted a savage attack on his nonagenarian mother Nellie (a Lyons cornerhouse cleaner and barmaid) in a TV interview with Melvyn Bragg (q.v.) after the publication of his autobiography, *A Better Class of Person*, in which he wrote that he despised and hated her. She replied, 'My fault may have been loving him too much.' Moved from Edenbridge, Kent, to Wales with Helen, a former programme compiler for the National Theatre, with whom he fell in love, 'Because she lets me eat all the onions I want'.

O'TOOLE, (SEAMUS) PETER, *born* 2 August 1932.
Educated Royal Academy of Dramatic Art. Son of an Irish bookmaker from Leeds, he married, 1960 (dissolved 1979), Sian Phillips (two daughters). With the Bristol Old Vic Company 1955–8. Debut on London stage in 1956 as Peter Shirley in *Major Barbara* at the Old Vic. Won an Oscar for *Lawrence of Arabia* in 1962, which was his fourth film and has been nominated, without success, six times since. His much-vaunted return in 1980 to the classical theatre in the Old Vic's *Macbeth* was one of the disasters of the decade, making the front pages of newspapers as audiences rolled in the aisles at the sight of actors wading through gore and bumping into the scenery. Gave up as a legendary drinker in 1975 after his liver packed up and he underwent an extensive abdominal operation. He has a son, Lorcan, (Irish for Lawrence), born 1983, by a two-year affair with American actress Karen Somerville, who obtained a warrant for his arrest after he allegedly kidnapped the boy during a prolonged custody battle. In August 1988 a judge ordered that Lorcan should go to school in England and spend the holidays with his mother in America. O'Toole's Hampstead house, where he lived with Sian (who left him to marry actor Robin Sachs, seventeen years her junior, in 1979), was put on the market for £900,000 in January 1989 and later that year he returned successfully to the West End in *Jeffrey Bernard Is Unwell*, a Keith Waterhouse play about an alcoholic journalist trapped overnight in a pub.

Pp

PACKER, KERRY FRANCIS BULLMORE, *born* 17 December 1937.
Educated Cranbrook School, Sydney, Geelong Church of England Grammar School, Victoria. Married, 1963, Roslyn

Weedon (one son, one daughter). Inherited the Consolidated Press Holdings media empire from his father, yachtsman Sir Frank Packer, who twice challenged for the America's cup with yachts named after his wife, Gretel. In 1972 Sir Frank had sold the family newspapers in Sydney to Rupert Murdoch, leaving a business of television, magazines and newspapers. In 1987 Kerry sold Channel Nine to Alan Bond, who had just been defeated in his bid to defend the America's Cup in Fremantle, for £458 million, and decided to 'retire' to play polo. He spent £30 million constructing seven polo grounds and buildings at Ellerston, his property in New South Wales, bought 100 ponies from Argentina and moved to London for the summers to play, taking eight suites, filled with his own furniture, at the Savoy. A ferocious gambler who has bet £1 million on a horse race, he has wagered £7 million in a night playing blackjack in London gaming clubs and when he won £2.4 million at the Clermont Club in May, he gave each of his seven polo professionals a £100,000 'present'. A partner with Sir James Goldsmith (q.v.) and the Hon. Jacob Rothschild (q.v.) in their aborted £13.5 billion bid to take over British American Tobacco, he regained Channel Nine from the beleaguered Bond in June 1990, who owed him £100 million in preference shares, which were converted to give Packer a fifty-five per cent holding. In 1979 Packer turned the world of cricket upside down by forming a rebel tour, managed by former England captain Tony Greig, after Channel Nine failed to win the rights to test matches. He pioneered floodlit games with white balls and players attired in blue and pink colours.

PALMER, Sir (Charles) Mark, **fifth baronet,** *born* 21 November 1941, educated Eton and Oxford, a page-of-honour to the Queen 1956–9.
Born posthumously the son of the fourth baronet, his mother, Lady Abel Smith, was lady-in-waiting to the Queen 1949–87, and has been an extra lady-in-waiting since 1987.

The original aristocratic hippy, he led a band of drug-taking travellers in the sixties in a brightly painted gypsy caravan pulled by a carthorse, dropping out in the West Country saying, 'We are really on the path to the Kingdom of Heaven. It's not easy, it's not comfortable, but any bad scenes we have to go through we are grateful for. One can only benefit from divine wrath.' In 1968 he was fined £20 by Glastonbury court for having 'dangerous' drugs. In 1976 he married the Hon. Catherine Tennant (one son, one daughter), heiress sister of Lord Glenconner (q.v.) but has given up his ambition to become a vicar. He once rang the Queen from a pub pay-telephone to reply to an invitation but was cut off by the pips in mid-conversation, an experience hitherto unknown to Her Majesty.

PALMER-TOMKINSON, Charles, *born* 4 July 1940, educated Eton and Royal Agricultural College, Cirencester.
Married, 1966, Patti Dawson (one son, two daughters). **Jeremy Palmer-Tomkinson,** *born* 4 November 1943, educated Eton, Second Lieutenant, Royal Green Jackets. Married, 1982, Clare Leveson (two daughters). Sporting sons of stockbroker James Palmer-Tomkinson, the Captain of the British ski team at the 1948 St Moritz Olympics, who was killed in Klosters training for the 1952 Olympic Games. Charlie captained the British team at the 1964 Innsbruck Olympic Games and acts as adviser to the Prince of Wales, with whom he was skiing, with his wife, Patti, and Major Hugh Lindsay in March 1988 when the party was buried by an avalanche, killing the Major and causing multiple fractures to Patti's legs. Jeremy, who became British ski champion in 1965, competed in five Olympics and was the standard-bearer for the British team in Lake Placid in 1980. He dubbed the thrilling skiing sequences in the James Bond film, *On Her Majesty's Secret Service*. Charlie owns a 500-acre farm at Dummer, next to Major Ronald Ferguson, and farms 1,200 acres on a cooperative, while Jeremy works for the

International Management Group.

PALUMBO, PETER GARTH, *born* 20 July 1935. Educated Eton and Worcester College, Oxford. Married first, 1959 (dissolved 1978), Denia Wigram (one son, two daughters), secondly Hayat Morowa (one daughter). An art connoisseur and collector who spent twenty-five years buying thirteen freehold properties and 348 leasehold interests around the Mansion House, London, at a cost of £25 million, in order to erect a skyscraper designed by his hero, Ludwig Mies van der Rohe (similar to his Seagram building in Park Avenue, New York). Given initial planning consent, this was overturned and refused after a public enquiry costing £2 million. Palumbo, who played polo with Prince Philip and the Prince of Wales, was not aided by Charles's description of the project as 'a black stump more suited to downtown Chicago'. Palumbo, left a property empire by his late father Rudolph (long criticized for having razed historic Norfolk House in St James's Square to make way for a modern office building), then commissioned James Stirling. After another public enquiry, the then Environment Secretary Nicholas Ridley, granted permission. This was successfully challenged by the conservation group Save Britain's Heritage and the matter is being appealed. In the meantime the delay is costing Palumbo, who was appointed Chairman of the Arts Council in 1989, £1 million a month. He was on the point of remarrying his first wife when she died of cancer in 1986 after collapsing in Venice. His Ascot home, Buckhurst Park, was sold to King Hussein of Jordan (q.v.) for £4.2 million. He owns the Farnsworth House, in Plano, Illinois, the only private house designed by van der Rohe (for his mistress) and is having built an underground house in a hillock on his deserted Hebridean island of South Ascrib.

PARKER BOWLES, Colonel ANDREW HENRY, *born* 27 December 1939. Educated Ampleforth and Royal Military

Peter Palumbo

Academy, Sandhurst. Married, 1973, Camilla Rosemary Shand (one son, one daughter). Colonel Commanding the Household Cavalry and Silver Stick-in-Waiting to the Queen since April 1987 (when a head of state visits Britain, Silver Stick greets him as he arrives at Buckingham Palace carrying an ebony walking stick with a silver knob on it). Camilla, niece of Lord Ashcombe, head of the Cubitt building family, is regarded as the closest confidante of the Prince of Wales, whose name features regularly in their visitors book. By coincidence her great-aunt, Violet Trefusis, was the mistress of his great-great-grandfather, King Edward VII. An escort of Princess Anne in 1970 (the romance came to nothing because he is a Roman Catholic), Parker Bowles was ADC to Lord Soames when he was the last Governor-General of Southern Rhodesia 1979–80 and caught the eye of his younger daughter Charlotte, then married to merchant banker Richard Hambro (see Jocelyn Hambro, q.v.). That marriage was dissolved in 1982 and in

Michael and Mary Parkinson

1989 she married Earl Peel. In 1986 Parker Bowles sold, for £600,000, Bolehyde Manor near Chippenham, in the flower garden of which the Prince of Wales proposed marriage to Lady Diana Spencer.

PARKINSON, MICHAEL, *born* 28 March 1935. Educated Barnsley Grammar School. Married Mary Heneghan (three sons). A Yorkshire miner's son, he started journalism on the local paper, before entering Fleet Street with the **Guardian**, moving to the **Daily Express** and, finally, the **Sunday Times**. From 1971 until 1982 he was host of his own BBC TV chat show, having previously presented 'Cinema' and 'The Movie Quiz'. He would spend winters in Australia, where his show ran 1979–84. Back in Britain, he was one of the Famous Five (with David

Frost, Robert Kee, Angela Rippon and Anna Ford) who launched TV-am in 1983, which had to be rescued six months after its launch when viewing figures had plummeted to 200,000. He was also less than successful hosting 'Desert Island Discs', which he called a 'silly little programme', being replaced in 1988 after two years by Sue Lawley. His Thames-side home in Bray was put on the market for £1.4 million in May 1990 and the Parkinsons, both golf fanatics, were looking at other properties convenient for a good course.

PARKINSON, NORMAN, *born* 21 April 1913. Educated Westminster. Married, 1945, Wenda Rogerson (one son). A photographer for more than fifty years, whose greatest feat was making Princess Anne look beautiful when he photographed her for her twenty-first birthday portraits. A great favourite of the Royal Family, he also photographed Queen Elizabeth, the Queen Mother, on her eightieth and eighty-fifth birthdays – Prince Charles for his Investiture as Prince of Wales was his first Royal portrait. Lived with Wenda in Tobago, where he produced his own sausages. These were later marketed in Britain as Porkinson's Bangers and are on the menu of several London West End restaurants. Soon after Wenda died in 1987 their house in Tobago was burned to the ground and he was in the process of rebuilding it exactly as it had been when he collapsed with a brain haemorrhage in February 1990 while photographing top American model Debra Harris in the Sarawak jungle for *Town and Country* magazine. His friend Mohamed Al-Fayed, owner of Harrods, ordered a hospital plane to fly 'Parks', as he was universally known, to Singapore for expert medical attention. He died without recovering consciousness. Princess Anne sent her hairdresser Michael Raser of Michaeljohn, to represent her at his Westminster Abbey memorial service in June 1990 – it was 'Parks' who had originally introduced her to the crimper.

PEARSON, the Hon. MICHAEL ORLANDO WEETMAN, *born* 17 June 1944.

Educated Gordonstoun. Married first, 1977 (dissolved 1984), Ellen 'Fritzi' Erhardt, secondly, 1987, Marina Cordle (two daughters). Known as 'The Gunner' because of his fondness for firearms, is the elder son and heir of Third Viscount Cowdray (q.v.), inherited £7 million on his twenty-first birthday, bought an Aston Martin and a house in Elystan Street, Chelsea, close to the police station, and installed two close friends as lodgers, insurance broker Anthony McKay and artist Willie Feilding at £5 per week. Ended affair with Miranda Quarry (*see* Peter

Norman Parkinson and Lisa Butcher

Sellers) by tipping her clothes onto the pavement. Bought a Camper and Nicholson yacht, *The Hedonist*, for £250,000 and moved to a £1 million mansion in the Boltons, before selling to an Arab and going into tax exile in Monte Carlo in 1978, spending half the year on his Ibiza property, Can Bonnet, set in twenty-five acres, from where he went deep-sea fishing. When he became engaged to Fritzi he tried to buy the negatives of nude photographs of her taken by Gunther Sachs, a former husband of Brigitte Bardot, but Sachs refused to hand them over. Lost her in June 1983 to the mystic Marquess of Northampton (q.v.). Following his second marriage he returned to Britain from tax exile in April 1988, buying a large house in London's Gloucester Road and a country residence, close to the 17,000-acre Cowdray estate, which he will inherit. By his sixties romance with former model Barbara Ray, he has a son, Sebastian, to whom he has remained close, but who cannot inherit the Cowdray title as his parents never married. He has a controlling interest in Bardsey, the leading British machine tool company, named after Bardsey Island off the Welsh coast, which he once owned as a retreat.

PEMBROKE, Seventeenth Earl of, HENRY GEORGE CHARLES ALEXANDER, also Fourteenth Earl of Montgomery, Hereditary Grand Visitor of Jesus College, Oxford, *born* 19 May 1939.

Educated Eton, Christ Church, Oxford, Second Lieutenant, Royal Horse Guards. Married, 1966 (dissolved 1981), Claire Pelly (one son, three daughters), secondly, 1988, Miranda Oram (one daughter). Better known as Henry Herbert, the film and television director, he inherited historic Wilton House, Salisbury, and 14,000 acres and used the estate for the location shots for the soft-porn film, *Emily*, in which Koo Stark (q.v.) made her topless debut. Shakespeare was a visitor to Wilton when Henry's ancestor Mary, wife of the Second Earl, gathered around her the nation's outstanding intellectual, social and artistic talent, including her

brother Sir Philip Sydney. The house was rebuilt in the seventeenth-century by Inigo Jones and his assistant John Webb, with the Double Cube room, highlighted by Van Dyck's portrait of Charles I's children and works by Rembrandt and Van Leyden.

PETERSHAM, Viscount, CHARLES HENRY LEICESTER STANHOPE, *born* 20 July 1945, son and heir of the Eleventh Earl of Harrington.

Educated Eton. Married first, 1966 (dissolved 1983), Virginia Freeman Jackson (one son, one daughter), secondly, 1984, Anita Fugelsang, former wife of the Twenty-first Earl of Suffolk and Berkshire. Heir to a family estate in London's South Kensington including the Gloucester Road and adjacent acres, he was brought up in Ireland to where his bloodstock-agent father moved, becoming an Irish citizen in 1965. Used to work as a stable lad, barefist fighting co-workers on Friday evenings for the week's wage packet. Now based in Monte Carlo with a home in Wiltshire, he bought the 104ft yacht, *Surama*, following his second marriage, and spent 800 days sailing 35,222 miles around the world with his photographer wife and her daughter, Lady Katherine Howard.

PHILLIPS, Captain MARK ANTHONY PETER, *born* 22 September 1948.

Educated Marlborough College and Royal Military Academy, Sandhurst. Married, 14 November 1973, Princess Anne (one son, one daughter). Joined first the Queen's Dragoon Guards, July 1969. Became Company Instructor at Sandhurst 1974–7, when his officer cadets named him Fog ('Because he's thick and wet'), and retired in 1978. Has been Personal ADC to the Queen since 1974. Team gold medallist Munich Olympic Games 1972, team silver medallist Seoul Olympic Games 1988, winner, Badminton Three Day Event 1971, 1972, 1974, 1981. Managed by Mark McCormack of IMG (whose other clients have included Bjorn Borg and Arnold Palmer), earning an estimated £250,000 annually from conducting equestrian clinics in Australia, New Zealand

and Canada. In 1988 he invested £100,000 in the Gleneagles Mark Phillips Equestrian Centre and his own sponsor has been Range Rover. Instituted the Gatcombe Three Day Event to produce income for the 1,400-acre Gatcombe Park estate (a wedding present from the Queen) of which he is manager. In August 1989 Princess Anne announced her separation from her husband, who moved out of Gatcombe into a small flat up a lane at the rear of the house. Banned from entering Gatcombe, he had to send a friend to collect his possessions for the move. His name has been erroneously linked romantically with several women, most frequently Canadian Kathy Birks, who acts as his press adviser. In April 1989, rumours surfaced about the marriage when letters couched in affectionate terms sent to the Princess by the Queen's Equerry Commander Timothy Lawrence were stolen and offered to the *Sun*.

PIGGOTT, LESTER KEITH, *born* 5 November 1935.

Married, 1960, Susan Armstrong (two daughters). Known as 'The Long Fellow' because of his unusual height (5ft 8½ins tall) for a top jockey. Eleven times champion jockey, he retired in 1985 to become a trainer with his bloodstock-agent wife Susan, daughter of the late 'Sam' Armstrong and sister of Robert Armstrong, both Newmarket trainers. Legendary for his tightfistedness, he was known for his 'cash' deals long before he received a three-year jail sentence in October 1987 for defrauding the Inland Revenue of £3.75 million. When Charles Clore (q.v.) asked Lester how much he wanted to ride his filly, Valoris, in the 1966 Epsom Oaks, he replied 'all the prize money'. He duly won. In June 1988 the Queen took away Piggott's OBE, awarded in the 1975 New Year's Honours List. He has not reapplied to the Jockey Club for a licence to train and Susan remains officially in charge. In December 1989 he became a grandfather when his elder daughter, Maureen, wife of Newmarket trainer William Haggas, gave birth to a nine-pound daughter, Mary Anne.

Lester Piggott

PIGOTT-BROWN, Third baronet, Sir WILLIAM BRIAN, *born* 20 January 1941.

Educated Eton. Champion amateur jockey 1960–1, 1962–3, runner-up 1961–2. A member of the Brown Shipley banking family who inherited £750,000 on his twenty-first birthday (his father, a Captain in the Coldstream Guards, was killed in action in Tunisia on 25 December 1942). He bought a 1,200-acre Berkshire estate and stud farm at Aston Upthorpe, down the road from where his horses were trained by Frank Cundell. His home, Orchard House, was famous for its two-way mirror into the main guest bedroom, giving the host and his cronies endless hours of pleasure. In 1966 he was one of the backers of Sybilla's, a discotheque in Swallow Street, Piccadilly, and a shop called Brown's in South Molton

Street and owned twenty-five per cent of Island Records (*see* Chris Blackwell). The following year he bought **Look of London** magazine and installed Christopher Collins (q.v.) as Editor, but it folded within a year. Urged by his family to go to work, he went into business with former racing driver Michael Taylor (q.v.) who ran a property company called London Bridge. After rejecting a £3 million takeover bid, London Bridge fell down with debts of £3,208,632 in the wake of the 1973 property crash, bankrupting Taylor and decimating Pigott-Brown's fortune, because he gave personal guarantees for bank loans. Among his earliest loves was Virginia Lyon (later Viscountess Royston, q.v.) and he became engaged to model-cum-potboiler novelist Patsy Booth in the seventies. Other romances include Aldine Honey (q.v.), Dido Goldsmith and Hollywood heiress, Wendy Stark. In the eighties he bought a beach-side house outside Cape Town and now spends half the year in South Africa after his Lloyd's syndicates, managed by Charles St George (q.v.), crashed with estimated losses of £30 million. He is ever hopeful of marriage one day.

PLUNKET, The Hon. SHAUN ALBERT FREDERICK SHERIDAN, third son of Sixth Lord Plunket, *born* 5 April 1931.
Educated Eton, the Institute de Tourraine, Lieutenant, Irish Guards. Married first, 14 December 1961 (dissolved 1979), Judith Power (one son, one daughter), secondly, 1980, Elisabeth Drangel, who died 1986, thirdly, 1989, Andrea Milos, former wife of Sheldon Reynolds. His eldest brother, Patrick, the Seventh Lord Plunket was Deputy Master of the Royal Household from 1954 until his death in 1975. He was extremely close to the Queen with whom he was in daily contact and his grave is in the Royal burial ground of Frogmore. Shaun met Andrea, for five years the love of Claus von Bulow, in January 1989 in the foyer of the Theatre Royal, Haymarket, when they joined mutual friends to see **Orpheus Descending**.

POLANSKI, ROMAN, *born* Paris 1934.
Educated Poland. Married, 20 January 1968, actress Sharon Tate at Chelsea register office with a reception at the Playboy Club in Park Lane. Began career as an actor before entering Poland's film school at Lodz. He made six short films before, in 1961, he wrote and directed **Knife in the Water**, which earned him an Oscar nomination and the front cover of **Time** magazine. After moving to a mews house in Chelsea, he made **Cul-de-Sac**, which won the 1966 Golden Bear best film award at the Berlin Festival, and **Repulsion**, both seminal films of the sixties. **Rosemary's Baby**, starring John Cassavetes, Mia Farrow and Ruth Gordon, about the occult and devil worship, set in Manhattan, opened in January 1969, seven months before his wife, who was eight months pregnant, was one of four people murdered by the Charles Manson gang in a ritual killing in Beverly Hills, Los Angeles. In 1977, after directing **Chinatown**, he was charged in Los Angeles with having unlawful sex with a thirteen-year-old girl in the house of the film star, Jack Nicholson. Two weeks before he was due to be sentenced in February 1978, he fled from California and has never returned to the United States, where he would face a prison sentence. Later that year he made **Tess** in France with Nastassia Kinski, who was aged seventeen and became his lover. In 1988 he married twenty-three-year-old actress Emmanuelle Seigneur in Paris, where he lives. He moves around the Continent, but if he comes to England, he faces arrest.

PREVIN, ANDRÉ (GEORGE), *born* Berlin 6 April 1929.
Educated Berlin and Paris Conservatoires. Married first Betty Bennett, secondly, 1959 (dissolved 1970), Dory Langdon, thirdly, 1970 (dissolved 1979), Mia Farrow (three sons, three daughters), fourthly, 1982, Heather Jayston (one son). Winner of four Oscars for film scores, Music Director of the Houston Symphony Orchestra 1967–9, Principal Conductor of the London Symphony Orchestra 1968–79, Music Director

Roman Polanski and Sharon Tate

Pittsburgh Symphony Orchestra 1976–84 and Los Angeles Philharmonic Orchestra 1986–9, Principal Conductor, Royal Philharmonic Orchestra since 1987. In 1971 and 1972 tours and performances of the LSO were enlivened by the presence of Miss Gillian Widdicombe, music critic of the *Financial Times*, who formed a close attachment to the conductor and accompanied the orchestra to Moscow. She once enlivened a Royal Festival Hall rehearsal of the orchestra when involved in a furious altercation with Mia Farrow (formerly married to Frank Sinatra), which was described by one of the violinists as, 'Handbags at dawn'. Farrow and Previn lived at a large house near Dorking with their twin sons, Sasha and Matthew, and in 1973 Previn applied for British citizenship. They divorced after Mia spent six months on a South Pacific island making a film, and she now lives with Woody Allen. The fourth Mrs Previn is the former wife of actor Michael Jayston.

PUTTNAM, DAVID TERENCE, *born* 25 February 1941, educated Minchenden Grammar School.
Married, 1961, Patricia Mary Jones (one son, one daughter). Began career in advertising in London in 1958, working for five years at Collett Dickenson Pearce before becoming a photographer and agent in 1966 and starting in film production in 1968, making *That'll Be The Day* and *Stardust* with David Essex in the lead roles. *Bugsy Malone*, 1976, was his first award winning film and *Midnight Express*, 1978, won two Academy Awards. *Chariots of Fire*, 1981, won four Oscars, *The Killing Fields*, 1985, three, and *The Mission*, 1986, one. In 1986 he was hired on a three-year contract as Head of Production of Columbia Pictures, owned by Coca Cola, but left in acrimonious circumstances after eighteen months, collecting a £2.7 million payoff. Chairman of the Society for the Prevention of Rural England, he ruffled local feathers after buying a £1 million Wiltshire

André Previn and Mia Farrow at her sister's wedding

millhouse and attempting to reroute a public footpath away from the front of it. His daughter, Debbie, married to Lloyd Grossman, the super-snoop of TV's 'Through the Keyhole' programme, presented him with a granddaughter, Florence, in August 1989. When it was revealed that he was a member of the Wigmore Club in the wake of disclosures about Major Ronald Ferguson (q.v.), Puttnam claimed to be unaware of its unsavoury reputation and says he was a client for strictly medical reasons, needing massage to relieve back pains.

Qq

QUEENSBERRY, Twelfth Marquess of, DAVID HARRINGTON ANGUS DOUGLAS, *born* 19 December 1920.
Educated Eton, Lieutenant, Royal Horse Guards. Married first, 18 July 1956 (dissolved 1969), Ann Jones (two daughters), secondly, 1969 (dissolved 1986), Alexandra Sich (three sons, one daughter). Great-grandson of the Marquess who gave the name to the Queensberry Belt and the Rules of Boxing and persecuted his third son, Lord Alfred, for his association with Oscar Wilde (who called him 'an infamous brute'), he was Professor of Ceramics at the Royal College of Art 1959–83 and helped found the Reject China Shop in Beauchamp Place. His first wife went on to marry Robert Bolt (*see* Sarah Miles) but before their divorce, Alexa gave birth to two sons, Sholto (1 June 1967) and Milo (1968). Queensberry, whose title is Scottish and dates from 1682, petitioned Lord Lyon King of Arms, Sir James Monteith Grant, and under the Scottish Legislation Act 1968, was allowed to legitimize his sons, making them heirs to the title, the first ever ruling under the act. In 1985 Alexa gave birth to a daughter, whose father was Wiltshire landowner Nicholas Yeatman-Biggs, formerly a close friend of the Marquess and married with two children, and who refuses to divorce his wife.

Rr

RADZIWILL, Prince STANISLAS, *born* 1914.
Educated Poland. Married secondly, 1946 (dissolved 1958), Grace Kolin (one son), who, in 1961, became the third wife of the Third Earl of Dudley, twenty; thirdly, March 1959 (dissolved 1974), Lee Bouvier (one son, one daughter), former wife of Michael Canfield. Arrived penniless in Britain at the end of the Second World War, having been invalided out of the Polish army in 1940, spending the rest of the War in Geneva, working for the International Red Cross. Became associated with Charles Clore (q.v.) in property deals and became a partner with Felix Fenston (q.v.) telling him, 'If you cheat me, I kill you.' Lived in a Georgian house close to Buckingham Palace, in which President John Kennedy and Lee's sister, Jackie, stayed on a visit to London in June 1961 and in 1966 he bought, for £55,000, Turville Grange, a seven-bedroom house with forty-nine acres (later the home of Henry Ford II, q.v.). Mystery surrounds his first marriage, which was annulled by Sacra Rota shortly before his third marriage (Roalyne, his first wife married Swiss banker Baron de Chollet), and which invalidated, he claimed, his second marriage at Caxton Hall, thus enabling him to marry Lee in a Roman Catholic ceremony. He died in June 1976, leaving his twenty-eight-year-old mistress, American Christine Weckert, £40,000 in his £624,000 will.

RAMPLING, CHARLOTTE, *born* 5 February 1946.
Educated Jeanne d'Arc Académie pour Jeunes Filles, Versailles, St Hilda's, Bushey. Married, 1972 (dissolved 1977), Brian Southcombe (one son), secondly, 1978, Jean Michel Jarre

(one son). Daughter of Colonel Godfrey Rampling, who won a gold medal in the 440 yards in the 1936 Berlin Olympic Games. Made film debut in **The Knack** and won acclaim for her role in **Georgy Girl** and scandalised London society by living with both Southcombe, her manager, and male model Randall Laurence before choosing to marry the former. Now lives in Versailles with her second husband, son of Maurice Jarre, the Oscar-winning composer, the noted electronic composer and musician, whose two laser concerts in the Docklands in October 1988 lost backers £1 million.

RAWLINGS, PATRICIA ELIZABETH, *born* 27 January 1939, educated Oak Hall, Haslemere, Le Manoir, Lausanne, Florence University, University College, London and the London School of Economics.
Married, 1962 (dissolved 1967), David, Wolfson. Daughter of textile manufacturer, she was one of the first girlfriends of the Aga Khan (q.v.) and the model for the Pietro Annigoni (q.v.) portrait **La Strega** (The Witch), shown at the 1960 Royal Academy summer exhibition. Unhappy and ill-advised dynastic marriage to David Wolfson (knighted 1985) lasted a few months and in 1971 she was sued in the high court by American Ralph Stolkin, head of RKO Pictures, for the return of jewellery and other goods worth £224,000 (including a £68,000 engagement ring), given, he claimed, on the promise of marriage and that he had been jilted. In mid-hearing, the case was settled out-of-court and the judge, the late Mr Justice Melford Stevenson, was then heard to say in the Garrick Club, 'Silly bitch. If she'd held on, I'd have given her the lot.' A trained nurse, Patricia contested Sheffield Central for the Conservative Party in 1983, Doncaster Central in 1987 and was elected Euro MP for Essex South West in 1989.

RAYNE, Lord, MAX (life peer), *born* 8 February 1918.
Educated Central Foundation School, University College, London. Married first, 1941

(dissolved 1965), Margaret Marco (one son, two daughters), secondly, 1965, Lady Jane Vane-Tempest-Stewart (two sons, two daughters), sister of the Ninth Marquess of Londonderry (q.v.). Jane was maid-of-honour to the Queen at her Coronation and changed to the Jewish religion to marry philanthropist Rayne (knighted in 1969, ennobled for charitable works in 1976) after a lengthy and secretive romance. Chairman of London Merchant Securities since 1960, the self-effacing Rayne is the opposite from his brother-in-law Sir James Goldsmith (q.v.), for whom he has little time, having served on numerous charitable boards and seventeen years as Chairman of the National Theatre.

READING, Third Marquess of, MICHAEL ALFRED RUFUS ISAACS, *born* 8 March 1916.
Educated Eton, Balliol College, Oxford, Major, the Queen's Bays 1939–45 War. Married, 7 June 1941, Margot Duke (three sons, one daughter), with John Profumo as his best man. Grandson of Rufus Daniel Isaacs, a London merchant's son who was 'hammered' from the Stock Exchange and was called to the Bar, taking silk in 1898 and, ten years later, such was his gift for cross examination, earning £50,000 a year. He became Solicitor-General in Asquith's ministry, Attorney-General in 1912, Ambassador to Washington 1918–21 and Viceroy of India 1921–6. Michael Reading has a less controversial career in the stock exchange where his late father, Percy Duke, was a larger-than-life character, qualities passed down to his daughter, Margot. She once threatened to castrate the Earl of Snowdon, her neighbour in Sussex, after she learned that he was having an affair with her daughter, Lady Jacqueline, in 1969. She gave her dogs nursery names like Pardon and Toilet, and once, to avoid an unwelcome visitor, put her whole houseparty under her enormous kitchen table where they were discovered by the intruder. Reading died in July 1980 and was succeeded by his eldest son Simon, a born-again Christian who met his wife

during a bible class at Holy Trinity, Brompton.

REDGRAVE, Sir MICHAEL SCUDAMORE, *born* 20 March 1908.

Educated Clifton College, Magdalene College, Cambridge. Married, 1935, Rachel Kempson (one son, two daughters). Worked as a modern languages master at Cranleigh School, Surrey, before joining Liverpool Repertory Theatre 1934–6. A long and distinguished career on stage and in films was occasionally overshadowed by the political affiliations of his son Corin (born 1940) and elder daughter Vanessa (born 30 January 1937) with the Trotskyite Workers Revolutionary Party, which finally expelled them after twelve years, in November 1985, for supporting the party's ousted founder Gerry Healey, who had been booted out over bizarre allegations of sexual debauchery involving at least twenty-six young WRP women. Younger daughter Lynn (born 8 March 1943) wisely moved to California in 1976. Sir Michael, suffering from Parkinson's disease, appeared as the incapacitated father in the 1979 National Theatre production of Simon Gray's **Close of Play**. He died on 21 March 1985, having sold his beloved Hampshire woodland house for £150,000 to move to London for treatment.

REED, (ROBERT) OLIVER, *born* 13 February 1938.

Educated Aisle Castle. Nephew of film producer Sir Carol Reed, he married first, 1960 (dissolved 1970), Kate Byrne (one son, one daughter), secondly, 1985, Josephine Burgin.

The Redgraves

Left school to become a bouncer, boxer and taxi driver before first break on the BBC TV series 'The Golden Spur'. Made film debut in 1960 in *The Rebel*. Acting life punctuated by brawls, drunkenness and other macho confrontations, including arm wrestling. Lived for many years in Broome Hall, a forty-seven-room former nunnery in sixty acres near Dorking where his companion in the seventies was former ballerina Jackie Daryl, the mother of a daughter born in 1970. In 1980 he became involved with a fifteen-year-old Surrey schoolgirl who became his second wife five years later. Now based in Guernsey, where there are no licensing hours. Claims to have conquered many of his leading ladies, including Faye Dunaway, Carol Lynley and Susan George, but not Raquel Welch, preferring her hairdresser, Charlene.

Oliver Reed

REGINE, *born* REGINE ZYLBERBERG, in Brussels of Polish parentage, 1930.
Married, 1970, Roger Choukroun. Began in the fifties as a cloakroom girl in the Whiskey-A-Go-Go club in Paris, a branch of which became the world's first discotheque in 1959 in Cannes (previously clubs had live bands). In 1963 she opened her own club, Jimmy's, in Paris and by the early eighties had a chain of nineteen, from Europe to South America. Known as 'Queen of the Night', in January 1978 she opened Regine's, backed by Indian businessman Nandkishore Ram, on the roof garden of the Derry and Toms store in High Street, Kensington, with Princess Caroline of Monaco (Regine had two clubs in Monte Carlo) as guest of honour. Asked what she thought of the venture as she left, Viscountess Rothermere (q.v.), said: 'It's too far out of London.' Regine severed her connection in December 1980 after receiving £400,000 in commission and expenses from Ram, who put the company into liquidation in May 1981 with debts of £1.1 million. The premises were bought by Virgin Records boss Richard Branson and renamed The Gardens. In January 1987 Regine opened up again in Berkeley Street, Mayfair, backed by Lebanese gambler Elie Abou Taka, at a cost of £4.2 million. It closed five months later and became a Chinese restaurant. Her ghosted autobiography was published in 1988, titled *Call Me By My First Name*.

RENDLESHAM, Lady, (CLAIRE MCCRI-RICK), *born c.* 1923 and who married, as his second wife, the Eighth Lord Rendlesham (one son, three daughters) on 3 November 1947.
A colonel's daughter, she claimed to be descended from Rurik, the Viking founder of the Russian nation. For twelve years from 1952 she worked on *Vogue* before being appointed Fashion Editor of *Queen* by Jocelyn Stevens (q.v.) in 1966, remaining for a year. She became fashion consultant to the Wallis shops until being made director of Yves St Laurent's first Rive Gauche boutique in this country. With a sharp eye for up-and-

coming designers, she launched Karl Lagerfeld with a Chloe boutique on Bond Street and expanded Rive Gauche to five other locations, which she owned. In 1983 Duncan Roy, aged twenty-two, who claimed to be the bastard son of Lady Rendlesham was jailed for fifteen months for obtaining property and services by deception, having asked for 211 other offences to be considered – he had worked for three months as her general assistant before being dismissed. She died of a heart attack in the King's Road, Chelsea on 30 January 1987 and left nearly £2 million.

RICE, TIMOTHY MILES BINDON, *born* 10 November 1944.
Educated Lancing College. Married, 1974, Jane Artereta McIntosh (one son, one daughter). With Andrew Lloyd Webber (q.v.), discovered by impresario David Land, the partner of Robert Stigwood, and paid £20 a week to produce a musical, coming up with *Joseph and the Amazing Technicolour Dreamcoat* in 1968, *Jesus Christ Superstar* in 1970, and *Evita* in 1976, before the partnership broke up. Fell in love with Elaine Paige when she was cast as Evita Peron for its West End run, but remained with his wife while conducting a public, decade-long affair. In 1989 Tim and Jane commenced divorce proceedings on the grounds of two years' separation and she was to be found sharing her Holland Park, London house with Eton-educated Nick Bartle, who was half her age. Later that year Elaine opened in the West End in *Anything Goes*, the Cole Porter musical she co-produced with her lover. In June 1990 Tim sold their country home, Romeyns Court, Great Milton, for £1.5 million. A cricket fanatic and slow left-arm bowler, he formed the Heartaches XI in 1973, which tours around the country. He has translated and adapted *Starmania*, a French rock opera about a Donald Trump-type tycoon, which he plans to put on in London in 1991 at a cost of £1.5 million.

RICHMOND, Tenth Duke of, CHARLES HENRY GORDON-LENNOX, also Fifth Duke of Gordon, *born* 19 September 1929.
Educated Eton, William Temple College, Second Lieutenant, Sixtieth Rifles. Married, 1951, Susan Grenville-Grey (one son, two daughters, and two daughters adopted). Better known as the Earl of March, he succeeded his father, Freddie, in November 1989, who had made over Goodwood House and its 12,000 acres to him in 1969, moving to a smaller house on the Sussex estate best-known for its racecourse where the five-day Glorious Goodwood meeting is held at the end of July. A motor racing enthusiast, Freddie also constructed a formula one course on a disused fighter airfield on his estate in 1948, but it was closed in 1964. In the sixties March and his wife adopted two black baby girls, Maria and Naomi. The latter, renamed 'Nimmy', was the daughter of a Zulu musician and a white woman and became an actress, with parts in the Lenny Henry series, and the 'Albion Market' soap opera. Maria has been married twice, the first time to a welder. Heir to the dukedoms is Charles Henry Gordon-Lennox, Earl of March, born 8 January 1955, who has one daughter by his 1976 marriage (dissolved 1989) to Sally Clayton, a former dancer with the Pans People group.

ROCKSAVAGE, Earl of, DAVID GEORGE PHILIP CHOLMONDELEY, *born* 27 June 1960, succeeded father as Seventh Marquess of Cholmondeley in March 1990.
Inherited Cholmondeley Hall, Cheshire and 12,000 acres when his father died after a heart-bypass operation, while he was in the process of renovating the family's Palladian palace, Houghton Hall, Norfolk for his own use. A tax exile from 1979 in Monte Carlo, along with fellow bachelor Earl Jermyn (later the Marquess of Bristol, q.v.). With the title he became Lord Great Chamberlain of England, a largely ceremonial position involving little more than walking backwards in front of the Queen at the State Opening of Parliament. Worked as aide-de-camp to Robert Stigwood in the mid-eighties.

Tim Rice and Elaine Paige

RONSON, GERALD MAURICE, *born* 26 May 1939.

Educated Clark's College, Cricklewood. Married, 1967, Gail Collard (four daughters). Built up a family furniture business into the Heron Corporation with interests in property, petrol and car showrooms (H.R. Owen) as well as land in Arizona, worth an estimated £750 million, and Britain's second largest private company after Littlewoods. Names his yachts *My Gail* (*I*, *II* and *III*) after his wife, a former model. Has made over sixty per cent of his company to a charitable foundation that contributes to Zionist and other causes, while also raising millions for other charities from friends and associates. He became involved in the Guinness trial after agreeing to support the brewing firm's takeover bid in Distillers in 1986, buying Guinness shares and receiving £5.8 million as a 'success fee', which he handed back before being charged with theft of that sum. He called the trial, which he attended at Southwark Crown Court every day, after putting in three hours at his Marylebone office, an 'aggravation'. Nonetheless, he was sentenced to·a year in jail, which he is now serving at Ford open prison in Sussex.

ROOTES, First Lord, WILLIAM EDWARD, *born* 17 August 1894, educated Cranbrook School.

Married first, 15 March 1916 (dissolved 1951), Nora Press (two sons), secondly, 9 August 1951, Ruby Joy 'Ann' Duff, widow of Sir Charles Mappin, Bt, and formerly wife of Sir Francis Peek, Bt. Son of a cycle and motor engineer, he went into the family workshop and started in 1913 with Singer Cars in Coventry. After the First World War, he started a motor business in Maidstone with his brother Reginald, borrowing £1,500 from their father. In 1929 they acquired the Hillman and Humber factories, adding in the thirties Singer and Sunbeam, all of which became the Rootes Group, Britain's third largest car manufacturers after Ford and Vauxhall. With his second wife Ann, he lived at Ramsbury Manor (sold in 1965 for £350,000

to Harry Hyams, q.v.), built in the reign of Charles II, with 460 acres, having sold nearby Stype Grange to Charles Clore (q.v.). Ann once assaulted a customs officer with a dildo when her personal luggage was searched on a trip to France and the sexual aid was discovered in her case. When asked what it was, she grabbed it, hit the man over the head and said, 'Any prick should know.' Lord Rootes had to make a substantial out-of-court settlement. His elder son, Geoffrey (born 14 June 1917), who became the Second Lord Rootes in December 1964, sold a minority interest in the family firm, which had been crippled by a three-month strike, to Chrysler in 1964, and the American company became the sole owner in May 1970, after several years of heavy losses.

ROTHERMERE, Third Viscount, VERE HAROLD ESMOND HARMSWORTH, *born* 27 August 1925.

Educated Eton, Kent School, Connecticut. Married, 1957, Patricia Evelyn Beverley Matthews (one son, two daughters), the former wife of Captain Christopher Brooks (one daughter). Grandson of the First Viscount and great-nephew of the legendary Viscount Northcliffe, who invented popular journalism, owning *The Times*, *Daily Mail* and many other newspapers and periodicals. After becoming Chairman of Associated Newspaper Holdings in 1970, merged his two ailing daily newspapers, the *Mail* and the *Sketch*, and relaunched the new *Daily Mail* on 3 May 1971, exactly seventy-seven years after the original *Mail*. Launched the *Mail on Sunday* in 1982 and after acquiring, in December 1985, the fifty per cent interest in the London *Evening Standard* that he did not own, became the only Fleet Street proprietor with a twenty-four hour, seven-day-a-week operation. In 1989 the *Daily Mail* and General Trust, in which the Harmsworth family holds seventy-two per cent of the votes, made a £511 million bid for the 50.05 per cent of Associated Newspapers it did not already own, taking the company private at a value of £1.05 billion. Rothermere travels the world exclusively from his Paris base in the Rue Bude, Île St Louis, while his first wife, Pat, (dubbed 'Bubbles' by *Private Eye*), moves between homes in Sussex (burned down and rebuilt), Eaton Square, Round Hill, Jamaica, Fifth Avenue, New York and Beverly Hills, Los Angeles. As actress Beverley Brooks, she was discovered by director Lewis Gilbert who cast her in *Reach For The Sky*, the 1956 classic starring Kenneth Moore as Sir Douglas Bader.

ROTHERWICK, Second Lord, (Herbert) Robin Cayzer, *born* 5 December 1912.
Educated Eton and Christ Church, Oxford, served 1939–45 War with Royal Scots Greys. Married, 4 April 1952, Sarah Jane Slade (three sons, one daughter). Head of the Cayzer family whose company, British and Commonwealth Shipping Co., which ran the Union Castle boats to the Cape, was transformed into a £2.5 billion business after John Gunn was hired as Chief Executive in 1985 from Exco, the money-broking house. Lord Cayzer, whose ancestor founded the Clan Line, moved out (he was Deputy Chairman) selling the family interests for £427.5 million. Following an ill-advised foray in July 1988 buying Atlantic Computers for £407 million (later found to be worthless), B&C had its shares suspended in April at 53 pence, down from a peak in 1978 of 564 pence. In June 1990 its debts were estimated at £1.3 billion. In 1967 Rotherwick, whose wife committed suicide in 1978, paid £600,000 for the 6,000-acre Cornbury Park estate in Oxfordshire, close to Blenheim, putting his nearby 2,846-acre Bletchington Park estate on the market for £575,000. In September 1989, after losing a twenty-four year battle over a right of way through part of his land, the 1,300-acre Wychwood Forest, he demanded £1.6 million compensation from Oxfordshire County Council – nearly £1,000 a yard for the mile long path – for loss of shooting rights, logging activities and increased maintenance costs.

ROTHSCHILD, Third Lord, Nathaniel Mayer Victor, *born* 31 October 1910.
Educated Harrow and Trinity College, Cambridge. Married first, 28 December 1933 (dissolved 1946), Barbara Hutchinson (one son, two daughters), secondly, 14 August 1946, Teresa Mayor (one son, two daughters and one son deceased). At Harrow he opened for the First XI with Terence Rattigan, gained a Blue at Cambridge and played county cricket for Northamptonshire, and faced bowling from Larwood, which he described as the most alarming experience of his life. Served during the Second World War in the anti-sabotage section of MI5 and became a research scientist for Royal Dutch Shell in 1963. He was head of the 'Think Tank' in Edward Heath's Government 1971–4. In 1987 he became involved in the controversy over the Government's attempts to ban publication of former MI5 agent Peter Wright, who claimed that Rothschild would have known that former MI5 chief Sir Roger Hollis was a Soviet agent, and when Sir Anthony Blunt, another former member of MI5, was exposed as being a Soviet agent it was put about that Rothschild was the Fifth Man – he had been a contemporary at Cambridge and a member of The Apostles society, as had been another traitor, Guy Burgess. He quit the family bank after two months declaring the job 'dull'.

ROTHSCHILD, Fourth Lord, (Nathaniel Charles) Jacob, *born* 29 April 1939.
Educated Eton and Christ Church, Oxford. Married, 20 October 1961, Serena Dunn (one son, three daughters), although he was once close to Lady Antonia Fraser. In 1955 he passed at his third attempt for training as an officer-cadet at Sandhurst, after starting his National Service as a trooper in the Royal Horse Guards. The legend has it that he turned up for training in a chauffeur-driven Rolls Royce and when the Regimental Sergeant Major bellowed out, 'Who do you think you are, a bloody Rothschild?' he replied simply 'Yes.' After becoming a partner in the family bank, he left following

Lord (Jacob) Rothschild and family

a disagreement with his cousin, Sir Evelyn de Rothschild and started his own, J. Rothschild Holdings, in 1971. He was one of the three principals in the BAT takeover. He owns a fifteen-acre estate in Kanona, North Corfu, which is rented out to friends like insurance magnate Sir Mark Weinberg (q.v.). He inherited much of his cousin Dollie Rothschild's estate – she left £93 million and the last private house in St James's Place, in which he gave a flat to Sir James Goldsmith (q.v.).

ROUTH, JONATHAN, *born* 1923.
Educated Cambridge University. Married first, 1949, Nandi (two sons), who died in 1972, secondly, 1975, Shelagh Marvin. A journalist with the London *Evening*

Standard, in 1960, with Bob Monkhouse hosting the ITV programme, he devised 'Candid Camera', a half-hour show on which his face was never seen while he hoaxed the public. In 1968 he started a lengthy romance with oil heiress Olga Deterding (q.v.), moving into her triplex Piccadilly penthouse for which he bought a flock of rocking horse sheep, under the tails of which he would sprinkle raisins bought from nearby Fortnum and Mason. In 1969 he was named as co-respondent when millionaire publisher Paul Hamlyn divorced his wife Eileen, and ordered to pay costs. Six months before his second marriage he was living with Mrs Susie Allfrey, half-sister of the Earl of Caithness and had previously been attached to Australian journalist Gillian Robertson (later the Duchess of Hamilton). In 1980 he began painting, featuring Queen Victoria as a nun in exotic settings, living five months of the year in Jamaica. With Shelagh, the former Public Relations Officer to the Aga Khan (q.v.), he lives between Tuscany and the Caribbean.

ROXBURGHE, Tenth Duke of, GUY DAVID INNES-KER, *born* 18 November 1954.
Educated Eton, Magdalene College, Cambridge and Royal Military Academy, Sandhurst, Lieutenant, Blues and Royals. Married, 1977 (dissolved 1990), Lady Jane Grosvenor (two sons, one daughter), sister of the Sixth Duke of Westminster (q.v.). Inherited title, Floors Castle and 60,000 acres near Kelso on the death in September 1974 of his father, the Ninth Duke, known as 'Bobo', a crashing snob who said it was *infra dig.* to eat in other people's houses, let alone restaurants. Guy met Jane when he was stationed in Northern Ireland, where her father, the Fifth Duke lived, and they became engaged after a year. It was at 200-room Floors in March 1986 that Prince Andrew proposed marriage to Sarah Ferguson. In 1989 Lothario Guy announced his separation from Jane, who had discovered that her husband was romancing three other women at the same time, and she has moved to a six-bedroom Georgian house, set in 530 acres near Kelso, with the children. The couple divorced in March 1990 on the grounds of his admitted adultery.

ROYSTON, Viscount, PHILIP SIMON PROSPERO LINDLEY RUPERT YORKE, son and heir of the Ninth Earl of Hardwicke, *born* 20 April 1938.
Educated Eton, Able Seaman in Royal Navy 1956–8. Known as 'Pips', he married, 20 November 1968, Virginia Lyon (one son, one daughter), who had previously been involved with Sir William Pigott-Brown (q.v.) and Calcutta-born bandleader Confrey Phillips, who played at deb. dances and Royal parties. Pips died of a congenital heart disease in January 1973 and Virginia, accompanied by Emma Soames, went on holiday to Mustique in August 1975, falling in love with Basil Charles, formerly the barman at the Cotton House Hotel on the island. Basil, who came from neighbouring St Vincent, was then working as assistant general manager to Colin Tennant (the future Lord Glenconner, q.v.) who owned Mustique, and later took over Basil's Bar on the marina. Tennant had saved his life in the sixties when he found Basil, who had been run over, in a ditch in St Vincent and paid for his hospitalization after he lost a kidney. The following August Virginia moved permanently to Mustique, buying a house, where she brought up her son (who became the Tenth Earl of Hardwicke on the death of his grandfather in 1974) and daughter. Basil left her in 1984 and she died four years later from liver and kidney complications, aged forty-six. Her children live with their aunt, Lady Amabel Lindsay, widow of the Hon. Patrick Lindsay (q.v.).

RUSSELL, Sir JOHN WRIOTHESLEY, *born* 22 August 1914.
Educated Eton, Trinity College, Cambridge. Married, 1945, Aliki Diplarkos (one son, one daughter). Entered Diplomatic Service 1937, Ambassador to Ethiopia 1962–6, to Brazil 1966–9, to Spain 1969–74. His wife, a former Greek beauty queen (Miss Europe 1931) divorced her first husband, millionaire French aircraft manufacturer Paul Louis Weiller (one son, Paul, who in 1965 married Princess Olympia Torlonia, a cousin of the King of Spain) in Nevada in 1943 while he was imprisoned by the Germans. In 1947 Weiller went to court in Paris requesting that the divorce and subsequent remarriage should not be recognized in France. Weiller won the case which meant that on the Continent the Russells' marriage was considered bigamous. Finally in 1961 after claim and counter claim, the Weiller finally gave up. The couple's daughter, Georgiana, was more than a passing fancy of the Prince of Wales in the early seventies and is now married to baronet

Sir Brooke Boothby (two daughters).

RUTLAND, Tenth Duke of, CHARLES JOHN ROBERT MANNERS, *born* 28 May 1919. Educated Eton and Trinity College, Cambridge, Captain Grenadier Guards. Married first, 1946 (dissolved 1959), Ann Cumming Bell (one daughter), secondly, 1958, Francis Sweeny (two sons, one daughter), daughter of Charles Sweeny (q.v.) and Margaret, Duchess of Argyll. His first wife, who bred Palomino ponies, was framed by a crooked private detective when actress Zena Marshall (who starred in the James Bond film *Dr No*) sued her millionaire husband Reggie 'The Anteater' Ward, cousin of the Earl of Dudley (q.v.), for divorce, citing the Duchess. Zena's society solicitor, homosexual David Jacobs, later committed suicide. Rutland has not spoken to his mother-in-law, Margaret Argyll, since 16 March 1970, when his wife received a letter from her over the silly matter of who sent flowers to Marg of Arg when she was in hospital (Margaret thought they came from her daughter who did not deny it, but they did not). Lives at Belvoir Castle, set in 15,000 acres under which the Coal Board have found some of the greatest deposits in the country. His heir, elder son of the Marquis of Granby (born 8 May 1959), has a mental disability and lives in the stable block, dealing in antique firearms.

S s

SAINER, LEONARD, *born* 12 October 1909. Educated Central Foundation School and London University. A leading London solicitor who was the business partner of the late Sir Charles Clore (q.v.), taking over from him as Chairman of Sears Holdings in December 1977, which owned Selfridges, most of Britain's shoe shops and the William Hill betting business. His father, Archie, lived to 101. In 1955 Sainer became engaged to musical star Elizabeth Webb, but never married, and in June 1985 he set a wedding date with Wendy Harris, thirty years his junior. The couple, who had been together for twenty-four years, inexplicably cancelled the ceremony and Ritz Hotel reception for 100, because, it was thought, of family pressure, but have remained together. In 1989 their Farm Street, Mayfair house burned down the night before they were due to move in after a year's renovation. Wendy, once a buyer for Selfridge's, had previously called off her marriage, in 1962, to Lex garages heir, Trevor Chinn.

SAINSBURY, Lord, JOHN DAVAN, (life peer), *born* 2 November 1927. Educated Stowe, Worcester College, Oxford. Married, 1963, Anya Linden (two sons, one daughter), the ballet dancer. Joined the family firm in 1950, the year it opened its first self-service store, to work in the bacon department, and became Chairman of J. Sainsbury in 1988 (Finance Director since 1973). He has been Chairman of the Royal Opera House since 1987. The family owns shares worth £1.6 billion in the company and have endowed a charitable trust worth £350 million. They donated £50 million to the National Gallery extension, which opens in April 1991. As one of three sons of Lord Sainsbury of Drury Lane, John's fortune is split three ways, unlike that of his cousin, David Sainsbury, (born 24 October 1940), the only son of Sir Robert Sainsbury, who owns £800 million in shares, which paid £17,040,097 in dividends in 1989. Sir Robert and Lord Sainsbury of Drury Lane are the sons of John James Sainsbury, who founded the business as a small dairy shop at 173 Drury Lane in 1869, and each received an equal inheritance.

ST GEORGE, CHARLES ANTHONY BARBARO, *born* 21 June 1925. A baron in the Nobility of Malta, along with his younger brother, **Edward Gerald Patrick St George,** *born* 6 March 1928. After serving in the Coldstream Guards,

Charles joined Lloyds and became a leading racehorse owner. In 1981 his firm, Oakeley Vaughan, was censured and his son James, by his first marriage, was banned from holding a directorship for five years, losing his seat on the board. By his second wife, Christine, he has two Eton-educated sons. In March 1985 St George's Syndicate 551, among whose 200 investors were friends like Lester Piggott (q.v.), Henry Cooper and Sir William Pigott-Brown (q.v.), collapsed with losses incurred in the American market that could ultimately reach £30 million and many 'names' have started a legal action, due to begin in the High Court in October 1990. Oakeley Vaughan became the first company in the 302-year history of Lloyds to be put into receivership. Owner of the Sefton Lodge stables in Newmarket, from which Henry Cecil (q.v.) trains his forty-two horses, Charles briefly owned Fort Belvedere, from where King Edward VIII made his Abdication speech, selling it in 1980 after six months for a £200,000 profit to Galen Weston. Edward, whose first wife, Kathleen, was the daughter of legendary bookmaker, William Hill (she died in 1961), married, in 1979, Lady Henrietta FitzRoy (born 14 September 1949), eldest daughter of the Duke of Grafton (one son, one daughter). He lives in Grand Bahama where he has business interests with Sir Jack Hayward, the philanthropist known as 'Union Jack', and who was the financial saviour of the Liberal Party when Jeremy Thorpe was leader. Maurice 'Mo' Dalitz, said by the FBI to be a leading member of the Mafia, attended the second weddings of both Charles and Edward.

ST GERMANS, Tenth Earl of, PEREGRINE NICHOLAS ELIOT, *born* 2 January 1941.
Educated Eton and Millfield. Married, 9 October 1964 (dissolved 1989), the Hon. Jacquetta Lampson (three sons). The original motorbiking aristo, he was left Port Eliot, St German's, Cornwall and 6,000 acres when his father, a former bookmaker, trading as Nicky Eliot, went into tax exile in 1962 to take up residence in Tangier, thereafter living

on a boat, sailing around the Mediterranean. Perry was once financially involved with the Beatles, helping form Seltaeb (Beatles backwards) to market the group's names in America in 1964. Surprisingly it failed to make money. Jacquetta, daughter of the late Lord Killearn (q.v.), posed nude many times for Lucian Freud with whom she had a lengthy affair in the seventies – she featured in several of his full-frontal nude paintings that were exhibited at a retrospective at the Hayward Gallery for the world to see. During the hippy years, gipsy caravans and travellers were welcome at Port Eliot where Perry hosted, every July, an annual Elephant Fayre, so named because the family crest is an elephant's head. Some years afterwards, Perry just happened to be at his lodge gates when a lone Romany caravan drawn by a horse pulled up and the fading occupant asked if it was still possible to linger awhile at Port Eliot. 'Certainly not,' snapped back the owner. 'I'm not into freaks this year.'

SANGSTER, ROBERT EDMUND, *born* 23 May 1936.
Educated Repton College. Married first, 1960 (dissolved 1978), Christine Street (three sons, one daughter), secondly, 1976 (dissolved 1984), Susan Peacock, former wife of Australian Foreign Minister Andrew Peacock, thirdly, 1984, Sue Lilley (two sons). Leading British racehorse owner and breeder 1977, 1978, 1982, 1983 and 1984, and heir to the Vernon Pools fortune started by his grandfather. Went into tax exile in the seventies in the Isle of Man to protect a £10 million fortune and eventually sold the business for £90 million. In 1982 he was captured by Jerry Hall, who had been with Mick Jagger for five years – she told her friends, 'He could buy Mick ten times over.' But after a dalliance in America, he went back to Susan, known as 'The Sheila', eventually leaving her for another Isle of Man resident, who was married to Peter Lilley, heir to the Lilley and Skinner shoes fortune. With around 850 thoroughbreds in Britain, Ireland, South Africa, Australia and America,

Robert and Susan Sangster

his annual outgoings are £8 million. Bought Manton, with 2,050 acres, in 1984, and turned it into British racing's finest training centre. But put it up for sale in 1989 at an asking price of £13 million as neither he nor his family were able to spend even one night there because of tax reasons.

SELLERS, PETER (RICHARD HENRY), *born* 8 September 1925.
Educated at St Aloysius College, Highgate, served 1939–45 war in the RAF. Married first, 1951 (dissolved 1964), Anne Howe (one son, one daughter), secondly, 1964 (dissolved 1969), Britt Ekland (q.v.) (one daughter), thirdly, 1970 (dissolved 1974), Miranda Quarry, fourthly, 1977, Lynne Frederick. Began career at the Windmill Theatre in 1948 and graduated to the BBC radio show 'Ray's a Laugh' for five years before a meeting with Spike Milligan in 1951 led to the 'Goon Show', which ran for nine years. Believed in spiritualism and communicated with his mother, Peg, from 'the other side'. During

his marriage to Britt became close to the Earl of Snowdon (q.v.) and Princess Margaret and used to claim that he had had an affair with the Princess – the two couples spent holidays together and were constant guests in each other's homes, posing for indiscreet happy snaps. Best known for his portrayal of Inspector Clouseau, although his last film, *Being There*, was regarded as one of his finest. In May 1979 he announced that his fourth marriage was over but there was a reconciliation in the July. He was on the point of changing his will when he suffered a heart attack at The Dorchester Hotel on 22 July 1980 and died the following day. It was later revealed that he had again decided to seek a divorce from Lynne, who was in America when he collapsed, and who inherited his estimated £4 million fortune, with his three children receiving just £750 each.

SHAND KYDD, WILLIAM, *born* 12 May 1937.
Married 1962, Christina Duncan (one son,

Peter Sellers and friends

one daughter). A wallpaper heir, his elder half-brother, Peter, married, in May 1969, Viscountess Althorp, whose ex-husband became the Eighth Earl Spencer (q.v.). An amateur jockey and permit holder, Bill won forty-seven races and seventy-eight point-to-points and bred and co-owned Brown Windsor, third in the 1990 Grand National and winner of the 1989 Whitbread Gold Cup. His sister-in-law Veronica married the Seventh Earl of Lucan in November 1963 and, following his disappearance on 8 November 1974, the Shand Kydd's brought up the three Lucan children, paying for their schooling. He believes that Lucan did not murder the family nanny, Sandra Rivett, and that the fugitive peer (there is still a warrant for his arrest) is alive. A gambler, he once won just over £100,000 at the Clermont Club and went home to Regent's Park, but decided to go back to collect a receipt for the Inland Revenue. He was sucked back into a *chemin-de-fer* game and quickly lost, to Newmarket trainer Bernard van Cutsem, £183,000. 'I should have stayed in bed,' he said afterwards.

SHRIMPTON, Jean, *born* 1943.
Educated Lucie Clayton modelling school. Married, 1979, Michael Cox (one son). A Buckinghamshire builder's daughter, in 1963 she shocked the Melbourne Cup crowds by appearing in a shift four inches above the knee, and became engaged that year to photographer David Bailey, after he had helped her to become Britain's leading model, earning £8,000 a year, but called off their 6 June 1964 wedding. Known as 'The Shrimp' her agent was David Puttnam, and a romance with Terence Stamp followed. When that ended she moved to New York to be with American photographer Jordan Kalfus, but returned to London in 1969. She retired in 1972 to 'disappear' with a man simply known as 'Malcolm The Poet' and opened an antiques shop in Marazion, Cornwall. She met her husband, Michael, who was five years younger, when he walked into the shop in 1975. He was married and worked restor-

ing and selling old houses and when, a few months later, Malcolm The Poet left to join a Buddhist community, Michael left his wife and moved in with Jean. Their wedding reception was celebrated with fish and chips at the Abbey Hotel, Penzance, which they later bought for £85,000 and which they both run. Their son, Thaddeus, was born in 1980 after she almost died in pregnancy from a rare disease called hyperemesis gravidorum. The Abbey gained an award in the **Good Hotel Guide** for 'utterly acceptable mild eccentricity'.

SMITH, Dame (Margaret Natalie) Maggie, *born* 28 December 1923.
Educated Oxford High School for Girls. Married first, 1967 (dissolved 1975), Robert Stephens (two sons), secondly, 1975, Beverly Cross. Studied at the Oxford Playhouse School, made debut in June 1952 as Viola in the Oxford University Dramatic School's **Twelfth Night**. Won Oscar for **California Suite**, 1977. Jilted her first love, author and playwright Beverly Cross after a three year engagement, to marry actor Robert Stephens, but they divorced at the height of his involvement with Lady Antonia Fraser. Almost immediately she went on a sight-seeing tour of America with Beverly, whose second marriage had ended in divorce the previous year. They had met in Oxford when he was at Balliol College reading history and she later appeared as a chorus girl in his play **Strip The Willow**, preceding their engagement.

SNOWDON, First Earl of, Antony Charles Robert Armstrong-Jones, *born* 7 March 1930.
Educated Eton and Jesus College, Cambridge, where he won a Blue coxing the Cambridge boat to victory against Oxford. Married first, 6 May 1960 (dissolved 1978), HRH The Princess Margaret Rose (one son, one daughter), secondly, 1978, Lucy Davies (one daughter), former wife of Michael Lindsay-Hogg (q.v.). Constable of Caernarvon Castle since 1963. A noted photographer who

Jean Shrimpton at the Melbourne Cup

has walked with a limp after catching polio at Eton, he met Princess Margaret at the Chelsea home of Lady Elizabeth Cavendish, sister of the Eleventh Duke of Devonshire. He was previously involved with Trinidadian-Chinese actress, Jacqui Chan. When he was ennobled on his marriage, Welsh baronet Sir Michael Duff said, 'They have made a mountain out of a molehill.' In 1966 he discovered that his best man, Anthony Barton, whose family owned vineyards in Bordeaux, had fallen in love with Princess Margaret, but he returned to his wife, Eve. In September 1973 the Princess met Roddy Llewellyn, seventeen years her junior, at a houseparty in Scotland given by Colin and Lady Anne Tennant. Snowdon met Lucy working on the BBC TV 'Great Explorers' series and she accompanied him to Australia in February 1975, when he made a film on the ill-fated explorers Burke and Wills, working as a production assistant. A champion of the disabled, he helped design a motorized wheelchair for his friend, Quentin Crewe (q.v.), which went into limited production.

SOAMES, Lord, (ARTHUR) CHRISTOPHER JOHN, (life peer), *born* 12 October 1920.
Educated Eton, Royal Military Academy, Sandhurst, Lieutenant (later Captain), Coldstream Guards, 1939–45 War. Married, 1947, Mary Churchill (three sons, two daughters), youngest daughter of Sir Winston Churchill. MP for Bedford 1950–66, Secretary of State for War 1958–60, Ambassador to Paris 1968–72, the last Governor of Southern Rhodesia 1979–80, Lord President of the Council and Leader of the House of Lords 1979–81. Was credited with once having been discovered making love on a banquette at Annabel's with the wife of a racing peer. Dogged at White's through the years with the rumour that he had not done all he could have for his soldier-servant when he was killed during the war. He died, after seemingly recovering from a four-and-a-half hour intestinal operation, in September 1987, leaving £2,102,337.

SOPWITH, THOMAS EDWARD BRODIE, *born* 15 November 1932.
Educated Stowe, Lieutenant, Coldstream Guards. Married first, April 1972, Rainey, who died in 1975 in a helicopter accident, secondly, 1977, Gina Hathorn (two daughters). Only son of aviation pioneer Sir Thomas Sopwith, 'Tommy' raced cars and powerboats and has owned a series of luxury yachts called ***Philante***. Known as being careful with his cash, a club was formed for people who had been bought a drink by Sopwith. Second wife, Gina, the former British Olympic skier, is a close friend of the Prince of Wales, accompanying him (without Tommy) on skiing holidays. After the death in 1989 of his father, aged 101, Tommy sold his King's Somborn, Hampshire estate, with 2,200 acres and 6.4 miles of the River Test for £12 million.

SPENCER, Eighth Earl, EDWARD JOHN, *born* 24 January 1924.
Educated Eton, Royal Military Academy, Sandhurst, and Royal Agricultural College, Cirencester. Married first, 1954 (dissolved 1969), the Hon. Frances Roche (one son, three daughters), secondly, 1976, Raine McCorquodale, former wife of the Ninth Earl of Dartmouth. Won custody of his children when his first wife left him to marry Peter Shand Kydd, which led to charges that she was a 'bolter'. Inherited Althorp House and 12,000 acres in three counties from his father, the Seventh Earl and married Raine, who had three sons and one daughter, after she left Dartmouth because, it was said, she wanted to be chatelaine of a grand country house. Clearly it was love – giving a lift to someone staying at the same weekend house party, Spencer stopped his Rolls at a petrol station with a motel and booked into a room, leaving their passenger to twiddle her thumbs! In 1981 Raine saved the life of Johnny Spencer when he suffered a brain haemorrhage from which doctors did not expect him to recover – she had heard of an experimental drug and obtained supplies. Raine angered her stepchildren by selling

£2 million heirlooms to refurbish Althorp. 'When we ask where a picture has gone, we're always told it has been sent for cleaning and we never see it again,' said one. In the eighties Johnny bought three seaside homes near Bognor for his grandchildren to use for bucket and spade holidays, but Princes William and Harry have yet to visit. In July 1990, heir Charles, Viscount Althorp, announced that his model wife, Victoria, was expecting their first child in the New Year.

SPENCER-CHURCHILL, Lord CHARLES GEORGE WILLIAM COLIN, *born* 13 July 1940, the younger son of the Tenth Duke of Marlborough (q.v.).
Educated Eton and Vanderbilt College. Married first, 1965 (dissolved 1968), Gillian Spreckles Fuller, secondly, 1970, Jane Wyndham (three sons). Known as 'Nutty', he promoted line of Lord Churchill clothes in America, before becoming promotions representative for the Trusthouse Forte group, signing them up to sponsor the Prix de L'Arc de Triomphe, Europe's richest race at Longchamp in October (in 1988 the sponsorship was taken over by the Aga Khan's (q.v.) CIGA hotels group). In 1988 left his wife, Jane, for Irish beauty Elaine Lawlor, known as 'Legs', two years after meeting her at Deauville races. But, soon after Legs, who works as a racing manager in California, left him for Ned Evans, former head of Macmillan, New York, which he sold to Robert Maxwell. Leading London interior decorator Jane, who had put up with her husband's previous peregrinations, started divorce proceedings and in 1989 became involved with former world backgammon champion Philip Martyn, whose ex-wife, Nina, married Viscount Bridport (q.v.) in 1979.

SPENDER, LIZZIE, *born* 1950.
Educated St Clare's, Oxford. Married, 25 June 1990, Barry Humphries, creator of Dame Edna Everage. Daughter of poet, Sir Stephen Spender, by his second wife, Russian ballerina Natasha Litvin. At 5ft 10ins tall, she was nicknamed 'Big Spender' by the late Mark Boxer, and enjoyed several lengthy romances, in the seventies with Iranian diplomat Parviz Radji, who was the Shah's last Ambassador to London, and Hollywood art director Dick Sylbert, and in the eighties with actor Gerald Harper and Peter Jay, former Ambassador to Washington. An actress and author of the cookbook *Pastability*, she became the third wife of Barry in Spoleto, where, two decades earlier, she studied with composer Gian-Carlo Menotti.

STARK, KOO (KATHLEEN DEE-ANNE NORRIS), *born* 29 April 1956.
Married, August 1984 (dissolved 1989), Tim Jefferies. Sometime actress whose first major film, *Emily*, was directed by Henry Herbert, Earl of Pembroke (q.v.). In February 1982, when involved with Turkish-born textile businessman Touker Suleyman (marriage had been discussed), she met Prince Andrew. During their eighteen-month affair she was introduced to the Queen, who was said to approve of the relationship although Koo was four years older. After the Falklands War the Prince, who piloted a Sea King helicopter in the thick of the action, and conducted a correspondence with Koo (locked now in a Knightsbridge bank vault), ended the romance because it was not going to lead to marriage. She married Tim Jefferies, eight years younger, whose grandfather, Richard Tomkins, made a £50 million fortune through Green Shield stamps, after a three month romance. His mother, Hilary, disapproved. They separated after fifteen months and Koo, who has also worked as a photographer, has successfully sued several Fleet Street newspapers for libel over her association with Prince Andrew. In November 1988 she was awarded £300,000 and costs against a Robert Maxwell publication, one of nine victories.

STASSINOPOULOS, ARIANNA, *born* July 1950, educated Girton College, Cambridge, where she became President of the Union. Married, April 1986, Michael Huffington (one daughter). Dubbed 'The Gigantic Greek

Pudding' by *Private Eye* (she was 5ft 10ins tall and prone to overweight), she published a modest best seller at age twenty-three (*The Female Woman*) and spent five years in the seventies with Bernard Levin, following a spell with a curious Californian religious cult. Her 'Saturday Night at Pebble Mill' TV show, with Harriet Crawley, was taken off because few could understand her thick Greek accent. In 1981 she moved to New York, had her teeth capped, lost weight and wrote the biography of Maria Callas, earning an estimated $1 million, followed by a controversial biography of Picasso in 1988. She was introduced to Huffington, whose father, Roy, put the family liquid gas and property firm up for sale in January 1990 for $1 billion, by Ann Getty in September 1985 at a charity ball in San Francisco. Their marriage and reception in New York was a media circus (paid for by Mrs Getty) with TV star Barbara Walters as matron-of-honour. They now live on a large estate in Santa Barbara, California with their daughter, Christina, and Michael has been discussing a political career.

STEVENS, Jocelyn Edward Greville, *born* 14 February 1932.
Educated Eton, Trinity College, Cambridge, Lieutenant, Rifle Brigade. Married, 1956 (dissolved 1979), Jane Sheffield (one son, two daughters, and one son deceased). Maternal grandson of Sir Edward Hulton, who owned the London *Evening Standard* until selling it to Lord Beaverbrook in 1923. His mother died shortly after his birth and he likes to joke, 'For two weeks I was poor!' As a twenty-fifth birthday present to himself he bought **Queen**, poached Mrs Betty Kenward (Jennifer) from *Tatler* and turned it into the magazine of the late fifties and early sixties. Tony Armstrong-Jones (*see* Earl of Snowdon) was one of his photographers and was paid 19s 6d per photograph. When he was thirty-five he sold **Queen** to Michael Lewis, who ran a printing company, and joined Beaverbrook Newspapers, becoming Managing Director and later, after the company was sold to Lord Matthews (q.v.), Deputy Chairman. In the seventies his wife, Janie, a lady-in-waiting to their close friend

Arianna Stassinopoulos and husband

Princess Margaret, went off with David Davies (q.v.). In 1984 Stevens was appointed Rector and Vice-Provost of the Royal College of Art and for the last decade he has been involved with heiress Vivien Clore. They live in a Chelsea apartment overlooking the Thames and Jocelyn's Longparish, Hampshire country home, although she has a residence in Gstaad, Switzerland. Marriage, they say, is not on the agenda.

STEWART, (John Young) Jackie, *born* 11 June 1939.
Educated Dumbarton Academy. Married, 1962, Helen McGregor (two sons). A clay pigeon shooting champion, and reserve for the two-man British Olympics team in 1960, he first raced in 1961, competing in four meetings, and the following season won fourteen out of twenty-three starts. Formula One debut in 1964 for BRM, and was world champion in 1969, 1971 and 1973. Retired, 1973, to home in Switzerland from where he manages his considerable investments. A close friend of Prince Rainier and the late Princess Grace, as well as Princess Anne and the Duke of York, who are frequent guests of his and Helen. Known as an international Fixit, he is on first-name terms with King Hussein of Jordan and ex-King Constantine of Greece as well. In June 1990 he held his last annual charity celebrity clay pigeon shoot at Gleneagles, which had been attended over the years by the great and the good, because of problems of organizing such a high-profile event.

Archie Stirling and Diana Rigg

STIRLING, ARCHIBALD HUGH, *born* 18 September 1941.

Educated Ampleforth, Lieutenant, Scots Guards. Married, November 1964 (dissolved 1977), Charmian Scott (two sons), niece of Princess Alice, Duchess of Gloucester, secondly, 1982, Diana Rigg (one daughter). Worked for the family drilling company, Keir and Cawdor, but went into theatre production after meeting Diana, who was then married to Israeli artist Menachem Gueffen. Left with the remains of the Keir estate, he put a 8,600-acre deer forest on the market in 1984 for £1.25 million, to concentrate on his 5,000-acre farm. In 1989 he separated from Diana after falling in love with Joely Richardson, twenty-five years his junior and daughter of Tony Richardson and Vanessa Redgrave.

STIRLING OF KEIR, Lieutenant-Colonel, WILLIAM JOSEPH, *born* 9 May 1911. Educated Ampleforth and Trinity College, Cambridge, Lieutenant, Scots Guards 1932–6. Married, 1940, Susan Bligh (two sons, and two sons deceased), whose sister, Jasmine, was one of the two first women television announcers. Elder brother of Sir David Stirling, who founded the SAS, he commanded a regiment during the Second World War. A fearless gambler and racehorse owner who inherited two great estates, Keir and Cawdor, and a large part of Glasgow, which he sold to Lord Rayne for £1 million, only to see its value multiply eight times in a short period. In 1974 he forfeited 4,000 acres of farmland on the slope of Mount Kilimanjaro when it was nationalized by President Julius Nyerere. Old Masters and acres vanished over the years to pay debts to bookmakers and gaming clubs and in 1976, without telling his wife, he sold Keir and 200 surrounding acres to Mahdi Al-Tajir (q.v.), moving to another part of the estate. Mrs Stirling refused to move and said, 'The estate has been sold because my husband needed the money but gambling debts simply did not come into it. My husband is, by nature, a gambler but not in the sense that he could lose gigantic sums at the tables.' Only on her death, in November 1983, did Al-Tajir get possession. Bill Stirling died in January 1983 having lain for thirty-six hours undiscovered with a broken leg in his Park Lane home after a fall. In 1970 his elder daughter, Hannah, married Robert Cecil, now Viscount Cranborne and the eldest son of the Marquess of Salisbury.

STOCKTON, Second Earl of, ALEXANDER DANIEL ALAN MACMILLAN, *born* 10 October 1943.

Educated Eton, University of Paris and Strathclyde University. Married, 1970, Birgitte Hamilton (one son, two daughters). Grandson of 'SuperMac', Prime Minister 1957–63 who resisted accepting a hereditary peerage while his son, Maurice, held political ambitions – 'SuperMac' finally became an Earl in 1984, the year Maurice, an alcoholic, died. Alex, a former foreign correspondent with the *Telegraph*, is also an alcoholic, giving up drink after waking up in a Paris hotel after a binge and thinking he was paralysed – in fact he had, in a haze, put both legs in the same pyjama leg. The problem appears to have come from the Devonshire family – Harold Macmillan married Lady Dorothy Cavendish and her children and grandchildren have been afflicted by drugs and drink addiction – Alexander's younger brother, Joshua, died, aged twenty, while at Balliol. In 1988 Alexander fell in love with Miranda Nuttall and left his wife 'Bitte'. They were reconciled within months, after he said, 'I am the pig that loved the leopard,' but separated for good in 1989, when he sold Birch Grove House and its 1,234-acre estate for £5 million. Chairman of Macmillan (ninety-five per cent owned by the family) from 1980 until ousted in February 1990, and given the titular role of President. Now devoting time to a career in the Lords.

SUFFOLK, Twenty-first Earl of, MICHAEL JOHN JAMES GEORGE ROBERT HOWARD, also Fourteenth Earl of Berkshire, *born* 27 March 1935.

Educated Winchester and Le Rosey, Sub-

Lieutenant, RNVR. Married first, 1960 (dissolved 1967), Simone Litman (one daughter deceased). Secondly, 1973 (dissolved 1980), Anita Fuglesang (one son, one daughter), thirdly, 1983 Linda Paravicini (two daughters), former wife of Fourth Viscount Bridport. Known as 'Mickey', his grandmother was the daughter of American millionaire Levi Leiter and her brother went bust attempting to corner the United States corn market. Suffolk, the senior descendant of the last Plantagenet King, Richard III has a 5,000-acre estate near Malmesbury and met his second wife, Anita, when she came to photograph a horse he had bred (his first wife was declared bankrupt in 1970 and received a fifteen-month suspended jail sentence in 1975 for deception). His third wife came to live in a cottage a few yards from his house after the end of her marriage and love blossomed following his divorce from Anita – he left her in a hotel foyer in Manila in May 1979 as they were about to fly back to London, saying he was going to Hong Kong 'on business'.

SWEENY, CHARLES, *born* 3 October 1909.
Educated Loyola School, Canterbury School, New Milford, Connecticut, and Wadham College, Oxford. Married first, 1933 (dissolved 1947), Margaret Whigham (one son, one daughter), who later became the Duchess of Argyll, secondly, 1957 (dissolved 1966), Arden Sneed. An all-round sportsman who arrived in England with his younger brother, Robert (born 1911), who was the better golfer of the two, winning the British Amateur Open Championship in 1934. Formed the Eagle Squadron in 1940 for American pilots to fly with the RAF and later became an Intelligence officer with the United States Air Force. Remained in London, where he became a noted clubman, playing backgammon daily at first the St James's, then the Clermont and finally Aspinall's. Daughter Frances married the Tenth Duke of Rutland (q.v.). In July 1990 he published his autobiography, *Sweeny*.

T*t*

TAVISTOCK, Marquess of, HENRY ROBIN IAN, heir to the Thirteenth Duke of Bedford. *Born* 21 January 1940.
Married, 20 June 1961, Henrietta Tiarks (three sons). Known as Robin, he and Henrietta (dubbed 'Deb of the Year' in 1957) reluctantly took over Woburn Abbey, dating from the seventeenth century, and 13,000 acres when his father, the Duke of Bedford (q.v.) went into tax exile. The mansion contains magnificent collections of paintings, including one room full of Canelettos, and works by Rembrandt, Van Dyck, Gainsborough, Reynolds, Velazquez and Holbein, and French and English eighteenth-century furniture. One of their treasures, Antonio Canova's **Three Graces**, was sold by the family in 1985 to a mysterious Cayman Island's company, who resold it for £7.6 million to the Getty Museum. It was refused an export licence in 1990 and there have been two offers to keep it in Britain. In February 1988 Robin was given just hours to live after suffering a stroke, but has recovered fully and his family rewarded the National Hospital for Nervous Diseases with a £250,000 donation to its Development Foundation. The Tavistocks are also successful racehorse breeders and have a Newmarket home – producing prize-winning progeny from their mare, Mrs Moss, formerly owned by Sir William Pigott-Brown and named after his ex-love Elaine, second wife of Stirling Moss (q.v.).

TAYLOR, MICHAEL JOHN CLIFFORD, *born* 1934, known as 'Slippery'.
Educated Wellington College. Married first, 1959 (dissolved 1980), Charlotte Lyon (one son, one daughter), second, 1980, Elaine Barbarino, former wife of Stirling Moss (q.v.). Son of a Mercedes car salesman, who founded Taylor and Crawley in Mayfair, he became a racing driver in 1958 but his career ended

when, practising for the Belgian Grand Prix at Spa in May 1960, the steering wheel came away in his hands at 130mph and the car hurtled into a wood, finishing wedged between two trees, eight feet off the ground. Taylor, with a broken neck, back, five ribs and an ankle, was found, by the farmer of the land, face down in mud and had his life saved when turned over. Two years later he sued Colin Chapman (q.v.) and Lotus and won an out-of-court settlement of £100,000. He founded London Bridge as a private property company in 1970, took Sir William Pigott-Brown (q.v.) in as a partner and the shares reached a peak of 192p before the property crash in 1973, when the price plunged to 9p. The company was wound up in 1977 with an eventual deficiency of £8,208,632 and the Official Receiver, Mr James Christmas, blamed the collapse on 'expensive, ill-judged, speculative ventures'.

THATCHER, MARK, *born* 15 August 1953, two minutes before his sister, Carol.
Educated at Harrow. Married, 14 February 1987, Diane Burgdorf (one son). Became a racing driver, finishing third in the European SuperVee championship and famously losing his way in the Sahara during the Paris-Dakar Rally. He set up Monteagle Marketing with Steve Tipping (best man at his wedding) in 1979. It was into that firm's bank account that the very controversial consultancy fee of £50,000 was paid after Mark helped in a £300 million deal to build a new university in Oman, where Mrs Margaret Thatcher, the Prime Minister, was on an official visit at the time the contract was secured. In the eighties Mark moved to America to sell Lotus Cars for David Wickens (who also employed Denis Thatcher on one of his boards), moving to Dallas to work in the motor trade and meeting Diane, whose father, Ted, runs

Mr and Mrs Mark Thatcher

a new and used-car business. Since setting up as a wheeler-dealer, he has made an estimated £5 million, enough to employ a full-time butler, Graham, who travels the world with him. In Britain Mark has a three-man Scotland Yard bodyguard, a result of IRA threats following a statement he made about the organization in America. In contrast, his sister Carol, educated at Queenswood, Hatfield, St Paul's School for Girls, Hammersmith and University College, London, travels alone, working as a freelance writer, broadcaster and author. Her first lover was Conservative MP Jonathan Aitken, who joined her for a skiing holiday in the Austrian Alps in the spring of 1977. Romances with tennis writer Richard Evans (biographer of McEnroe) and BBC TV producer Mike Begg ended short of the altar and she says she doubts she will ever marry or have children.

THEODORACOPOULOS, TAKI (PETER), *born* 11 August 1937.
Educated Blair Academy, the University of Virginia. Married, 1980 (dissolved 1985), Princess Alexandra Schoenburg-Hartenstein (one son, one daughter). Greek-born, American educated sportsman, who played at Wimbledon and represented Greece in the Davis Cup and was Greek karate champion for many years. Began a writing career in the early seventies, living in a Mayfair flat while his elder brother, Harry, went into the family shipping business in New York. Their father, John, was also an industrialist (he owned the Caravelle Hotel in Athens as well) whose fortune was estimated at one time at £250 million. Taki used to paper his study walls with cheques for his freelance writings and became the permanent High Life correspondent for the *Spectator*, interrupted for a three month period from December 1984 to March 1985 while he languished at Pentonville, serving a sentence for attempting to smuggle 24.1 grammes of cocaine for his 'personal use' after being stopped at Heathrow after a flight from New York. In 1989 his father died leaving him all his money, estimated at £75 million, which he sport-

ingly offered to share with his brother (the offer was refused). He was divorced because of his constant philanderings with young English aristocrats, including Lady Cosima Fry and Lady Anne Somerset, but continues to live with his ex-wife for much of the year in New York and Gstaad. He has two yachts on which he spends part of the summer in the Mediterranean and still has an eye for nubile English women.

THYSSEN-BORNEMISZA DE KASZON, BARON HEINI (HEINRICH), *born* 13 April 1921.
Educated Realgymnasium, The Hague, and the University of Fribourg. Married first, 1946 (dissolved 1953), Princess Therese de Lippe (one son), secondly, 1953 (dissolved 1955), Nina Dyer, thirdly, 1955 (dissolved 1964), Fiona Campbell-Walter (one son, one daughter) fourthly, 1967 (dissolved 1984), Denise Shorto (one son), fifthly, 1985, Carmen 'Tita' Cervera (one son adopted), widow of Tarzan actor Lex Barker. Owner of the world's finest private art collection, mainly housed at his Swiss home, the Villa Favorita on Lake Lugano. Grandson of the Ruhr steel baron whose factories armed the German forces in two World Wars, Heini was born in Holland and became a Swiss citizen in 1950. In her divorce action, Brazilian-born Denise, who was claiming an £80 million settlement, put her husband's worth between £400 million and £1.2 billion. He counter-sued for the return of family jewels worth £50 million. In December 1988 Heini signed an agreement with the Spanish Government to display 787 of his paintings at the Villahermosa Palace for ten years, turning down pleas from Mrs Thatcher and the Prince of Wales to house them in London. It was reported that he hoped that his wife, 'Tita', a former beauty queen, would be rewarded with a title of her own by her country.

TIKKOO, RAVI, *born* 1933.
Educated Punjab University, served Indian Navy. Married, 1958 (dissolved 1979),

Taki Theodoracopoulos

Baron Heini Thyssen and wife

Mahrukh (two sons). Son of the Finance Secretary to the Rajah of Mundi, he moved to London in 1964, becoming a British citizen five years later, and made his fortune by ordering two giant supertankers, the *Globtik Tokyo* and the *Globtik London*, which, at 438,000 tons each, were then the largest ships ever built in Japan, and carried forty-three million barrels of oil a year from the Gulf to Japan. His fortune was estimated at £50 million and he became a substantial racehorse owner moving his string, because of arguments with turf authorities, from Britain to France and finally America, where he bought an estate in Greenwich, Connecticut for £2.5 million. In 1982 he became involved with Mrs Denia Palumbo, former wife of Peter Palumbo (q.v.) and introduced her as his fiancée, but she called it off and became reconciled with Palumbo, who was on the point of remarrying her when she died of cancer. In racing circles, Tikkoo was famed for his arrogance – when he employed Old Etonian Ben Hanbury as his trainer, he sent him a list detailing how he should be addressed, when he could be spoken to and other points of etiquette! In 1988 Tikkoo unveiled his most ambitious project, choosing the beleaguered Belfast firm of Harland and Wolff to build for him the world's largest liner, with accommodation for 3,108 passengers, at a cost of $500 million. The project never got off the ground.

TOWNSEND, Group Captain PETER WOOLRIDGE, *born* 22 November 1914.
Educated Haileybury and Royal Air Force College, Cranwell, Royal Air Force 1933–56. Married first, 1941 (dissolved 1952), Rosemary Pawle (two sons), secondly, 1959, Marie Luce Jamagne (one son, two daughters). Equerry to King George VI 1944–52, Deputy Master of the Royal Household 1950, Equerry to the Queen 1952–3, Air Attaché, Brussels 1953–6. Unofficially engaged to Princess Margaret in 1955, he bowed under pressure, and, says the Princess, 'It was Peter who said no.' He went abroad and married a Belgian tobacco man-

ufacturer's daughter and they set up home in France, where he became a best-selling author, eventually writing his autobiography, *Time and Change*, in 1978. In 1988 he sold his medals, a DSO and two DFCs for £22,000 to launch a fund to help children who have suffered in war. Of his sons by his first marriage to a brigadier's daughter (later Marchioness Camden), Giles is a wine merchant who buys all the wines for the Savoy Hotel group and the younger is Father Hugo, a Carmelite monk.

TOWNSHEND, Lady CAROLYN ELIZABETH ANN, elder daughter of Seventh Lord Townshend, *born* 27 September 1940.
Married first, 13 October 1962 (dissolved 1971), Antonio Capellini (one son), secondly, 1973 (annulled 1974), Edgar Bronfman. Publicist who numbered Bob Hope and Jack Benny among her clients, she became Public Relations Officer for Seagrams, the world's largest distillers, and married the boss, Edgar Bronfman, whose family fortune was estimated at £2 billion, as his second wife. They celebrated their January 1974 wedding with a dance for 300, at London's Inn on the Park, with a Russian theme, serving vodka and caviar, but the couple almost immediately became estranged. Two months later Bronfman, whose Canadian-born father was a twenties bootlegger, demanded she hand back her wedding presents – $1 million and a mansion in New York's Yorktown Heights. 'I thought we were happy,' said the bride. 'He chased me round the world for two years asking me to marry him and when I did, he didn't want me anymore.' The case was heard in Manhattan in November 1974, when Bronfman asked for an annulment on the grounds of non-consummation. He said in court that on their wedding night she told him she had 'a hang-up about sex'. In an out-of-court settlement, after Bronfman was granted an annulment, she received £17,000 a year for ten years, jewellery valued at £50,000, but gave back the $1 million and the house. She returned to live in London and resumed her career in public relations.

Twiggy in 1966

TRYON, Third Lord ANTHONY GEORGE MERRICK, *born* 26 May 1940.

Educated Eton, Lieutenant, Royal Wiltshire Yeomanry. Married, 1973, Dale Harper (two sons, two daughters, of whom a son and daughter are twins). Son of Second Lord Tryon (died 1976), who was Assistant Keeper of the Privy Purse to King George VI 1949–52, and Keeper of the Privy Purse and Trea-surer to the Queen, October 1952–71. The family house, The Manor, at Great Durnford, near Salisbury, was turned into a girls' school, but Anthony Tryon inherited 2,000 acres and retired from merchant banking (he remains a director of Purdeys, the gunsmiths) to look after his interests and country pursuits when his Australian wife, nicknamed 'Kanga' by her close friend the

Prince of Wales, for whom she acted as hostess on two of his Antipodean trips before his marriage, started a successful clothes operation called 'Kanga and the Dale Tryon Collection' – now sold in Britain, Japan, America, Hong Kong, Australia, Sweden and Spain. The Prince is godfather to the Tryons' elder son Charles, born May 1976, who is also a page-of-honour to the Queen. Kanga, who has also made a small fortune in London property through buying and selling her town flat, has remained in close touch with the Heir to the Throne, but it is only a rumour that she curtseys when he telephones.

TWIGGY, (NÉE LESLEY HORNBY) *born* 19 September 1946.
Educated Cricklewood. Married, 1977, Michael Whitney (one daughter), who died 1983, secondly, 1988, Leigh Lawson. Followed Jean Shrimpton (q.v.) as the most famous model in the world, managed by former hairdresser Justin de Villeneuve (née Nigel Davies), with whom she lived for a decade. She retired to pursue an acting career in 1971, being cast in *The Boy Friend*. In 1973 she met Michael Whitney and they made the film *W*, but after their marriage, as her career took off, culminating in the broadway smash-hit *My One and Only*, he took to drink and they separated. He died in a McDonald's hamburger outlet in New York, taking their daughter, Carly, out for the day. In 1986 she met Leigh Lawson, who had a ten-year-old son, Ace, by Hayley Mills, and they married three years later. He co-starred with Dustin Hoffman in London's West End and on Broadway 1989–90 in *The Merchant of Venice*.

VENTURA, VIVIANE, *born* 5 December 1947.
Educated at the Lycée Français, Bogota, New York, London, and the Ada Foster Childrens' Drama School, London. Married, 1966 (dissolved 1978), Frank Duggan (one daughter) and one daughter, Scheherazade, by John Bentley (q.v.). Became a child actress aged fourteen, made *High Wind in Jamaica* with Anthony Quinn, *Finders Keepers* with Cliff Richard and *Promise Her Anything* with Warren Beatty, who became something more than her leading man. Retired at twenty-four. Rather than write her autobiography, she penned a *roman-à-clef* in 1982, featuring the men in her life, thinly disguised, including King Hussein of Jordan whose large, personally inscribed, colour portrait occupied pride of place on her bedside table for most of the seventies. She lives in a Chelsea house bought for her by Adnan Khashoggi (q.v.) and for the last ten years has run a promotions company, setting up international events – she opened Sun City in Bophuthatswana for Sol Kerzner. Bids for her address book have reached £25,000, but she still ain't selling.

VESTEY, Third Lord, SAMUEL GEORGE ARMSTRONG VESTEY, *born* 19 March 1941.
Educated Eton, Lieutenant, Scots Guards. Married first (dissolved 1981) Kathryn Eccles (two daughters), secondly, 1981, Celia 'Cece' Knight (two sons). Member of Britain's second-richest family, owner of 1,330 Dewhurst butchers shops, beef producing land in South America and Australia and shipping and insurance companies. Lives at 4,000-acre Stowell Park in Gloucestershire, commuting to offices in Smithfield by helicopter, landing on a pad in the Thames by his Oxo building – at Eton he was known as 'Beef' and later nicknamed 'Spam'. A polo enthusiast like his younger brother, Mark, he employed Argentinian professionals Hector Barrantes (now stepfather of the Duchess of York) and the late Eduardo Moore. The first Lady Vestey, Kate, daughter of a Heinz 57 director and who once worked on the candle counter of Fortnum and Mason, formed an attachment for Moore and the couple separated in September 1971 (Moore, then the

Viviane Ventura

Lord and Lady Vestey

best player in Britain, stayed on at Stowell). Sam's younger brother, Mark, also a polo player and all-round horseman, is paralysed from the waist down following a hunting accident in February 1984.

WARD, GERALD JOHN, *born* 31 May 1938. Educated Eton, Royal Military Academy, Sandhurst, Royal Agricultural College, Cirencester, Captain, Royal Horse Guards. Married first, 20 March 1967 (dissolved 1983), Rosalind Lygon (two daughters), secondly Amanda Vincent, former wife of Barry Dinan (*see* Lady Charlotte Curzon). Father 'Jackie' Ward was Colonel Commanding the Household Cavalry 1953–6 and Silver Stick-in-Waiting; his mother was the society beauty Susan Corbett, who created a scandal in the sixties by having an affair with the Spanish Ambassador, the Marquis Miguel Primo de Rivera. Her husband was infuriated to catch them in bed together, not least, he told fellow members at White's, on a matter of form, because she was 'wearing a vest'. Gerald inherited the 2,000-acre Chilton Foliat estate and in 1979 Ros left him for London-based banker Count Gian-Luca Salini-Amorini. But after a divorce, she married Sir Charles Morrison, Conservative MP for Devizes and son of Lord Margadale. Gerald, who was once Colin Tennant's (q.v.) partner in Mustique, is a godfather to Prince Harry and a born-again Christian, friendly with the Fourth Marquess of Reading (q.v.).

WAUGH, AUBERON ALEXANDER, *born* 17 November 1939.
Educated Downside, Christ Church, Oxford, Lieutenant, Royal Horse Guards. Married, 1961, Lady Teresa Onslow (two sons, two daughters), only daughter of the Earl of Onslow. Retired from the army while serving in Cyprus and catching twenty-nine bullets when his machine gun accidentally went off – he miraculously survived severe abdominal wounds and has only a lost finger to show for the mishap. Britain's most prolific journalist, and Editor, since 1986, of the *Literary Review*. His most successful column was his outrageous Diary in *Private Eye*, which he gave up in 1986 after sixteen years. Known to have an eye for a pretty girl, he developed Tina Brown (q.v.) as his protegée, after receiving a fan letter from her while she was at Oxford. The friendship cooled after she married Harold Evans, whom he nicknamed 'The Dame' in *Private Eye*. Evans was libelled so many times by the satirical organ that he has a lifetime agreement that he will never again be mentioned in the *Eye*. Auberon's wife took an adult degree at Exeter University and has become a successful author herself. Waugh, son of Evelyn, entertains liberally at Combe Florey House, which he inherited, along with his father's overcoat and suits, giving guests fine wines – he is an expert and writes about wine for the *Spectator*. In 1990 he began work on his autobiography.

WEINBERG, Sir MARK (AUBREY), *born* 9 August 1931.
Educated King Edward VII School, Johannesburg, University of the Witwatersand. Married first, 1961, Sandra Le Rioth (three daughters), secondly, Anouska Hempel (one son). Insurance marketing genius who has made two fortunes out of the business, starting Abbey Life in 1961, then setting up Hambro Life (now Allied Dunbar). With his second wife, former actress Anouska, known as the most upwardly mobile couple in London. Princess Margaret graces their table in their magnificent Holland Park house and holidays with them every August in Corfu, when they take the house of Jacob Rothschild (q.v.). Dress designer Anouska, who was briefly married to Bill Kenwright (q.v.), has made a property fortune and owns the fashionable Blake's Hotel in South Kensington. She inherited it on the death of her first husband, Constantine Hempel, whose father was the German Ambassador to Ireland. A former journalist with the *Sunday Dispatch*, he started dabbling in London property after meeting Ned Ryan in a £5-a-week Earl's Court boarding house. Ryan, who became Princess Margaret's most constant escort in the eighties, was the passenger in Constantine's Porsche when it crashed into a Pimlico basement, killing Hempel. He had met Anouska, New Zealand-born, on her first weekend in London after flying in from the Antipodes, picking her and her sister up in Belgrave Square and inviting them to a pub for a drink. In February 1987 Weinberg was blackballed by the ultra-exclusive Corviglia Club in St Moritz, despite being proposed by the Duke of Marlborough – the German faction in the club objected.

WESTMINSTER, Sixth Duke of, GERALD CAVENDISH GROSVENOR, *born* 22 December 1951.
Educated Sunningdale School, and Harrow. Married, 1978, Natalia Phillips (two daughters). Passed up on a promising football career – he was given a trial for Fulham Football Club – after his father objected to 'all that kissing' and concentrated on the family holdings; 300 acres of Mayfair and Belgravia (Pimlico was sold to meet death duties in the fifties), 13,000 acres in Cheshire and the centre of Chester, 14,000 acres in North Wales, 900 acres in Shropshire, 12,000 acres in Vancouver and a 10,000-acre sheep

Sir Mark and Lady Weinberg

Duke of Westminster

farm near Wagga Wagga, Australia, conservatively worth £3 billion. When he was fined £120 for speeding in March 1990, he accepted the magistrates' offer of seven days' time in which to pay the fine. After his family pulled down Gothic Eaton Hall, near Chester and built Britain's first post-war modern Bauhaus-style stately home, Gerald moved out in 1989 so that architects could create a more sympathetic exterior (the family called the house Zimbabwe Airport) in two shades of pink sandstone with a natural slate roof. A tireless campaigner for charitable causes, Gerald spends most weekends dressing up in uniform and exercising with the Territorial Army. The couple are best friends with the Prince and Princess of Wales – Diana is godmother to their younger daughter, Lady Edwina, and 'Tally' is godmother to Prince William. After a ten-year gap, she is expecting a third child in 1991.

WHITE, Michael Simon, *born* 16 January 1936.
Educated Lyceum Alpinum, Zuoz, Switzerland, Pisa University, Sorbonne, Paris. Married first, 1965 (dissolved 1973), Sarah Hillsdon (two sons, one daughter), secondly, 1985, Louise Moores (one son). Known as 'Chalky', he became assistant to leading

Lady Virginia White

impresario Sir Peter Daubeny in 1956, working for him for five years before branching out on his own, staging **The Rocky Horror Show**, **Oh! Calcutta**, **Sleuth** and many other successes, interspersed with some disasters, before becoming a film producer, responsible for **The Comic Strip**, **Supergrass**, etc. The only man in Britain to have won the pools without having filled in a coupon, he married Littlewoods heiress Louise Moores (daughter of the late Nigel Moores and granddaughter of the founder). A well-known gambler, playing blackjack at gaming clubs and tilting at the bookies on race-courses.

WHITE, Sir (VINCENT) GORDON (LINDSAY), *born* 11 May 1923.
Educated De Aston School, Lincolnshire,

Captain SOE Force 136, 1939–45 War. Married first, 1958 (dissolved), Elizabeth Kalen (two daughters), secondly, 1974 (dissolved 1979), Virginia North (one son). Became friendly with James (later Lord) Hanson through his younger brother, Bill Hanson, an Olympic showjumper who died of cancer at the age of twenty-nine and first teamed up with James in a business importing amusing greeting cards from America. Hanson Trust (now Hanson PLC and valued at £11 billion) was founded in 1973 and the following year White left for New York with his second wife to drum up business in America, starting with £3,000, all that was permitted under exchange controls. Dubbed 'The White Knight', he is desperately keen for a peerage to match that of his partner, who was knighted by Harold Wilson and ennobled by Mrs Margaret Thatcher and is involved in high-profile patronage – his conglomerate's Ever Ready offshoot sponsors the Derby and other major races at Epsom during Derby week, attended by the Royal Family. White (6ft 6ins tall, as is Hanson) has spent an estimated £20 million chasing success as a racehorse owner. He lives in America between a Park Avenue apartment and a Beverly Hills house close to LA Lakers basketball star, Magic Johnson. His escort, since 1984, has been Californian model Victoria Tucker, four decades his junior, but he says of marriage, 'Never marry a young girl, they want babies.' In June 1990 he put his 176ft yacht, *The Galu*, on the market for £8.5 million, twice what he paid for her.

WIMBORNE, Third Viscount, IVOR FOX-STRANGWAYS GUEST, *born* 2 December 1939.
Educated Eton. Married first, 1966 (dissolved 1981), Victoria Vigors (one son), secondly, Venetia Quarry (one daughter), former wife of Captain Fred Barker. Chairman of the Harris and Dixon group of shipping and insurance companies, he went into tax exile in Paris 1976, and quickly became involved with exotic Pierre Cardin model Anjali Mendes, born in Bombay. But in August 1983, five months after he shelved plans to marry her, he became engaged to statuesque mother-of-five Venetia, stepdaughter of the Second Lord Mancroft (q.v.). He inherited 32,000 acres. In 1972 he was offered £26 million for just 575 acres of land he owned adjacent to Poole, Dorset, for development. In January 1986 a Madrid court ordered the arrest of three people over the alleged smuggling out of Spain of Goya's *Marquesa of Santa Cruz*, which Ivor Wimborne had bought in good faith through a family trust three years earlier in Zurich and had put up for sale at Christie's. Spain acquired the masterpiece three months later for £4.2 million, substantially below the valuation of £10.25 million, but Wimborne said he was happy at the price. Later that year he announced he was setting up a fighting-bull

farm in Spain 'to get to know fighting bulls better'. His American cousin Raymond Guest, former Ambassador to London, named his 1966 Epsom Derby winner Sir Ivor after the family first name.

WINTOUR, ANNA, *born* 3 November 1948. Educated North London Collegiate. Married, 1984, Dr David Shaffer (one son, one daughter). Daughter of Charles Wintour, Editor of the London *Evening Standard* 1959–76, and his first wife, American heiress Noni Baker, daughter of a Harvard professor. Worked in the fashion department of *Harpers & Queen*, before going to America to write for *New York* magazine. Ultimate ambition always was to edit *American Vogue*, in which she succeeded in July 1988 after being Editor-in-Chief of *Vogue* in London. Among her former loves were Australian anarchist Richard Neville, impresario Michael White (q.v.), milliner James Wedge, writer Jon Bradshaw (with whom she spent six years) and backgammon player Claud Beer (one week). It was she who discovered her father's long-standing affair with Gaia Servadio, wife of Willie Mostyn-Owen, which led *Private Eye* to call him Sir Charles Mostyn-Wintour.

YATES, PAULA, *born* 1959.
Educated St Clare's, Oxford. Married, 1986, Bob Geldof (two daughters). Daughter of TV producer Jess 'The Bishop' Yates, who lost his Sunday-night religious programme in 1973 because of an affair with dancer Anita Kay (almost half his age) despite the fact he was long separated from Paula's mother, raunchy novelist Heller Toren, a former Bluebell Girl. Aged eighteen Paula was taken to hospital in Oxford for treatment to cuts on her wrists and began an affair with Boomtown Rats lead singer Geldof in 1978. She

Paula and Bob Geldof

Princess Elizabeth of Yugoslavia and young family, 1974

co-hosted 'The Tube' with Jools Holland and in 1989 launched her first book, **Good Times With Bad Boys**. In February 1990 she revealed that her husband has had two baths in six years, the first when they got married and the other in 1988. Awarded an honorary knighthood for Live Aid in 1986, Dublin-born Geldof cannot use the title while retaining Irish nationality. But Paula's own cheque book bears the legend 'Lady Geldof'.

HRH Princess ELIZABETH JELISAVETTA **of Yugoslavia,** *born* Belgrade, 7 April 1936. Married first, 21 May 1960 (dissolved 1966), Howard Oxenberg (two daughters),

secondly, 23 September 1969 (dissolved 1974), Neil Balfour (one son), thirdly, 1987, Manuel Ulloa. Often referred to as a cousin of the Queen, she is, in fact, the niece of the late Princess Marina, Duchess of Kent and her mother, Princess Olga of Greece, was married to Prince Paul of Yugoslavia. Her elder daughter, Catherine Oxenberg, became an actress who starred in the eighties soap series 'Dynasty', playing the daughter of Joan Collins, and her younger daughter, Christina, married Damian Elwes, artist and son of the late Dominic Elwes (q.v.). A close friend of Lady Annabel Goldsmith, Elizabeth ran off in the seventies with Richard Burton, leaving Balfour (later the Euro MP for North Yorkshire) with their son, but the romance ended because of Burton's alcoholism. In the autumn of 1989 she separated from her third husband, a Peruvian, and was briefly escorted by *soi-disant* billionaire Donald Trump, who also numbered Catherine among his closer friends.

Zz

ZILKHA, SELIM KHEDOURY, *born* 7 April 1927.
Educated English School, Heliopolis, Egypt, Horace Mann School for Boys, USA, Williams College, USA. Married (dissolved) Diane Bashi (one son, one daughter), who later married Lord Lever of Manchester (q.v.). An American of Iraqi extraction born in Baghdad, he went into partnership with James (later Sir) Goldsmith (q.v.), launching on his own the first Mothercare shop in Kingston, Surrey, in December 1961. Within two years there were twenty-eight shops and in 1981 he sold out to Sir Terence Conran of Habitat, leading to jokes that the new company should be named Mothertat, pocketing £19 million, having previously raised £33 million by selling shares. In 1982 he moved with his longtime mistress Mrs Mary Hayley to New York, taking a $5,000-a-week apartment in the Waldorf Towers and founded the Zilkha Energy Company in Houston in 1987, before settling in Los Angeles. A passionate bridge player and fourteen-handicap golfer, he was once in partnership in racehorses with Sir Gordon White and used to give an annual Christmas dinner, when the pudding was liberally impregnated with gold sovereigns, rather than token pieces of silver.

Photographic Acknowledgements

Alpha: 178

Arts Council: 141

Luis Basualdo: 23

Alan Davidson: 3, 10, 16, 21 *above,* 27, 40, 42 *above,* 47, 51, 65 *above,* 67, 72, 85, 96, 97, 99, 100, 102, 104, 106, 107, 109, 124, 126 *left,* 130, 137, 142, 143, 145, 151, 154, 157, 161, 167, 168, 171, 173, 174, 179, 180, 183, 185

Financial Times: 138

Patrick Lichfield: 174

Popperfoto: 53

Press Association: 57

Rex Features: 69, 70, 75

Peter Sellers Collection: 162

Sports & General: 129

Spooner/Gamma: 38 *left,* 92, 147

Syndication International: 15, 18, 19, 21 *below,* 28, 30, 31, 33, 34, 38 *right,* 39, 42 *above,* 42 *right,* 43 *above,* 43 *below,* 44, 52, 61, 63, 65 *below,* 73, 74, 77, 81, 82, 84, 86, 95, 111, 113, 117, 121, 126 *right,* 127, 133, 136, 148, 152, 176, 182, 186

Universal Pictorial Press: 14

Weidenfeld Archive: 17, 78, 88, 90, 164